WE COULD BE CONTENDERS

To my good friends

Gordon & Beverley

Sincere Best Wishes

Ray Piggott

DEC 2008

For a complete list of Management Books 2000 titles,
visit our web-site on http://www.mb2000.com

WE COULD BE CONTENDERS
or
What a British Management Education Doesn't Teach You

Ray Piggott

2000

Copyright © Ray Piggott 2000/2006

All rights reserved. No part of this publication may be reproduced, stored in a retrieval system, or transmitted in any form or by any means, electronic, mechanical, photocopying, recording, or otherwise without the prior permission of the publishers.

First published in 2000 by Management Books 2000 Ltd under the title
'What a British Education Doesn't Teach You'

This completely revised 2nd edition published in 2006 by Management Books 2000 Ltd
Forge House, Limes Road
Kemble, Cirencester
Gloucestershire, GL7 6AD, UK
Tel: 0044 (0) 1285 771441
Fax: 0044 (0) 1285 771055
E-mail: info@mb2000.com
Web: www.mb2000.com

Printed and bound in Great Britain by 4edge Ltd of Hockley, Essex – www.4edge.co.uk

This book is sold subject to the condition that it shall not, by way of trade or otherwise, be lent, resold, hired out, or otherwise circulated without the publisher's prior consent in any form of binding or cover other than that in which it is published and without a similar condition including this condition being imposed upon the subsequent purchaser.

British Library Cataloguing in Publication Data is available
ISBN 1-85252-526-6
ISBN13 978-1-85252-526-2

Contents

Preface to the 2nd Edition	7
Introduction	20
Part 1. Our Industrial Heritage: An Insider's View	
1. 'Them' and 'Us'	30
Part 2. A profit 'Park and Ride' for Overseas Investors	
2. 'Education, Education, Education' – But Will It Do the Trick?	42
3. Do Our Institutions Serve Us Well?	52
4. Run the Business and Let the City Take Care of Itself	60
Part 3. The Way Ahead	
5. Becoming a team player	78
6. The Designer	87
7. The Marketer	109
8. The Salesman	142
9. The Financial Controller	159
10. The Human Resources Manager	164
11. The Production Manager	169
12. The General Manager	173
Part 4. Conclusion	
13. Can You Get There?	190
Appendices	
I. Comparing Companies	193
II. Corporate Operational Procedures	209
III. Strategic Marketing Group	220
IV. Bexley Business Academy Presentation	
Index	227

Preface to the 2nd Edition

When the first edition of this book was published in the year 2000 under the title 'What a British Education Doesn't Teach You' (ISBN 1-85252-309-3), it was sufficiently well-received to merit half a dozen broadcasts by the author on Radios 4 & 5 and the World Service of the BBC. Since then there has been more publicity given in the media to business, with programmes such as *The Apprentice*, hosted by Sir Alan Sugar. Whatever the merits of Sir Alan's programme, it unquestionably put business in a better, more attractive and stimulating light than hitherto. Furthermore, the participants in the programme were all young which illustrated in part that it is possible to engage young people in business issues if the subject matter is put across in an engaging manner. However, there is a very real danger that such programmes, with their emphasis on entrepreneurialism, together with some of the measures introduced by HM Treasury to encourage the formation of new businesses, will lead those interested in a life in commerce, or those who simply have no choice but to enter it, to believe that only those blessed with an entrepreneurial flair can succeed. Furthermore, that those not so blessed will believe that success in industry will be denied them.

But there is unquestionably a difference between the skill set displayed by the entrepreneur and the management skill set required to bring that entrepreneur's new product or service to market in a successful and sustainable fashion. Too often, in one person, these two skill sets are mutually exclusive but both are vitally necessary to a business for its success. As a consequence, a lack of entrepreneurial flair by an individual does not inhibit that individual from developing skills in management of a team, a department or a company.

It is to such individuals that the book is aimed, the intention being to provide some education to the readers aimed at showing how they can still develop, and achieve success, with the one business open to them – themselves!!

Why is such an education necessary or desirable?

To make comparisons between the inherent talents – be they entrepreneurial or managerial – of the American individual and his UK counterpart would have little validity, particularly in today's climate where many more entrepreneurs are being created on both sides of the Atlantic. But a recognition of the value of management, as distinct from entrepreneurship, and a willingness to reward those with management talent is still more advanced in the USA than in the UK. If the UK is to be a contender on the global stage, it must change its attitude and current practice to prevent the waste of energy and talent that exist within its ranks. The attitude of the USA is not altruistic but a recognition of the value of good managers and good disciplined management structures, to fully expoit their potential. The USA has Microsoft, Dell, Google – the list goes on. Where are the comparable UK enterprises?

The author feels that the climate in the UK to engage people in examining their role in industry is now better than ever, as it has become increasingly apparent to all that the 'job for life' regime is, to all intents and purposes, extinct. We've also seen some well-publicised manifestations of how *the British way of doing things is not adequate for the task of competing in today's global market*, and therefore it is a very high risk strategy indeed for a young employee just starting out on his career, to join one of the bastions of British commerce in the hope that they will still be there at retirement; the company itself might not be there. As a consequence, all employees need to take responsibility for their own development in a manner that is independent of their employer.

Marconi

We have seen Marconi, once a giant in the British electronics industry almost brought to its knees by bad management to the point where it cannot compete against global competitors, all of them foreign. Earlier another casualty of bad management was Ferranti, covered in Appendix 1 later in the book; a classic case of engineers whose technical wizardry could be recognised by being member of the company's Inventors Club yet, quite deliberately, be held in total ignorance of the financial significance or otherwise of their creativity.

Marks and Spencer

We have seen, and are still seeing, Marks and Spencer (M&S), make great efforts to regain its place as the country's leading retailer. Not long before it lost this illustrious position, the company blithely assumed it could clone its UK business in overseas ventures. Most of them closed before they were really established. On June 26 2005, Lord Tebbit, former Chairman of the Conservative Party, was asked on Radio 4's Today programme, to comment on the processes then being undertaken to find a leader for the party. He drew parallels between his party and their methods of appointing leaders, and the new management regime of M&S. He said that M&S had appointed 'apparatchiks' to manage the company and was still not focused on the market. Whether one agrees with his assessment of the new M&S management regime or not, it is almost certain that Lord Tebbit, given the party to which he belongs, would not have condemned M&S in such terms 10 years previously, such was the nation's collective faith in these household names. It illustrates graphically that, at last, there are questions being asked about the country's way of doing things, not least by people who hitherto would have assumed that the success gained in a less competitive era would be sustainable forever. The nation would have overlooked the fact that the successful founders of these companies were replaced by 'apparatchiks'. It can take, and has taken, years for the shortcomings of this methodology, to become apparent.

Vodafone

Vodafone, the mobile telephone company, in its early formative years found growth relatively easy to achieve when the industry was new and exciting and almost everybody over the age of 12 was a potential customer. Thus the company, in its attempts to become a global player, acquired many complementary companies and overseas companies. In 2006, Vodafone announced the biggest loss in British corporate history and claimed they had to put a realistic value on the companies they had acquired at an unrealistic price when the mobile telephone business was perceived as a licence to print money. It is difficult to escape the conclusion that hubris rather than prudent business management determined the business culture, particularly when one views the proliferation of very expensive professional sports sponsorship that Vodafone undertook. It could indicate yet another example of a company management being dazzled by the sheer excitement of the phenomenal income the company was enjoying in its early days rather than an objective assessment of the market realities. Another example of a company looking inward at its success, rather than outward at its market and its competition, real and potential? It is all too easy for any company during good times, when examining its strengths, weaknesses, opportunities and threats (SWOTS), to be selective about which of these criteria are going to be accorded significance.

Not all the signs are negative

In the retail sector, Tesco has set a pace for all of its competitors to match. But as soon as these competitors show signs of matching the Tesco performance, Tesco moves ahead with a new strategy for growth and tactics to match. The Post Office, long written off as a commercial 'basket case', has experienced a remarkable turn-around despite union opposition, and the turn-around has resulted in bonuses being paid to the rank and file workers as well as to the management; an excellent example of enlightened management responding to the imminence of the end of a monopoly together with a realisation that the company must first address the concerns of its customer base if it is to retain its revenue in the face of future competition. A noteworthy feature of the Post Office turn-around is the management's acceptance that everyone on the payroll goes to work for money, and the consequent bonuses have been voluntarily awarded and not extracted as a result of duress from union pressures. Mention should be made of British Airways that has also brought about a remarkable transformation in the face of long-standing opposition from entrenched trades union attitudes; another case of survival wrought by the threats from low-cost carriers such as Ryannair who, because of their relative newness, have not had to shake off the industrial relations baggage that burdened British Airways.

One relatively recent phenomena that has provided a very public education into the ways of business is the conversion of previously privately owned professional football (or soccer as it is called in the USA) clubs into publicly listed companies. The sport, created in the UK, has become a huge global business. In this transformation from privately owned plaything of parochial business men, to publicly listed enterprises with investors ranging from the professional investor to the fan attempting to own a piece of his beloved club, a whole host of business issues have been revealed. These issues, in turn, have provided a very clear, yet often vicarious, education in the ways of business to people who, in the normal course of events, would have shown and profess to have, no interest in business per se whatsoever. The soccer scene as a whole, when examining various facets, illustrates the tensions and conflicts inherent in most businesses, to an audience in a manner that captures the imagination of all; this 'all' runs the whole gamut from fan to team, to team management, to company management, to investors, to media, to government, to the public.

At the time of writing this book, an American, Mr Malcolm Glazer, had acquired the richest soccer club in the world, Manchester United. This acquisition will see the club that had become a publicly listed company return to its previous status of privately owned club; the first such return, although by no stretch of the imagination could Mr Glazer be described as parochial. As a result of this acquisition, the Government, fearful of the consequences of such a national institution as the professional soccer game falling into foreign hands, is considering what action, if any, it can take to prevent what it sees as a calamity.

The conflicts arising from this US acquisition could provide material for a book in its own right. This however, is not the purpose of allusion to it here. Different facets of the football (soccer) scene in general, and Mr Glazer's acquisition in particular, reveal a whole gamut of business issues. The conflict arising from the glamour of a sport versus the hard-headed approach to business has caused many casualties, perhaps the most prominent in the UK being the downfall of Leeds United. The conflict between demands of extremely highly paid workers, i.e players, who have no knowledge of, or regard for, a bottom line, and the club management; the conflict between the waywardness of extremely highly-paid players and the team manager who must instil a discipline if good results are to be achieved; the conflict between the team manager expected to produce results with a defined budget and the club management intent on producing acceptable results to its shareholders; the conflict between fans who believe they 'own' the club and the club directors (or owner in the case of Mr Glazer) who know they do. Quite apart from these considerations there is huge marketing potential in the sport and only relatively recently has this begun to be fully realised. Just recently one world-renowned footballer, David Beckham, who would not have been played in a particular game by the team coach, was included in the team on the orders of the club proprietor; the player's role as a marketing commodity and the resulting boost to income of the club business outstripped his value to the team as a player. It will be interesting to see how Beckham's worth is re-assessed following his being dropped from the England squad by the newly-appointed manager in post-Ericcson August 2006.

In July of 2004, the author of this book made a presentation to an audience of teenage schoolchildren; the purpose of the presentation and its content have been included as Appendix IV in this 2nd edition. Although largely fictional, the book illustrates the consequences for two clubs, Real Madrid and Manchester United, when the latter sold its star player, David Beckham to the former. The presentation showed how Manchester's income from sponsorship and merchandising could go down and that of Real Madrid could commensurately increase. Perhaps the presentation quite by accident was not so fictional, since the presentation was trying to make both a marketing point and a management point. In an article in the Sunday Times of September 2004, there was a quote, 'Manchester United had been persuaded, like Shakespeare's Othello, to throw away a pearl richer than all their tribe'. It further said, 'Beckham, the richest footballer alive, was a one-man global brand whose full money-making potential had yet to be tapped.' It is an illustration of the conflicts between a club as a football team and as a business. The conflicts between the team manager, Sir Alex Ferguson, and his star player, Beckham, have been well documented, but this is a graphic example of what can happen, and has happened here, when the personal friction between two very famous individuals transcends some very hard-headed business decisions that needed to be made. Ferguson, responsible for team selection, was allowed by management to dispense with the then captain of the England national side because ostensibly he, Ferguson, took exception to Beckham's glamorous lifestyle; the decision was purported to be unrelated to Beckham's playing ability. It is all the more surprising that club management allowed the team manager's prejudices to influence them to such an extent as to offload a very expensive 'piece of merchandise', given that the club that is arguably the most successful club in the world for marketing its image and its wares.

Returning to the Manchester United acquisition by Glazer, who would bet against him with his knowledge of the sporting scene in the USA, having yet another attempt at breaking into the world's largest untapped market for soccer, the USA, with the wealthiest club in the world. Already this market has been opened up by success in women's soccer and it can only be a matter of time before the man's game follows. If this comes to pass, it will yet again highlight, by comparison, the marketing imperatives observed by an American entrepreneur and those of his British counterparts. Because of its topicality and the illustrative education it provides, soccer provides a useful parable about business. Accordingly, from time to time throughout the book, there will be a return to this soccer scene as an illustration of different facets of the business world.

The 'British way'

However, although this book examines Britain's industrial and commercial culture, it is not dedicated to this examination nor is it the prime purpose of the book. This examination is included only to point out to individuals the dangers inherent in an instinctive belief that the 'British way' is the norm and that one must embrace this culture to succeed. The book is more concerned with illustrating to people engaged in Britain's industrial and commercial environment, that a good deal of this 'British way' is seriously flawed. That it is necessary for people working in this environment to develop their professional capability independently of the national culture and not to attempt to steep themselves in the culture as a way of making career progression. It is regrettably a fact that, despite many attempts to correct the imbalance, the worker in British industry and commerce is still less productive than his counterpart in many other countries. The author of this book suggests that it is not the British workers who are intrinsically less talented or less industrious than their counterparts, but that the culture mitigates against them achieving parity. Therefore if the workers are to achieve longevity in today's perilous workplace, they must undertake their own development for their own sake.

What is the evidence?

Is there any evidence to back up this assertion about the shortcomings of British industry and commerce? In July 2004, a BBC radio programme (BBC Radio 4, *Nice Work,* July 20 2004) examined British industrial and commercial productivity. The participants in the programme included a UK Professor of Organisation, an economics consultant from the USA, and people of other nationalities from different levels of management in a variety of organisations, some large some small. The programme coalesced into an examination of why, despite the presence of over a 100 business schools, British productivity still lags 15-20% behind continental Europe and even further behind the USA.

Evan Davies, economics editor of the BBC declared on the programme,

'On the whole, it's a bit of a mystery. We don't do that well when it comes to productivity.' Sadly, a year later Britain is still 30% less productive than France, despite the fact that France is a strict observer of the 35-hour week and Britain is not. Furthermore, Britain is 20% less productive than Germany, who despite its poor economy in the early part of the 21st century is still the largest exporter of Europe. In productivity terms, an OECD (Organisation for Economic Co-operation and Development) report (12/10/2005) ranks Britain 14th out of 30 OECD countries for gross domestic product per head and 15th for its rate of productivity growth. This despite Gordon Brown writing to the OECD in 1998 saying, *'Bridging Britain's productivity gap is the next national challenge.'*

An article in *The Times* (13/10/2005) suggests, *'Business productivity is hampered by unnecessary regulation, poor infrastructure and a poorly educated and underskilled workforce – all problems that the Government has recognised but not eradicated.'* But why should we look to the Government, any Government. The Thatcher government claimed to have freed up commerce from the unions and public utilities have been privatised. The Blair government has not reversed any of this new-found freedom and there have been countless tax incentives. Yet still the CBI wails at the Government.

This book contends that the problems are within industry itself; that the education necessary to improve the skill set of the workforce must also come from within industry. British industry needs to improve the motivation of its staff. It needs to discover the talent that lies in any workforce and nurture and develop the talent in the interest of the individual and ultimately the company. But companies can only do this when they change their current commercial culture – and this is a much bigger task.

A book written by three academics from the Royal Holloway College Management School in Surrey (*The Growth of Nations,* M Lewis, R Fitzgerald and C Harvey, Bristol Academic Press) speaks of 'Britain's relatively poor post-war performance' and draws comparisons with Japan's industrial success over the same period. In doing so, they seek to establish whether the differences have their origins in the different cultures of the two nations or in their institutional structures. The book does say, when speaking of the literature examining this phenomenon (p126), *'The culturist literature consists almost exclusively of the writings of historians or economic historians.'*

So there we have it. The perspective of academicians is used in both a radio programme and a learned book to analyse Britain's economic decline. The interest of both is the national economic performance and the factors giving rise to it. This book is written from a totally different perspective and its aims are much more modest than to suggest a solution to Britain's industrial woes. It is to illustrate that, from the perspective of one who has been employed in diverse cultures, particularly the UK and the USA, Britain's decline and lack of productivity is not a 'mystery' at all, to paraphrase Mr Davies. The business schools phenomenon is not a cause but a symptom of a much wider problem. When the link is made between graduates of over 100 business schools and poor productivity, the simplistic conclusion is that either the schools collectively are falling down on the job or the students are not up to the job etc. etc. etc.

Of course there will be some validity to this conclusion simply because the schools, being British based, will themselves inevitably be steeped to some extent in the British way of doing things. But such a conclusion quite naturally leads on to question the value of business schools and thence to find them wanting.

The author, who is not a business school graduate, nor does he have any links with business schools, does not subscribe to this view. Since this book by its very nature is attempting to correct the perceived shortfall in any form of commercial education to the thousands who enter industrial and commercial life, it would be contrary in the extreme to condemn those institutions and individuals devoted to correcting the shortfall. Therefore, the author would suggest that an education in the mechanics of business, whether it is in design, contracts, finance, human resources or marketing should be of benefit to the recipients, and their respective companies and ultimately the nation, particularly since the majority of people entering the workplace generally receive no education at all in such matters. But if the graduates of such schools enter into a culture that denies any form of individual creativity then they will be industrially impotent and their education nullified. Further, it is likely that in such a culture it will be not only the business school graduates that are 'punching below their weight' but all of their non-graduate colleagues as well, hence our poor national productivity performance.

Stopping the decline

Britain's decline is a direct result of the nation's history giving rise to an industrial culture, strong elements of which are still in evidence today. It is so deeply entrenched and inward-looking that even the long-term presence in the UK of American companies, such as IBM and Ford, seem not to have been adopted as role models that might have prevented the demise of say, the British national computer company, ICL, or that of the Rover car company to name but two, both of which have a comparable history in the UK with their American counterparts. The UK culture does not fully utilise the talents of individuals nor encourage the development of their talents. *In fact it is a culture that generally stifles individual creativity and as a result achieves lower productivity than could, and should, be the case if the collective talents of all individuals engaged in the enterprise were to be utilised.*

The purpose of this book

But this book has two purposes, neither of which is to solve Mr Davies' 'mystery', nor to illustrate some of the origins of the nation's industrial woes. Allusion to these is included merely to put the main purpose of the book into perspective.

The primary purpose is to point out to individuals in British industry and commerce how they can develop themselves despite the negative effects of British industrial culture. How they do not need to reflect the national scene when developing their own career.

A secondary purpose is of a more sociological nature. **Ageism** has become firmly entrenched of late in the British commercial arena and few people over the age of 55 can expect to be in full-time employment of any kind. It is extremely unlikely that any person joining a company upon leaving school or university can expect to be with that company at the current national retirement age of 65, even assuming that the company itself still exists. This ageism in the UK has, if anything, become more prevalent than in the USA, a country that has long held a 'hire and fire' reputation, often unjustified, around the world. The author would contend that ageism in Britain will have serious consequences in the short-term future but perversely may be of benefit to individuals in the longer term. It is undeniable that many people with outstanding mortgages, children in school or university, will face unemployment whilst still relatively young. Many of these people will have joined a company, done that which is expected of them, and then been made redundant in favour of those who are younger, more up-to-date with their knowledge of technology, and less expensive to remunerate.

The reason why ageism in Britain is more prevalent than in the USA is a direct consequence of the British society and the industrial culture mentioned earlier. In society, since the 2nd world war, we have seen the introduction and the increasing benefits of the welfare state. As a result, many of the support functions that well-established companies provided as employee benefits, i.e pensions, health care and so on, have been relinquished to the state. But with people having a longer expectation of lifespan, and with employment coming to an end earlier and earlier in an individual's life, the welfare state support is becoming unsustainable. More, and longer-term, demands for benefits from a system that has a narrower band of taxable earners to pay for it is simply not viable in its current form. So for the first time in two generations, the previously expected quasi-paternalism of an employer and the fall-back support of a welfare state will no longer be in place over the majority of what has customarily been an individual's working lifespan.

The USA does not have such an all-encompassing welfare state and an American employee does not look to his employer to provide the same degree of care that has been the norm in the British workplace; thus the American worker is accustomed to looking out for himself to a greater degree than his British counterpart; this is not to make a comparison between the talents or the industry of the two. Going forward, it will become ever more imperative that UK workers will also have to create for themselves a higher degree of self-dependence by undertaking a lifelong programme of self-development in order to extend, of their own volition, their contributory working life. By doing so, individuals can also ensure that, by adding to their skills throughout their lifetime, they will bring more valuable experience to their employers and will be less vulnerable to threats posed by later recruits who are merely younger and less expensive. Expressed another way, an employee employed for 20 years should aim, at the end of that term, to have 20 years experience, not 20 times one. Employees in the latter position are not only likely to be unemployed at the end of the 20 years but will be virtually unemployable – a situation that they have largely brought upon themselves. Since getting older is inevitable for all employees, this is a lesson for all to be aware of, and points to the need for an education for all to embark on as soon as possible in a working life.

This book aims to contribute to that education and comprises the author's collected observations, gathered over many years, of companies and departments in a number of countries but primarily in the UK and USA, and of managements and staff in those companies and departments. Unfortunately, if America is held up in the UK as an example to follow, it often evokes resentment, a latent anti-Americanism. Yet America is the most dynamic economy in the world and has long been so, and this dynamism shows no sign of abating. It is the role model that both the current Prime Minister, Tony Blair, and the Chancellor of the Exchequer, Gordon Brown, have admired and have tried without success to emulate using all manner of tax incentives. The book suggests later how these incentives are not the sole answer or even the most productive answer.

As has been said earlier, Britain still obstinately lags behind almost every other industrial country, including France, in terms of productivity. This despite the fact that compared to France, the UK economy is much more free to respond to market forces than France with its huge public sector employment. The author suggests that the fundamental cause of Britain's problem is that too often the aspirations of management in the professional environment is the same as that in the social environment. Professionally speaking, Britain 'worships false gods' in that the driving force behind the management of Britain's industrial scene is not the making of money, it is to seek a higher place on the company ladder as people are schooled to do in their social lives; the making of money thus almost becomes incidental.

Weaknesses and strengths

The book points out the weaknesses and strengths of observed company and departmental structures and behavioural patterns of people in them at various levels, and to make recommendations for the reader's personal development. Accordingly, the book includes details of how staff in various corporate disciplines such as sales, marketing, finance and human resources should function. How the staff are too often not properly focused on the task in hand, resulting in that task being carried out at less than maximum effectiveness. The book goes on to outline the functions of management at different levels and to include a comparison of a number of different companies in order to assist the reader to understand the different strategies and tactics employed by them and to make a judgment of them. Finally, there are some guidelines and procedures that should help the reader decide how to introduce some corporate disciplines, without which no company can be successful in the long term.

Of course, when making such observations and recommendations based on personal experience, it invites the criticism that the book is self-serving or self-promoting. If indeed, this is the perception in the eye of the reader, the author can only apologise because self-promotion is not intended. Before embarking on the task of writing this book, the author sought the views of various former colleagues, both peers and subordinates, and their overwhelming view was that unless the book reflected a personal chronicle of a lifetime's work, it would lack credibility. In mitigation, the author would say that his personal experiences have been moulded by observations of, and inputs from, many of the managers and peers with whom he came into contact during his professional life, and it is the task of any competent practitioner and manager to attempt to improve on the observed performance of such people and to avoid many of their pitfalls, whilst at the same time trying not to create others. It will be for the reader to judge to what extent the author has succeeded.

Introduction

Successful entrepreneurs and good managers are seldom one and the same. More often than not, they are spiritual opposites. So this book is not intended primarily for entrepreneurs, although some might find it useful when the first burst of customer enthusiasm for a brilliant new idea, or new product, or a less expensive solution for an existing idea or product, has passed. It is at this stage that an entrepreneur has to exercise other skills to take the business forward and keep it ahead of those coming along behind as, inevitably, they will. No, the book is about management – three forms of management, managing a business, managing other people but, above all, managing oneself.

In today's fiercely competitive world, some means of broadening an individual's appeal to a current or future employer becomes ever more necessary. No core skill learned at school or university, or in any other form of higher education, not even in the early days after entry into commerce or industry, will be enough in today's world to grant longevity to a career, the lifetime of which is constantly shrinking.

If he is to develop – and he must develop if he to survive longer than for the short term – he will need to do more than just carry out his allotted task without learning what part that allotted task plays in the overall scheme of things of his employer. The knowledge gained from this self-development will assist the individual to improve the manner in which he carries out his task. He will be able to be more efficient when he relates his own task to that of his peers and his management. It is such diligence to the task that separates him from others doing a similar task.

By the same token, some knowledge by the individual of the part played by his peer group in his own discipline, as well as in other disciplines, will make the individual concerned, for his own benefit, more commercially aware. A concomitant part of this process will be to understand the value judgement placed by the employer on the individual's activities.

Such an education about how to educate oneself within a corporate structure is rarely if ever taught in school where, metaphorically speaking, the focus is very much on obtaining qualifications for tomorrow's job, to the exclusion of what happens the day after tomorrow. Sadly, it is also true that corporations themselves too rarely undertake the task of educating their staff such as to increase their value to themselves and hence to the corporation.

Making money

The primary aim of business does not change; it is to make money and ultimately it has no other purpose. It never has had any other ultimate purpose. Such a bald statement is anathema or vulgar to many observers but there is no other sustainable means of judging a company's worth or success. Changes in the way business is conducted do not erode or diminish in any way this primary goal and all participants in the business are engaged directly or indirectly in achieving that one ultimate goal

Returning to the soccer metaphor referred to in the preface to the book, the only reason for playing soccer is to score goals. The design of boots, the design of playing kit, the weight and manufacture of the ball, even occasional rule changes over the years do not change the fundamental purpose of the game. A professional footballer knows that the rewards for his team for scoring more goals than the other teams in a league can be immense, but the consequences for doing otherwise can be nothing short of financially catastrophic; therefore the soccer player must constantly strive to improve his and/or his team's goal-scoring technique. Scoring goals in soccer and making money in business are analogous and all people in any given business should be very aware of their individual part in this process. To not do so is to render oneself very vulnerable indeed. The player who does not contribute to the process of scoring goals is dropped from the team.

Although not a game, it is apposite to draw the parallel between changes in the soccer world and those within industry and commerce. Techniques for bringing products and services to market are changing at an ever-increasing rate. Computer and telecommunications technology, more sophisticated design and production techniques, and the advent of the Internet can only accelerate the process. Products such as cars, computers and white goods will, sooner rather than later, be built to customer specifications generated on the Internet. Production times from concept to market readiness will be slashed from months or weeks, even days. But the ultimate purpose remains the same and individuals will ultimately be judged on their personal contribution and the mental energy they have brought to the task. Whatever new processes are employed nothing, absolutely nothing, will replace the power or value of thought – thought about products, about markets, about competition, about people and – about oneself. Thus equally irreplaceable for the foreseeable future will be the need by every individual to embark on a programme of continual self-education in order to develop an ability to earn a living for as long as possible and to benefit from this rapidly changing industrial world and not to be an early victim of it.

Until relatively recently, an individual in the UK could join a company, develop within the company, or more often not develop, and look forward to a reasonably comfortable retirement. Furthermore, there was always some form of safety net if things didn't quite work out as planned. Now, in this new global commercial world, it is not only unlikely that this scenario will obtain on this island for much longer simply because it cannot be afforded, but the British worker might find himself working for foreign employers who do not have their origins in such a comfortable environment and therefore see no reason to adopt it; thus the worker will have to be more and more self-reliant in a manner in which workers two generations hence will have had no experience. Furthermore, he will typically have to do so in an environment that not only does not encourage individual contributions but passively, and sometimes actively, discourages it.

The United Kingdom has shown in many fields – engineering technology, medicine, physics, aeronautics and many others – that it is able to match its 'brain-power' at the creative level with the best of other nations. What it has failed to do is to exploit this capability, and the opportunities presented, commercially. Whatever success has been achieved has been limited for the most part, to the national scene. With few exceptions, the UK national enterprise has failed to cover the globe in ways evidenced by Microsoft, Dell, Fedex, Avis and the Japanese automobile and electronics companies, and more recently the founders of Google. Can we envisage the UK producing an entrepreneur/technical wizard of the Steve Jobs ilk? Jobs has been making technical breakthroughs and funding world-wide businesses with which to bring them to market since the 1970s and is still doing so to this day. In a speech to Stanford University students in the summer of 2005 (*Sunday Times* 25 September 2005), Jobs was still concentrating on how he could technically stay ahead of competition, current and future. Among the companies aiming to frustrate his ambitions is Nokia from Finland, not historically a country known for its technological breakthroughs.

It is difficult to escape the conclusion that there is a direct correlation between the inward-looking business climate that obtains in the UK and the inhibitions on the exercising of individual talent within that climate. Even Vodafone, a successful company, depends largely on foreign-sourced equipment to provide its service. Of course, in the year 2006, the UK economy is booming and is said to be the envy of other countries in the European Union. But the euphoria that this gives rise to cannot disguise the fact that the 'product-producing' sector of the British economy is in serious decline. Recently, individuals in the defunct Rover car group were told by a government minister that they could find new jobs in a supermarket. Thus, at an individual level, it matters not whether the economy is buoyant or ailing; the same degree of self-development is called for if that individual is to be responsible for his own progress. There is no comfort zone.

The importance of self-development

As has been stated earlier, this book is aimed at providing some self-development assistance to the individual. However, an important step in this process is to understand the commercial methods of companies in a number of countries, including the UK in order that the individual can best decide how to develop himself as a global one-man business, albeit on a payroll. In other words to develop himself in such a manner as to make himself of increasing value over time, to an employer whose origins, and consequently whose cultural and commercial values may be located in any country in the world. It is regrettably a fact that a study exclusively of British companies or long-term employment by a British company will not provide this self-development opportunity. This book aims to provide a fundamental lesson in business by examining individual disciplines, some or all of which exist in almost all companies.

In order to better understand the need for such self-development and the possible inhibitions on doing so, an examination of Britain's industrial ills is included. This examination is not from an academician's, or economist's standpoint but from the standpoint of one who has worked in industry in the UK, North America and Asia at all levels from the factory floor to the boardroom. This, from a very practical standpoint, enables comparisons to be drawn between practices in the UK and other more successful industrial nations that seem to surround us, in order that we can examine ways by which to better exploit native skills in our own financial interest.

Although the United Kingdom gave birth to the jet engine, the computer, radar and 'brain and whole body' scanners, it failed to bring any of these products to market in any long-term, dominant manner. Britain once had thriving indigenous manufacturing industries, building world-beating automobiles, aircraft, motorcycles and televisions. Today, these products are either imported or manufactured under licence for foreign employers, by the same British workers who were once considered so unmanageable. In the 'softer' manufacturing environments, such as computer software or design, thousands of highly skilled young professionals are enjoying stimulating careers with overseas multinationals. Why have they proved such an invaluable asset to these foreign company owners? *Why can't Britain be the origin of such companies, the sponsor of such promising young people?* It is beyond doubt that Britain can invent and create and manufacture. But even companies founded by today's younger British entrepreneurs seldom seem to have the aptitude to become world class. James Dyson, the home appliances entrepreneur, and Sir Richard Branson of Virgin fame appear to be two individual exceptions that prove the rule. Even the latter of these two has been quoted as asking the question, *'How can we be global in our business aspirations when we are so parochial in our social aspirations?'*

Often the government of the day expresses gratitude for, and pays a high price for, inward investment of companies that manufacture and market the goods that the nation previously made for itself. But how clearly is it realised that these overseas companies repatriate all allowable profits? Should it not be of concern that, having spent considerable sums of taxpayers' money to attract inward investment, the government is powerless to prevent these foreign companies shutting down newly opened facilities, or not going ahead with planned expansions, because of external policy decisions? Is it not the economics of the madhouse to pay, as was the case in the not too distant past, vast sums of British taxpayers' money to German car companies or Norwegian shipping companies in order to protect British 'jobs', when at any time those 'jobs' may be used as a bargaining chip to extract even more money from the taxpayer? Is not enough being paid already for the goods these companies make? These 'jobs' are going to people who were not originally the employees of German or Norwegian companies, but of British companies, whose poor management has presided over their decline.

Regrettably, British taxpayers' money is no guarantee of long-term employment either. The employees, indeed the companies themselves, remain vulnerable to market forces way beyond their control. It is very

Introduction

possible that, for instance, a Scottish shipyard can be under the threat of closure, not because of a problem in Scotland, or indeed, a problem in shipbuilding, but because some other activity within the portfolio of its Norwegian conglomerate owners, but closer to its core business, requires that the owners consolidate around it. No company can resist market forces; but it can improve its management techniques and, if it is to fail, do so knowing that everyone in the company put their shoulders to the wheel and success was beyond them. Any other solution causes untold frustration, disappointment and bitterness; not to mention the loss of huge sums of taxpayers' money.

Governments of all political hues devise tax incentive schemes for young entrepreneurs, but unless these targeted people understand the fundamentals of organising for growth, incentives will be no more effective than all the other financial measures introduced over the years to stimulate a 'product-producing' industrial base. Economists and political pundits recognise this conundrum. Most of them call for the problem to be solved – and rightly so. However, recognition of symptoms does not reveal the origin of the problem nor suggest a cure.

The author contends that an understanding from within, of the structural problems of British industry, allied to an intuitive understanding of Britain's social culture will provide the key to the best solution for our ailing industrial base. However, such understandings will only point to a solution when comparisons are made with counterpart criteria in other countries, more successful from an industrial standpoint. It is the traditional, inward looking modus operandi of most of British industry, together with its inability to separate industrial structures and culture from those that determine the social structure of the country that has brought about its demise, particularly in the era since world-war II. To return to the soccer metaphor, when a footballer goes on to the pitch to play soccer, he abides by a set of rules appertaining to the game. When he comes off the pitch he leads his social life by a totally different set of rules, i.e. those of society at large. In industry there is but one set of rules that governs the lives of those involved. People at all levels in British industry seek to improve their position in 'the society' to the detriment of actually attempting to compete with others within the same industry but outside of 'the society'. Only when people in industry 'go on the pitch to score goals' rather than to just 'move around the pitch' will industry begin to catch up with foreign competitors.

Teaching the young

In reality, the only people we can expect to be motivated to change things in the interests of their own careers and their financial future are the young. Those who have already climbed some way up the corporate ladder can hardly be expected to kick the ladder away. But the young today need to be acquainted with a different method before they become entrenched in the traditional British way of doing things. This is particularly true as the government moves to take less part in the financial welfare of individuals. I believe Britain can produce a Bill Gates, a Steve Jobs (founder of Apple), a Michael Dell (founder of Dell) – but it needs to examine why the American system produces managers that can globally develop companies founded by these entrepreneurs and the British system does not. Certainly, Britain produces well-known entrepreneurs but few of them are world class. Richard Branson and James Dyson are two exceptions that prove the rule. Usually, as far as our British success stories are concerned, entrepreneurs they may be, managers of worldwide businesses they very rarely become; and they have no indigenously trained capable managers to take the business forward.

The USA produces not only renowned entrepreneurs but entrepreneurs who become profit-orientated managers of major businesses. Despite its pronounced emphasis on high-tech, since when has Britain produced computer industry stalwarts as Gates, Dell, Jobs, or even a Fred Smith, founder of low-tech Fedex? It should be borne in mind that entrepreneurs are usually born with a particular talent and in an era that enables them to exploit that talent in their own interest. They often enjoy both fame and fortune, not only because of their talent and their luck and their sense of timing, nor even because of the effort they have obviously expended. They attract attention as much because, relative to the entire working population, they are in a minority. On the other hand, the market for good managers, or even for good experienced practitioners of a given discipline, is huge. Almost all of the entrepreneurs mentioned above have been able at some stage in their company's development to hand on the reins of running and developing the company to others in their employ who are also commercially-aware, profit-orientated individuals. It is regrettable but true that typical British companies, because of the social dimension to their management thinking, do not produce naturally such commercially aware managers.

Introduction

By way of education, Britain's young people in industry need to learn those truths their American counterparts have instilled in them as part of their culture. Business is about offering, and supporting competitive products to a customer, at a price he is prepared to pay. Further, it is to conduct this business in a financially disciplined manner so that the complete enterprise runs at a profit. This is the fundamental difference between the UK worker and his American counterpart. This, contrary to the opinions of many, is saying nothing about the relative talents of the individuals from the two countries. Regardless of whether the US individual is capable of responding to market forces or competitive pressures, he is aware of those forces and pressures. The UK individual, on the other hand, is likely to be insulated from these same forces to such an extent that he is not only unaware of their existence, he is positively discouraged from knowing they exist. He is more likely to have instilled in him an unquestioning faith in his management, who are equally likely to be out of touch with market forces. Remember, the senior executive is also primarily concerned with his own position in the company hierarchy. Witness Marks and Spencer as a prime example of a once powerful company so out of touch with their core market that for a long time they were overtaken by much more agile competitors.

It is of crucial importance that everybody in business today – at whatever level – must appreciate the fundamental relationship between form and function; between making things that not only work well, but which have an eager and sustainable market. Only when British industry fully understands that each and every component part of business – product design, development and support, marketing, selling, customer liaison – must relate to the market place and not to its own internal processes, will it realise its full potential and achieve true greatness alongside other nations. Similarly, individuals within a company must understand that they too have a responsibility for looking out at the market in order to understand how their peers in competitive companies are behaving. It is this acceptance of his own responsibility in this process that will enhance his value to his current employer. Furthermore, this increase in his own worth will make him more attractive to an alternative, perhaps competitive employer, should he find his ambitions thwarted. He owes it to himself to seek rewards for the extra effort expended. It is this self-developing experience that can be the difference between having a job – and having a career.

There is no question that the UK workforce possesses the talent.

Unfortunately for the UK it is too often foreign companies that allows this talent to flourish. In an ideal commercial world this talent would be released in the UK's own national financial interest. In this fast-moving world no individual can afford to wait until this ideal world obtains. He must make a priority of developing his own potential in his own career and financial interest. If he cannot achieve recognition for this increase in his worth, he owes to himself to move on and gain recognition for it elsewhere. Better that than to become professionally institutionalised.

The purpose of this book is to spell out some of the steps, some of the thought processes that will assist in this self-development process within a product team, a corporate hierarchy, or in a commercially competitive international arena. It would be a bonus if the executives in some company or companies adopted some elements of the book as a way of breaking out of the traditional British way of doing things such as to compete with the best of foreign companies in this globalised business world. The contents of the book are drawn from actual practical experiences of working at a senior level in operations in a variety of cultures, British, American and Asian.

It is appropriate here for the author to offer an apologetic word on the subject of pronouns. In today's commercial world there are numerous women making their way to the top in industry. The author hopes that they – and you – will not take offence at the consistent use of the masculine pronoun, 'he'. It is intended merely as a literary convenience, not as a social comment.

PART 1

OUR INDUSTRIAL HERITAGE: AN INSIDER'S VIEW

1

'Them' and 'Us'

It is regrettably a fact that it is often only by working overseas for foreign companies that the British worker develops an awareness of how little the worker in the UK is prepared during his formative years for life in the commercial world. Culturally the worker appears to have accepted that it is up to 'them' to bring a job to 'us'. It is up to 'them' to ensure 'we' keep it and it is 'their' fault if we lose it ... Since this society is one where, historically, one privileged sector of society was educated to lead and manage, without necessarily having the ability to do either, this passive acceptance is hardly surprising. Unfortunately, this does not instil in the worker a feeling that he can fulfil his own potential, so too few try. As a result, a tenacious, aggressive will to win is sadly lacking. By the same token, those who have traditionally accepted their right by birth or privileged education to inhabit the upper echelons of society and commerce have not had to compete to get there or to stay there. Both attitudes have led to a lack of competitiveness. To paraphrase, the UK seems indeed, to be two societies separated by a common history. Although these boundaries have become less distinct of late, large elements of the cultural inheritance are still in place.

Since commercial competition often comes from foreign companies, it is hardly surprising that we are ill-equipped to compete with external forces such as the Americans, the Japanese and the Germans. You may ask, why does the author include the Germans, who have had their own troubles of late? Many years ago, when Germany was the industrial giant of Europe, I managed a German computer sales office for Rank Xerox. There, I met a German manager named Herr Droge. Something this gentleman said all those years ago left a marked impression on me. When asked, *'Why you? Why are the Germans so successful? (as indeed they have been for most of the period since World War II) You work no harder, you are no brighter, you are no more creative, yet you are more successful and wealthier than we British.'*

His reply was intriguing, and in many ways inspired some of the later comments in this book. *'When Germany and Britain entered the 2nd world war, we both drew our officers from the well-educated higher echelons of society. Germany emerged from the war as losers and Britain was deemed a winner. Consequently, our whole previous social structure disintegrated and we had to re-construct it as a meritocracy. Britain on the other hand, because its structure was perceived as having served it well, felt no compulsion or drive to change. This means that your social/industrial society has effectively stood still for many years and looks set to continue to do so for many years to come. It will be a long time before there will be another event or set of circumstances that will bring you face to face with the need for change in order to compete.'*

It is difficult not to see the truth of this observation when, even today, a half century later, foreign companies dominate the market for almost every market sector. UK economic commentators draw a peculiar comfort from the recent economic woes of Germany yet it is difficult to gainsay that Germany still produces world-class products in almost all sectors. Yet despite these economic problems, Britain remains 20% less productive than the Germans who remain the largest exporter in Europe. It is likely to still be doing so when it brings some long-overdue viability to its social welfare system. It is profoundly frustrating to see a nation with creativity, wit and energy, the equal of any nation, lose out to more aggressive foreign competitors.

Indeed, it leads to many of British professionals being employed by these very competitors where it is felt that only then can progress be made on merit, even if it does mean sometimes sacrificing 'Britishness' in favour of the cultural mannerisms and conversational idioms of foreign employers. This is preferable to trying to observe all the British social norms in the conduct of a professional life. Nevertheless, this choice is initially accompanied by a faint feeling of regret. This is not typical xenophobia but is an expression of frustration at seeing a nation's talented people not reaching their undoubted potential; or, very frequently, seeing this talent being used to aid the profitability of overseas employers.

Where the wealth is

There is little question that the wealth of the 21st century will principally belong, not to the countries with vast natural resources, but to those with brain power and the ability to exploit it. Manifestations of this phenomenon can already be seen in Japan and Singapore and the changing face of Hong Kong; China and India are taking their place among nations who do not see their future solely in terms of being the factory for the West.

Britain has a wealth of natural talent and has proved it for decades, but it has yet, in its own national interest, to realise fully this talent, particularly in a global sense. A former President of the Irish Republic, when asked on BBC radio, to explain her country's relatively recent economic success, said perceptively: *'We have set about removing the inhibitors of the natural expression of our talents'*. The United Kingdom must do the same! In the same way that rich industrialised nations exploit third world natural resources, so Britain, unless it too removes the natural inhibitors, will allow its natural resource of inventive brainpower, equal to that of any other country in the world, to be exploited by employers in those countries commercially smarter and more agile. Quite apart from its indigenous cultural inhibitors, Britain is part of Europe and as such is part of a society that *'suffers a number of discontinuities in the path from lab bench to profitable multinational, particularly in getting academia to work with industry, and in growing medium-sized enterprises into global businesses.'* (IEE Review, September 2005).

As it naturally looks to its traditional institutions to govern, Britain – and with devolution, England – is fast becoming the last outpost of the British empire, allowing itself to be increasingly economically colonised by many foreign companies whose own markets we once led. Assisting in the process is its own native wealth, employed by these same foreign companies. There are many notable economists and commentators who would expound the view that, as long as individuals and institutions can invest in these overseas companies, national ownership of these sources of product wealth is really of no importance. Most foreign-based companies do not subscribe to this view with regard to where profits ultimately come to rest. The author would suggest that the bulk of the profit from Britain's most precious resource should stay here. The nation can come again, in fact it must do so if it is to sustain its current standard of living.

Resources

Mineral based natural resources are not renewable; the natural resource, native creativity, wit and intelligence, is constantly renewable. In the new Millennium, Britain should exploit it commercially in its own national interest. If political influence is directly proportional to indigenous economic wealth, then Britain's influence in the world will be immensely increased if the intellectual strength of the nation is allied directly to its economic success. Tony Blair, Prime Minister, once stated that: *'We do not have an Empire, we do not have natural resources, but we do have knowledge, and this is the future.'* But it is a fact that *'Europe won't pay for the knowledge economy'* (IEE Review, September 2005), and Britain as part of Europe, is also falling behind in spending on R&D to bring new ideas to market. As a consequence it is difficult to escape the conclusion that British companies, with their management methods still for the most part those of the 19th century, will fall even further behind American companies and will, in the not too distant future fall behind the emerging Asian countries such as India, Japan and China whose percentage R&D spend is increasing year on year. Britain must grow a new breed of manager and each individual must embrace this change if they are to stay abreast of the demands of the 21st century.

Of course, there are those who would point to some of the problems that Germany, as an industrial society, has run into in the 1990s. Many economists have compared Germany's ills with the UK's recent economic success to draw favourable conclusions for the way the UK conducts its economy. Although not an economist, I would contend that an economist's view is too single-dimensioned and is statistically determined. Therefore the economist view does not satisfactorily explain the difference of living standards between Germany and the UK over many years following the 2nd world war, in fact up to the time immediately prior to German re-unification. Any frequent visitor to Western Germany cannot fail to see their higher standard of living. All the standard arguments about the assistance from the 'Marshall plan' are trotted out and may be, indeed, valid. However, it is undeniable that populations around the world have looked upon the ownership of a Mercedes or a BMW car or motorcycle, a Neff or a Bosch domestic appliance as a worthy status symbol. Conversely the UK's own flagship car, the Rover, built by British workers, only became popular – and profitable – after BMW bought the company – although closed down in

2006 with ongoing protracted discussions about possible Chinese ownership. As recently as March 1998, the company building Rolls Royce, the most prestigious cars in the world, designed by the British, hand-built by British craftsmen, and managed by the British for the best part of a century, has been bought – by Volkswagen, that once cheap-and-cheerful symbol of the German post-war economic 'miracle'.

Since British design and craftsmanship made these cars the most coveted status symbol in the world, with a name that is adjectivally synonymous with quality, it can only be inadequate management at Rolls Royce that has brought the company to this sorry state. There is no other excuse. Certainly, there is no God-given right for the Germans to have built Volkswagen, BMW and Mercedes into powerful companies with world wide markets, while our own Rover, Jaguar and Rolls Royce have been unable to sustain their once-formidable position, and have all been sold to overseas manufacturers, two of them German. There has to be a reason.

Trade unions – cause or scapegoat?

Is it treasonable to suggest that some of the timeworn utterances of British trade union leaders, bemoaning UK management practices and lack of investment, may, in retrospect, have been accurate? Will Hutton in his book, *The State We're In,* points out the dangers of using interest rates as the sole means of controlling, and presumably measuring, the worth of, the economy. It brings: *'...the danger of Britain becoming locked into a stagnant equilibrium of low investment, low growth and low skills.'* Surely, evidence that this is the way UK plc has operated for years is provided by the observation of the Vice President of Production for Ford Motor Co., shortly after Ford took over Jaguar cars. He stated that, in his career, he had never before seen such a 'Dickensian' factory as that building Jaguars in England. The workers may have built the cars, but they can hardly be held responsible for the condition of the production plant; it can only be laid at the door of poor management

The unions and their perceived responsibility for Britain's industrial decline arises from an instinctive reaction to UK management. Even today, deeply entrenched 'them' and 'us' working practices still exist to the exclusion of how the company needs to respond to competitive events in the market place. The more extreme manifestations of trade unionism have, on occasions, been inexcusable, but that is a far cry from holding them totally responsible for the nation's industrial decline.

Even now, in the 21st century, debates concerning the management and workers are heard as if they were two completely alien entities instead of a group of people that should be working together to beat the competition, foreign and domestic. It is not a cliché, but a fact that the most valuable commodity any company has is its workforce, and they are treated as an expendable commodity to the peril of the company. Undeniably, it is a fact that, in the more technically orientated industries, it is not unusual for 80 per cent of a company's overheads to be staff costs.

Knowledge workers

In any product-producing company, there is a large proportion of 'knowledge workers'. In most British companies, including often those that consider themselves to be high-tech, this knowledge is rarely used, meaningfully, in the actual management of the company. Furthermore, if the company is not doing too well, a lay-off is an easy way to cut costs and preserve profitability. When this happens the press applauds, the shareholders are happy and the Board saves its skin. Unfortunately, with this lay-off goes a good deal of the knowledge base and, perhaps more importantly, the co-operation of the remaining staff. The willingness of these people to believe any reassuring utterances about the future is seriously eroded, and with it the chances of true company success. There are other ways of behaviour and they must be explored. Of course, drastic change in technology or in the demands of the market place can sometimes make staff reductions inevitable, but it should not be restricted to 'us', the management, dismissing 'them', the workers.

Such a statement is not of a political nature but is merely pointing out that properly managed, properly motivated and better informed British workers at any level, working in a well-ordered company structure, are as good as their foreign counterparts. Conversely, treat that member of the workforce as someone incapable of adding two and two without supervision and he will respond appropriately. A serious side-effect of such treatment is that the British worker at both artisan and professional level is so conditioned by this management approach that any attempt to practice enlightened management is viewed by the worker with deeply ingrained suspicion. The task at hand becomes twice as difficult – sometimes impossible.

Putting a figure on it, most people in the UK are capable, with intelligent management, of raising their potential by some 30 per cent. Currently, American manufacturing workers are 60 per cent more productive than those in Britain. The British also trail significantly behind the French, Germans and Japanese in productivity. One does not have to be an economist to judge what a 30% improvement would do to the national economy. It is not overstating to say that an improvement in Britain's industrial performance is the only way to truly afford and sustain its standard of living. Furthermore, that improvement can only be brought about by a fundamental change in management attitudes and practices. All the share manipulation in the world is never going to do it. The nation has a wealth of talent and those in power with this deeply entrenched 'British' way of doing things must either release that talent, or be forced to do so by those with the talent. This new talent must, in turn, be enlightened if it is not to emulate the mistakes of their forbears simply because they have no other example to follow. The alternative is a slow decline and a continuation of the economic colonisation of Britain that has already begun.

In one quite substantial company known to the author, the CEO would personally call all the staff together, to what were called 'Awareness Days' at various locations around the world, and spell out the realities of their business. They were told there were three priorities: to give the shareholders a return on their investment, to keep the staff employed; and to increase their income. However that might be at odds with the order of priorities as perceived by the staff, it had to be order that the company would work to. To have stated it any other way would have been dishonest, and would not be treating the staff as adults. The shareholders had to be reassured that their investment in the company was a wise one. The company's growth and profit objectives cannot be achieved without staff. When these objectives are achieved – and only then – could everyone employed earn a share of the company's financial rewards. To demonstrate the point at these 'Awareness Days', the CEO would display company revenues and those of the major competitors. Similarly company profits and those of the competitors were shown, as well as costs, discipline by discipline, alongside the same competitors. Thus, every member of the staff, from office junior to director, could see what their company were up against and what each of them had to do in order to be competitive. Nobody had to be a financial genius to understand, it was just common sense; and, since no former management had ever taken the staff into their confidence in this way, it was very much appreciated. Recently, Jack Welch, former President of GE, the huge American engineering conglomerate, made exactly this point on the BBC Today programme (20 September 2005). He called for much more candour from management to the entire staff.

How can any management expect the staff to assist in achieving goals and overcoming obstacles if they do not know what the goals and obstacles are? To return to the professional soccer metaphor, the players train for a week to play for 90 minutes. Team strategy and tactics are examined and refined. Managers, coaches etc. are all involved and the players know exactly what is expected of them. They may not achieve it because the opposition is being similarly briefed but, without such methods, the team stands little chance of success. This approach can be adopted by any person responsible for managing staff. Any person too afraid of the personal ambitions and aspirations of his staff, to acquaint them with the realities of what is to be achieved, and the difficulties of so doing, should not be in charge of staff at all. All too often, one witnesses so many executives in British companies who seem to believe that relating directly to their staff is a sign of managerial weakness – it appears to make them feel more managerial to distance themselves.

The challenges of the global market place

As the world business community becomes more global, there has been some improvement in the commercial education of the British workforce. But the progress is much too slow, and has still not permeated sufficiently deeply into British society to tap the wealth of talent that resides there. An argument could be made in favour of Britain's membership of the EU on industrial and commercial grounds alone because many of the revered institutions of the United Kingdom, founded and developed during the latter part of the 19th century, were better suited to a society where the mass of the population accepted the status quo, and where the United Kingdom held dominion over three quarters of the world. Now, without a magnifying glass, one would have a problem locating that industrial sphere of influence on a globe of the world of less than 20 inches in diameter.

Nevertheless, there are many people in positions of power who have a vested interest in maintaining the status quo and who will resist change from within. Consequently, such influences can only come from outside, and they are doing so. Influences from outside, good or bad, such as globalisation plus business ownership from USA, Japan and the Far East, together with membership of the EU, will inevitably compel the nation to re-examine its place in the world and re-construct its institutions to match. In other words, there seems little point in changing, either by appointment or election, the people who manage the system when it is the system itself that needs examination and modernisation. Britain will be unable to sustain the existing commercial regime in the face of all the turbulence. However, it is still true that unless the workforce, and particularly the young workforce, understands the drivers behind the success of other nations around the world, then Britain's commercial infrastructure is as likely, indeed more likely, to be swept aside by the changes as it is to benefit from them.

Hope for the future

There is little of a tangible nature to confirm the view of many of the management and academic community that today's young are not the equal of their predecessors. They are less deferential then hitherto, they display wit and creativity and they are less willing to be intimidated by the conservatism of their elders. They live life at a pace undreamed of twenty or thirty years ago. Their zest in the creative worlds of music, the arts, journalism, fashion sets the pace for all of society. There is little to suggest that the young who enter industry today, particularly those who enter the high-tech world, are any less energetic or resourceful or creative. There's much more evidence of their striving to gain qualifications at GCSE level, at 'A' level, at graduate level and with occupational courses. The percentage of the young aspiring to be qualified is much greater than those of previous generations. They deserve better recognition from many self-appointed judges of their efforts than they currently receive. If the energy of the young is released and encouraged, instead of being denigrated and suppressed, then everyone, the young and the not-so young, will stay energetic and active longer.

There is little substantial evidence to confirm the view of many of the management and academic community that today's young are not the equal of their predecessors.

However there should be a concern for the young that business as practised, as opposed to that taught increasingly in colleges and universities, is still conditioned by the structure of a society cast in concrete for generations. As a result, many embryonic businesses of every type fail when the first spurt of creativity has run its course. Furthermore, many long-established businesses will not undertake the continuous process of renewal that is vital in today's global market place. This leads to many of those who choose to enter industry finding their initial zest gradually worn down by the grind of toiling in organisations, buried in bureaucracy, that allow no room for creativity to flourish. Again, the nation cannot afford for this to happen. But individuals need to take charge of their own lives, and not depend on an organisation to nurture, to recognise and to reward their talent. They need to have a better reason to get up in the morning than to face another day in an unyielding organisation where their creativity is subjugated to the unrewarding process of share price manipulation. Climbing a corporate ladder in such an organisation is the most soul-destroying, boring occupation there is, and can often be the cause of widespread premature ageing.

Being in business, whether as a proprietor, or as an employee, should be, and can be, exciting – and fun.

PART 2

BRITAIN – A PROFIT 'PARK AND RIDE' FOR OVERSEAS INVESTORS?

2

'Education, Education, Education' – But Will It Do the Trick?

The title of this chapter is deliberately provocative in order to draw attention to the dangers that confront the nation. Furthermore, it highlights two critical aspects of that danger. Foreign companies see a huge UK market to be exploited at the expense of less agile indigenous companies and the education is still provided within an out-dated commercial structure. There must be a sea change in the former if the latter is to be fully effective. There can be no other conclusion drawn from a close examination of British and American companies if the examination is allied to an observation of the social mores of both societies.

Many academic and media commentators and observers will proffer forensically constructed arguments for the national decline. Will Hutton, in his seminal book *The State We're In*, provides just such an excellent intellectual analysis. There are many such prognoses, but the common thread tends to confirm the view that Britain suffers from an historical inevitability that cannot be changed or reversed. That the country is victim to a natural evolution that means Britain has had its day, and it is now time for other countries to take a leading role. Allowed to prevail, this lack of a 'can-do' attitude will deny a huge proportion of the nation's young people, with formidable talent, the chance to achieve their potential. Even more serious, it denies these same young people the opportunity to contribute to a far more prosperous nation than is the case today. More and more there is talk of the 'tiger' economies and their quite natural progression to industrial prominence. The 'can do' attitude permeates countries such as Japan, Korea, Singapore, Malaysia, Hong Kong and more recently India and China and, of course, the United States. It is largely moribund here in the United Kingdom.

Education, Education, Education

The peoples in Singapore, Hong Kong, Malaysia, Korea and India, among others, display a hunger for success, for knowledge and the justified pride in national progress. **That it is lacking in the UK is a direct result of the management culture of the nation.** Instead of emulating the best of their practices, more comfort is drawn from news that these countries stumble on occasions, on their way to economic and industrial success. Tony Blair, British Prime Minister, and Bill Clinton, former President of the United States, have both declared 'education, education, education' as top of the priorities for their respective nations – and rightly so. However, if both are successful in their goals, the results for each nation will be different. Unless Britain examines, and is prepared to drastically change, its view of its internal institutions, that in turn reflects society's view of who is, and who is not, meritorious, then a better education, i.e better literacy and better numeracy, will not of itself, make us a more competitive nation, as Mr Blair assumes it will. Mr Clinton's exhortations on the other hand, are aimed at improving education in an already existing vibrant commercial structure.

The pressures to make high grades is enormous, on all levels of education in the USA, from primary school to university. Students at all levels are conditioned to believe that only by acquiring these grades will they enjoy a succesful career in industry or commerce.

Although the UK institutions and higher educational establishments are attempting to broaden their educational programmes in the commercial arena, they still cannot shake off their historical, elitist academic approach. They appear to have difficulties in measuring, and giving credit and recognition to those individuals whose talents do not fit some pre-determined criteria. Conversely too much credit, in the form of positions in the professional pecking order, is given to individuals whose talents are often limited to excelling in meeting the criteria. Industry for its part seems unable to metaphorically stand aside from itself in order to recognise that when comparing itself to foreign competitors, the problems of British commerce are more cultural than educational.

Britain is a nation whose creativity and inventiveness is beyond question. But unless that talent is turned into economic success, the decline must continue. Not so long ago, all of Britain's industry was indigenous and there was no outside example from whom the nation could learn. Now, success of companies and industries from other countries permeates throughout the nation – but the lessons have still yet to be learned.

We Could Be Contenders

This country once had a thriving indigenous automobile industry, a motorcycle industry, envied shipbuilding and aircraft industries and a leading position in electronics. Despite Mr Blair's exhortation for more education, it is unlikely that a lack of formal education caused the decline of these industries and therefore more of it is unlikely to reverse the trend. It is more likely that the young have instinctively felt that an education in the technical or engineering arenas, i.e. those disciplines which form the base of any industrial nation, does not provide the key to a bright future. Certainly, they have not been attracted in sufficient numbers to the more technical and scientific disciplines. Industry is (probably correctly) perceived by the young to be boring, bureaucratic and very unlikely to be exciting, fulfilling or financially rewarding.

If there is any enthusiasm for further education, it seems to be in the fields of finance, media, fashion, graphic design, law, etc. Yet Neil Kinnock, a European Commissioner and a former leader of the Labour Party, observed that, unless the country has a thriving manufacturing industry, it will not be able to afford all of the services the nation has come to expect. Here, a word of caution. Care must be taken in the use of the word 'manufacturing'. It should not always refer to the output of factories. In tomorrow's world, it will increasingly mean the bringing to market of products that customers want to buy, and using the very latest techniques to do so. In this regard, the American software giant, Microsoft is a manufacturer.

In the United States, there is considerable media and social interest in Bill Gates, founder of Microsoft and possibly now the world's wealthiest individual; in Ross Perot, the founder of EDS and erstwhile presidential contender; in Steve Jobs, founder of Apple Computers, in Michael Dell, founder of Dell Computers, and many others. They feature on the front page of Newsweek, Time and other journals. These people produce good role models for students because the companies they have founded have been exciting and dynamic. The companies have themselves been exciting to work for because there is a sense of purpose, a will to win. It is not overstating the case to suggest that working for these companies often instils in its employees worldwide, a feeling that one has joined a major soccer team. There is almost a religious zeal. A major order won, or a new product launch, is communicated to all and is seen as a triumph over the competition and is celebrated as such in the company. In the UK, in industry, there are no such role models, either companies or people. Sadly, the excitement engendered in American companies is often viewed with

Education, Education, Education

contempt. Young people in the UK currently draw their sense of excitement from entertainment, the media, soccer and even the financial sector. Industry, even in the high-tech arena is perceived, quite justifiably, as pedestrian and dull. Yet it is very often the case that once a British employee overcomes his cultural resistance and experiences energetic excitement in the industrial workplace, usually with American companies, he is actually stimulated by it.

It is regrettably a fact that industrial leaders in the UK are rarely recognised by the young, much less do they, as a result of their exciting demeanour, provide a role model for emulation. Sir Alan Sugar, founder of Amstrad, was largely invisible to the British public at large, until he took over Tottenham Hotspur football club and fired his coach, the former England team manager, Terry Venables, in a much-publicised boardroom putsch. Of course, his profile has increased since his television programme, *The Apprentice*, received good viewing figures. But even so it is unlikely that this exposure has done very much in terms of providing the industrial role model in the manner of say, the leading American industrialists. Perhaps it is significant that Sir Paul McCartney and Lord Lloyd-Webber, together with Sir Richard Branson, between them probably contribute more to the national economy and are more internationally recognised than many of our more prominent industrial concerns.

The purpose of drawing a parallel between these three gentlemen and the industrialist is not to disparage the educational attainments of Messrs McCartney and Co but to suggest that the young are more likely to want to emulate these three noted (non-University educated) talented individuals than any industrialist on the British scene. They, together with sports stars, are feted and praised and honoured by everyone from the Prime Minister and the Royal Family, to the press. Is any young person in industry in the UK likely to be so assiduously courted – even the relatively successful, young software and Internet entrepreneurs, many of them of Asian origin, who are now flourishing in our country? In the United States, on the other hand, it is very likely for the young there to wish to follow in the footsteps of Gates, Perot, Jobs and Dell. One could make a case for saying that both Gates and Dell are the natural industrial heirs of Henry Ford and Watson of IBM

Where are our natural heirs of Nuffield and Rootes, the founders of once-great British motor manufacturers? Not only have these gentlemen passed on in name and in fact, but the companies they gave their names to have also disappeared. In the UK we have Bamford, founder of the JCB earth moving equipment company, and Alan Sugar, founder of Amstrad, but neither of these are seen as role models for young students. Perhaps they should be. A sound technical education, allied to the entrepreneurial energy of these two gentlemen, plus some corporate sense of excitement, could provide a formidable formula. Should we not be concerned when Bill Gates undertakes to found a Cambridge University computer centre at a cost of £12m, because: *'Cambridge has built an outstanding computer science curriculum that has already become a training ground for entrepreneurs in this field around the world.'* (*The Times*, 26 Sept. 1997) Yet it has not produced even one such successful entrepreneur of our own? Of course, Sir Clive Sinclair achieved a fleeting fame, but here again, he was renowned for his inventive genius more than for his commercial acumen. Sir Alan Sugar is certainly not a product of Cambridge. Neither Sir Clive nor Sir Alan has had a significant impact beyond Britain's shores.

Perhaps some hope for the future is provided by James Dyson, the multi-millionaire inventor of the cyclone vacuum cleaner. So far, he has brought his own invention to market using only his own skills and his own money, and has had a tremendous impact on the more traditional manufacturers of vacuum cleaners – and he seems to be getting the right type of recognition for it. Nevertheless, it is sobering to note that Dyson did not willingly choose to use his own financial resources. He now expresses a cynical gratitude towards the venture capital industry. Their refusal to back him meant that he has remained the sole owner and beneficiary of his company's wealth.

It is always dangerous to select one or two examples, and present them as has been done here, as tokens of a whole nation, because it is a too sweeping generalisation. But not only is the general point valid but many other commentators have made similar points; furthermore political leaders of every hue have also expressed their concerns. The *Guardian* newspaper (14/9/2005) reported that, *'British productivity remains well adrift of the levels in France and the United States. The news will disappoint Gordon Brown, Chancellor of the Exchequer, who has made improving Britain's traditional poor productivity performance a key policy----. British productivity, or output per worker, is still well below the Group of Seven leading industrial countries.'* Is it fanciful to suggest that Mr Brown and his predecessors have been 'barking up the wrong tree' by relying on tax incentives to change the culture.

Education, Education, Education

Even in the reporting of this situation, the inference is that it is still the individual worker that is responsible and lurking behind this conclusion is one that lays the blame at the door of the unions. Yet a former Prime Minister, Margaret Thatcher, was hailed as the person who brought down the power of the unions and introduced new laws to curb their influence. Why did not all this hailed progress in industrial relations bring forth the new dawn of improved productivity. Could it be because management, who Mrs Thatcher never tackled, do not engage their staff fully in the endeavour of the company and thus are the real culprits? If this was done instead of spending time and resources on gimmicks such as 'Investors in People', which is mostly concerned with statistics gathering, the results could be remarkable. Individuals would be more personally motivated which, in turn, would create more corporate excitement. The industrial scene in America, particularly in the high-tech arena where Messrs Brown and Blair see our future, is exciting. The industrial scene in the UK-managed world by comparison is frankly dull, lacking in excitement or ambition, and uninspiring.

It cannot escape the notice of any observer that, along with many other countries, the US economy and trade base suffered severely from the Japanese commercial invasion. The country was flooded with manufactured goods of every description, the Japanese products being cheaper, more efficient, of better quality, and more attractive than their native equivalents. All this from a country that, not so many years ago, was mocked because it was deemed to be capable only of producing cheap imitations of other people's ingenuity. The Americans have spent years fighting back with a massive upheaval to their previous ways of doing things. Indeed, it is arguable that the Americans have, in many instances, overtaken the Japanese once more in the science of bringing products to a state of market readiness. The UK, on the other hand, has surrendered to the seeming inevitable; such that these foreign 'invaders' now own most of our industrial base, or we continue to import where there is a native shortfall. The reason for this lies, not surprisingly, in our history, which we cannot change; and in the maintenance of our industrial structure as a reflection of our social structure, which we can. However, for this to happen there has to be a will to change the structure, and a re-examination of our educational system; neither of these is there yet for three reasons.

First, because too many people in positions of influence, some of whom have worked very hard to attain their position, have, as a consequence, every reason to maintain the status quo; in any case they would, in all likelihood, not survive a change. Their advance within the current system is often less an indication of management competence than an ability to internally work the system. Thus, they would find it difficult to survive a more market-driven, 'bottom line' orientated culture. Of more concern is the fact that few of our middle and upper management in industry really know how a more successful system works. By the same token, most of the young are not aware of any other system; not aware that, given the right environment, there could be an exciting, productive future in industry. They are unable to articulate what changes could be wrought, such that they might be attracted in the future. Hence the attraction to media studies, for example, where life looks more exciting and in tune with society as a whole.

Finally, there is in the UK an almost instinctive belief that fundamentally the way of approaching issues is sound, and still the envy of the world. Since the approach to business reflects the orderliness of the social regime then, by definition, the commercial methods must be equally satisfactory. This flies in the face of a good deal of evidence to the contrary. The educational system needs to lead the way in ridding the nation of its view that the social and professional environments are synonymous. Ironically, many of the products of the system, that is those who enter the workplace, become over time acutely aware of its shortcomings. It's the perpetrators that have yet to see the light.

Teaching business studies

A start could be made at sixth form level. There have been moves of late to extend the curriculum to encompass knowledge of the civic structure. Why not include a commercial education? It's where almost everyone, professional and artisan, is going to spend most of their adult lives. The current education, as far as the realities of business is concerned, is woefully inadequate. This is particularly true in the immediate post-graduate environment. At the moment, there is no comparison between the American graduate in this regard, and his UK counterpart, even though there is little to choose between the two as far as the academic knowledge of their chosen subject is concerned.

This is not to say that Americans all leave school with an in-depth knowledge of business practice, but their society is a very business-orientated one and therefore, what they learn instinctively by being

Education, Education, Education

immersed in their society, the UK must do by more formal education. However, this education cannot be merely an extension of current educational practice, loosely termed the three Rs, but will call for a totally different educational regime allied to the commercial realities. The relatively recently established Business Academies sponsored by private individuals offers the best opportunity for introducing this regime. Of course, many British people learn American methods by working for American companies, but by definition, this means that an individual is likely to be well into his career for this to happen; the educational process should begin much earlier .

The structure of industry and its management methods must be changed to make it more dynamic. Only by doing so will industry be exciting enough to attract young people. Such a change would also create a sense of excitement and purpose and motivation for those already in industry. There is no question that a sense of excitement can be instilled into workers at all levels. If all workers can feel that they contribute to the overall excitement and sense of purpose, then productivity definitely increases. Most people would enjoy greater job satisfaction and being able to go to work for reasons other than to just pay life's expenses; this change must be undertaken. A government minister for trade, speaking on the radio, stated that: *'We must change the image of industry if we are to attract young graduates.'* It's not the image that must change, but the substance. To change only the image is merely to re-arrange the deckchairs on the Titanic.

Why is it so important? Primarily because there is an enormous well of talent waiting to be tapped in the nation's interest. The alternative is to lose these people to service industries or to foreign employers, or to see them choose to be unemployed. Unquestionably, many people are gainfully employed in Britain in enjoyable, stimulating careers for foreign employers. Nevertheless, it is inescapable that the profits from such endeavour go back to the country of the parent company and the profits retained in this country are those just sufficient to pay the local expenses and to satisfy the tax authorities. To digress, this phenomenon is not restricted to manufacturing industry. The profits from two outstandingly successful well-known British films, *The English Patient* and *The Full Monty* went to the United States. It cannot be expected or demanded that foreign companies change their methods, but those of the British companies must change. Once it was argued that 'invisible exports' was the nation's commercial claim to fame. It took great pride in its insurance and financial services income, and indeed it is substantial; but with the damage done to the invincible reputation of Lloyds, many of the major financial institutions falling into the hands of foreign banks, can the claim still be made? Does the damage done to Lloyds and the fall of Equitable Life and Barings, together with the inroads being made by foreign banks, financial houses and insurance companies, not suggest that our claim to be without parallel at such endeavours is really national self-delusion?

The concern is not xenophobic. The profits of the nation's endeavours need to be retained in the country if the services the country needs are to be afforded. Does anyone seriously continue to believe that major foreign manufacturers set up their manufacturing (product-producing) bases in the UK out of concern for the nation? In 1998, when the Far Eastern financial crisis occurred, many well-established companies suspended expansion plans, or closed their overseas HQs here, at the cost of many thousands of British jobs. American motor car manufacturers cynically engage governments in Britain, Germany and Spain in a Dutch auction, demanding huge grants in order to prevent factory closures or to have new factories opened. In other words, if all of the control of the manufacturing base and design capability is in foreign hands, then the economic base, not to mention employment, is always under threat. Quoted in the Sunday Times of 25 July 1999, Mr Terry Leahy, Chief Executive of supermarket chain Tesco, stated: *'We don't want to wake up one day to find that one of the few world class British industries has fallen into foreign hands. You have to ask who would really benefit from that?'* Given that Tesco, at that time, was not a renowned foreign exchange earner, it is not difficult to see how much more serious it is for a product based industry. Shortly afterwards, Asda was swallowed up by the US retailer, Wal-Mart.

The concern must be that if the nation, of necessity imports almost all of its high-tech needs, by far the biggest proportion of the profit margin made on these imported computers, software, cars, motor cycles, electronics, televisions and so on is retained by the foreign manufacturers. The same is true if the nation is merely the overseas production base for foreign companies, many of whom have received huge UK government grants as set-up costs. By definition, the resultant organisations are integrators, dealers, distributors, etc and they must content themselves with the margins of such endeavours. More importantly, these margins made in the UK when this role is adopted, are merely made from other UK companies and individual customers to whom the goods are sold. On the other hand, the profits made by the foreign manufacturers represent inward-flowing foreign capital from the UK to the country of company ownership. This could not be avoided if the country was an under-developed, colonised nation with no history of product design and manufacture; but, in just the industries referred to earlier, the UK once held a predominant position and could do so again in the emerging high-technology industries with their higher margin.

Far better surely, and more productive, that a nation with a long and glorious history of inventing world-changing products, the computer, penicillin, the steam engine – even the workaday vacuum cleaner – should add commercial awareness to the education of the young, such that they, in pursuing their own financial and career goals also contribute to the nation's economic interests. It is not a question of colonialism, but of competition. To succeed will call for changes on many fronts. These changes are all achievable, indeed imperative. Joe Kennedy the father of the late President Kennedy, said: *'Business is war'*. That may be carrying it to extremes, but nationally, the attitude still prevails that business is to be conducted by an 'old boys" network engaged in a game of cricket, with gentlemen and players. Even the 'young boys' in business can hardly wait to become 'old boys'; their behaviour is depressingly predictable.

The indigenous industries do not seem to be engaged in bringing profitable products to market – they have, in effect, become extensions of the financial services industry. It is legitimate to ask the question, 'Do UK industrialists know how to run an industry in an unprotected market environment?' Given the track record since the 2nd world war, the answer has to be in the negative. The institutions, relating to industry, including the educational establishment, need a major shake-up or they need to be in positions of less influence.

3

Do Our Institutions Serve Us Well?

Over the years, the DTI, the CBI and the bodies representing the various chartered professions have become ponderous bureaucracies providing yet another opportunity for self-eminent people, mostly men, to get even more recognition for less effort. How many young people aspire to membership of these 'professional freemasonries', just to add the initials to their calling cards or CVs, and then spend years wondering just what the particular body provides for its membership fees? The biggest change needed is to make industry more exciting for those engaged in industry, those actually working at the sharp end, not just those on the boards of directors with the task of presenting acceptable company results to the City and press. A better business education of all engaged in industry, graduate and non-graduate alike, will open up the 'closed book' that currently prevails in most of British industry, and will thus reveal that success in industry is not such a mystery. It might also reveal that success does not depend on the City and indeed, that the City has an influence out of all proportion to its competence.

Tongue firmly in cheek, the author of this book once suggested to an industrial grouping that, instead of the Chancellor of the Exchequer passing through the seated worthies of the City Of London at the annual Mansion House banquet in order to explain himself and his policies, it would be more fitting if the Chancellor was to sit on high while the worthies filed past him and explained how they have been instrumental in losing every one of our most significant industries. In his book, *The State We're In*, Will Hutton highlights the dangers of 'gentlemanly capitalism', a description coined by two historians. There is no question that the British worker engaged in industry, when exposed to the better focused working habits of his Transatlantic brethren is every bit as capable of the necessary commercial awareness – but the American is raised in a uniquely commercial world and knows the realities of business. The American knows instinctively that business is about making money, that every employee is an economic unit contributing to the process. There are many Americans working in industries with an entrenched trades union membership; the airline industry springs to mind. But even here the worker knows he is part of an organisation dedicated more to making money than it is in his personal welfare.

The UK is not such a society. There is still an instinctive belief that the employing organisation ought to look after the worker regardless of whether the individual actually makes a meaningful contribution to the success of the company. If the individual could be encouraged to participate meaningfully in the success of the organisation, he would not be in need of this artificial paternalism. Beneath this artifice, the UK society is certainly no more altruistic than the USA and it is time for all to embrace this reality..

The young at school, at college, at university are not a constituent part of the fabric of business education or practice. For this exclusion, the almost substantial decline of the product-producing industry is the price that has been paid. The situation is exacerbated by a system that encourages high-flying executives to be distracted from their proper objectives in the pursuit of honours given out by government or their chosen professional institution; only those who do not rock the boat are likely to be recognised or promoted. The cliché, 'If you cannot break the system – join it', is still in excellent working order. A secondary problem is that only those who feel they fit the stereotypical role are attracted to positions of influence, thus perpetuating a stagnant environment.

The lead for change can only come from government – is this not how Japan did it? The government cannot cure the industrial ills, but it can begin the searching questioning of the institutions that is so necessary. They need to be sceptical of the answers they receive, and to continually draw comparisons with other nations. Furthermore, they must seek a wider source of input to precipitate this change. Its current sources, the CBI, the IOD and the City are all part of the problem, being deeply entrenched in the current system, and have good reasons for ensuring that nothing changes that might loosen their grip. They have also become spokespeople for a commercial community that seeks to shift elsewhere, the responsibility for their own shortcomings.

In 1993, Mr Michael Heseltine, the then President of the Department of Trade and Industry, speaking at the annual dinner of the Institute of Directors, was highly critical of the performance and quality of British management. It was abundantly clear that the vast majority of the attendees did not feel he was addressing them personally. In fact, it was interesting to see one attendee, interviewed on television immediately after the dinner, state that he thought that Mr Heseltine was out of order, because: *'I have just reduced my costs by dismissing several of my staff'*. Spoken like a true captain of British industry, who has just chucked the purser and several of the crew out to lighten the lifeboat, and now finds himself having to take his turn rowing! The idea that the sole criterion for measuring management competence is the reduction of headcount is grotesque. Mr Blair, addressing the 1998 Labour Party conference, was equally scathing about the competence of our management.

The added danger from the institutions is that they appear to have an almost instinctive historical feel for where each layer of society belongs, and should stay; and for the relative importance of the various professional disciplines. This attitude, almost intuitive in our society, has led us to be, in effect, culturally imprisoned. In the social hierarchy of industry, finance people are deemed to be very important, as are corporate lawyers. Production management people are slightly more intelligent factory hands; who are, in turn, largely unintelligent, expendable units and a burden on the payroll. Design engineers are boffins with limited vision and absolutely no knowledge of commerce. Salesmen are 'cowboys', totally irresponsible and not to be trusted.

These attitudes have been held and expounded for so long, that people in each of these disciplines have come to accept them themselves as an unalterable fact. Thus, the industrial structure – reflecting, as it does, our social structure – still restricts advance in the former to those most able to emulate the demeanour of those with some standing in the latter. There is still to this day a divided attitude towards the professions and 'trade' which is archaic and no longer affordable. It leads to people in industry worshipping false gods, in a commercial sense. Instead of seeking to change things, professional British people in the work place seem more concerned with climbing the corporate ladder as a means of enhancing their position in the social pecking order, such that they can avail themselves of the benefits they see there. Often this is to the exclusion of actually doing anything radical to improve the business once they have made the advance.

In engineering companies in the not too distant past – and maybe today in some companies – the aspiration of a junior engineer was to be a senior engineer, a very laudable ambition. But very often the prime motive for this ambition was not necessarily to earn more money or even to work on more challenging work or to manage staff but simply because this advance automatically brought with it an armchair, as opposed to a chair without arms, an office shared by two instead of four. It might bring forth a more favourably positioned car park space. The final accolade to indicate this improved status would be access to the senior staff toilet, and rub shoulders with others whose urine was of an equally superior quality! Once on this higher rung in the hierarchy, the next rung has to be aimed for, and that usually means a full-time pre-occupation with cultivating others higher on the ladder. The actual business issues become secondary and sometimes totally neglected. More often than not, there is little awareness, even among those that are professionally qualified, that there is a business with commercial imperatives. In other words the aspirations were largely social and not professional.

The risk takers

Managing a business thus becomes secondary to managing a career. While each person is taking care that his own area of responsibility is 'clean', he is unlikely to take risks in any way. Furthermore, it is likely that, if he is adventurous, and the adventure fails, there are many others willing to exploit his misfortune and these will, of course, not be so foolish as to be adventurous. The people at the top of the company are also unlikely to take risks that endanger their position. All these attitudes emanate from looking down into the organisation in order to assess personal risks, instead of looking outward at where the market is going. Thus it is the management of careers that is the principle aim to the exclusion of managing the business. As a result, UK industry is, more often than not, playing catch-up to our foreign competitors, always a difficult and usually an impossible task.

Many years ago, there was an article in the business section of *The Times* that pointed out that this reactionary process reaches its culmination in the political honours system. As people reach a certain level of seniority their focus on the business becomes blurred by the possibility of receiving a knighthood, or even some lesser honour. People who might have demanded change become seduced by the possibility of receiving recognition from the Establishment, and so lose all incentive to demand change. Few can resist the seduction of such a society. Of course there are hierarchies in the companies of other countries, and many of them become deeply entrenched over time. Nonetheless, in most American companies few are allowed to get too comfortable and feel they are there for life. Many years ago one American senior executive was quoted as saying: *'When you reach forty in the States you need to keep your foot hard down on the accelerator or get out of the road'*. In British companies, on the other hand, the establishment of a pecking order seems to start early and remains set thereafter for life. This 'pecking order' mentality is part of the British cultural inheritance, dating back to the days of Empire and industrially it is proving very difficult to shake off this view of the world.

The civil service culture

In Asia, Britain once held dominion over many countries and colonies such as Hong Kong, Singapore, Malaysia and India. Despite moves for independence, there was a commonly held view that, whatever the shortcomings of colonialism, the British did at least create a civil service administration that enabled these countries, in post-colonial times, to grow their commercialism on a bedrock of Government and the rule of law. However, these countries have been able to combine these systems with an intense commercial orientation that Britain itself has not been able to match.

In an editorial in *The Times*, 'Asia On Line – Singapore and Malaysia struggle for Silicon Valley supremacy' (16 June 1997) an explanation was given of the competitive aspirations of these two nations, and their technological approach to the new millennium. India has emerged as a force to be reckoned with in software production, and not just because of its low labour costs or location on the international dateline. In Hong Kong before the colony was handed over to China it was tempting to make the observation, 'The Chinese make money, while the English run the place' As a nation, Britain seems to admire the United States, Hong Kong, Japan for their money-making propensities; yet seems to draw great comfort from being able to disparage the same 'pushy' qualities as somehow inferior to its own legendary sang froid.

The nation recognises that the creation of wealth will feed through society and improve the standard of living of the entire nation. Yet in industry, at the working level, it seems unable rid itself of the idea that the overt pursuit of money is vulgar and unworthy; this is in stark contrast with the investment community, where the ruthless pursuit of short-term gains is equally damaging to the nation's industrial prospects. Mr Geoffrey Dummer, 90-years-old veteran of British microchip technology, speaking on

Radio 4's Today programme (26 July, 1999), told of how he published, in America, a paper on the as-then unknown microchip. The device was patented by the American company, Texas Instruments – and the rest is history. Mr Dummer himself spoke of the 'innate American business sense'. He also talked of the more material connection in America between technical people and the commercial people, 'a connection which is missing in Britain'. It could be argued that the creation of a civil service is Britain's best industrial product, exported successfully to all corners of the Empire; but this is clearly a limiting and retrospective view. It is difficult to escape the conclusion that the nation will never be dynamic, never fulfil its intellectual potential until it shakes itself free of this enormous burden. Unfortunately, the country is now in a position where the young are more likely to be burdened by this history and they are to benefit from it.

Blaming the unions

In the same Times editorial quoted above, the leader writer inferred that the reason for the industrial demise was the trades unions, a view commonly accepted by many people abroad. It is so deeply entrenched that not only is it never considered that the view might be erroneous, but it is a view that management and professional staff have been conditioned to accept without question. As long as these people are allowed to see themselves as the victims of selfish trade unionism, and not made to accept their own responsibility, then the malaise will never be shaken off. Can anyone with an objective viewpoint really believe that anything other than poor management direction has led to the demise of the national industrial strength? Management that believed it only had to 'be' rather than 'do' has ill-served the nation.

The corporate ladder

Happily, the situation has improved in some measure, in that the right of entry to management ranks has been widened to be more meritocratic; but this, in turn, has led to another problem. Since, for most British managers, the only example to follow was that of their predecessors, it is hardly surprising that, for the most part, the new management copied the old methods slavishly. Authority for its own sake, the position in the pecking order, an almost exclusively obsessive preoccupation with improving that position, and a demand that recognition of that position be given as of right.

The mindset excludes the possibility of creative decision-making, or the offer of any opinion on the well-being or otherwise of the business. Thus everyone keeps their head down and hopes that they too will one day reach the next rung on that corporate ladder.

Of course, such ambition is part of any industrialised society and will always be so. However any objective observation comparing the UK with the USA is to see that, in the UK, this obsession with position and rank and accompanying perks is quite independent of any need to perform, to add value to the well-being of the company. In the United States such an ambition for upward mobility is not only recognised, it is encouraged; because ambitious people generally get things done, or at least try to get things done. Nevertheless, usually they must perform in a relatively short time if they are to keep, never mind improve, their place on the ladder – and they rarely take their eye off the market place.

An educated approach

It is undeniable that much of the infrastructure in former countries of the British Empire was put in place by well educated people from the upper echelons of British society, people like Lord Curzon, so well respected in India. However, it is a fact that the kind of education that enabled this system of administrative and management bureaucracies to be put into place, does not otherwise readily lend itself to success in the highly competitive world of industry as practised by, say, the Americans and the Japanese. In fact, the many excellent products of this same educational regime that have entered industry, now find themselves feeling vulnerable and defensive as the world changes around them in ways that they find difficult to deal with; another waste of talent, in short.

Thus we have in essence one level of society trying to hold on to their expected positions of influence and power, while a less well-endowed level of society tries to displace them, merely to emulate them and become a target for the new rising generation, whenever that may be. This, in social terms, will gradually change as the world changes, but there is too little evidence that the professional scene will change rapidly enough and unless the process is accelerated, the non-competitive nature of the nation will continue; to put it more succinctly, while staff are obsessed with competing with each other for their place in the industrial pecking order and the social rewards that go with it to the exclusion of the demands of the market, the

Americans and the Japanese and the Germans and others will continue to 'eat our lunch', as the expression goes.

Too often the order of priorities observed by the 'Brits' is a subject of much amusement for the Americans. For the 'Brits', it should not be a subject of amusement; it's a matter of survival. In the same newspaper editorial, referred to above, Prime Minister Blair said 'modernise or die'. But improving the 3 Rs, putting kids on the Internet with a computer in every classroom and berating the teachers and the trade unions might assist in the modernisation of the country, but it will do nothing towards modernising its attitudes. There is a need to examine the very structures being employed and to compare them with other nations. This should lead to an understanding of why the nation has fallen behind and why major industries in which we once held dominant positions are now, for the most part, in foreign hands. Unless this is undertaken, Britain could well become a national theme park with the population reduced to walk-on parts. The country's native creativity and wit should earn it a better fate.

4

Run the Business and Let the City Take Care of Itself

It is difficult to determine where the national industrial problem begins or to be precise which body of persons is, or has been, the major instigator – it's a collective responsibility. The source of the problem rests somewhere between the financial community, as represented by the City of London, and the board management of major industrial companies, aided and abetted by a compliant, accepting workforce.

The obsession of the financial press with share movements, as opposed to taking a more active, if complicated, interest in a company's market performance, is not helpful. Does the City demand unreasonable share performance, so that the management drives the whole company to comply, or does management feed the City with unrealistic expectations, thus leading to unsustainably high share prices? The answer is not important because both are culpable, and it is unproductive to explore who is the prime mover in this vicious spiral. What is undeniable is that the worker in the company is very often overlooked to such an extent that he becomes irrelevant to the cosy relationship developing between board level management and the City – yet, despite the fearsome reputation of the unions, the worker allows it to happen.

(The word 'worker' is chosen quite deliberately because it encompasses all denominations: including both shop floor workers and the professional staff as represented by designers, sales and marketing people, field service personnel and finance.)

It is indefensible that the messages often given to the City by the board, and thence via the city to the press, bear so little relationship to the view of the company held by their own employees at almost every level. Upbeat announcements about launch dates of new products, or news of a strategic relationship or joint venture are all made to the City primarily, and the analysts' recommendations to institutional and private investors alike reflect the board's optimism – not always justified by the inconvenient facts. Meanwhile, the staff are often embarrassed and outraged and frustrated because they are aware of the lack of realism behind the bland statements, often massaged by external image makers. They are aware that such false impressions reflect on their own competence, but seldom reflect their 'bottom-up' view of the performance of the board.

It is by no means unusual for a board of directors to engage their design and finance staff in a process of re-listing company assets and capitalising on product development; by this means the share price at the half year can be boosted. Hardly an appropriate role for engineers charged with bringing products to market. Another device used in times of poor performance is to make an acquisition to cover up the shortfall from expectations previously given out. A company might close down its entire manufacturing capability and then sub-contract the work out, thus pushing the costs a few months downstream into the next accounting period, merely to be able to tell the City that it had taken 'appropriate action', and so boost share performance.

The City, always willing to believe that manufacturing in Britain is a bad idea, applauds, and the share price is maintained. Sometimes this sub-contracting is to another British company with a similar cost structure and without the knowledge base. Production inevitably suffers serious disruption, affecting customers. But that is of little consequence when judged against the benefit of a good analysts report and increase in share price. Of course, a boost to the share price is always of value but when it is gained on the back of a manufactured myth, the edifice will eventually crumble.

Of course, such devices are used all over the world but what appears to be unique to the UK is that very often directors see them as solely their legitimate role quite divorced from market considerations. One President of an American company was quoted as saying that he could never make his company serve Wall Street, because: *'More often than not, the share price does not reflect the health, or otherwise, of the company. The only safe way for a company is to serve the market and the customers in it'*.

Who is running the show?

Some time ago an article in *The Sunday Times*, 'Why British firms inhabit the worst of all possible worlds' (5 October, 1997), made reference to this same problem from another viewpoint. Andrew Lorenz argued that strategic decisions are questioned by the investment community to such an extent that board decisions are changed and often abandoned to satisfy short-term demands. One might ask – who runs industry? Is it the Board, concerned with satisfying the City, and often having no consultation with those who will ultimately be responsible for providing the means of supporting the Board's utterances? Is it the investment community, with absolutely no regard for the long-term health of the company, as long as they sustain the resultant high level of profitability even if this profitability has been artificially produced? Can a supine middle management, and a 'nothing to do with me' compliant work force deny any responsibility? Of course, it is difficult for these latter entities to influence events, but surely a knowledgeable Board would be better advised to get closer to their workforce in order to establish a practical strategy; for that workforce to be closer to the market in order to properly advise the management. Then, for that management to tell the investment community what they intend to do, in what time scale and what returns the investors can expect. Then the company must adhere to these submissions – and perform. To do this, people at all levels and in all disciplines need to be engaged in the process.

In today's commercial world, the idea that such people would only be disruptive socialists, or not sufficiently educated to understand the problems, is outdated. Very often people engaged with the practical side of the business have a greater awareness of the realities than a Board of directors exclusively concerned with the share price. Yet British companies seem to 'ring-fence' each of its staffing layers with little communication, or at least filtered communication, between the layers. This 'ring-fencing' seems much less pronounced in American companies; their work force generally plays a much greater active role in the direction of the company, and in the face it presents to the outside world, than is the case with British companies.

By management and the workforce getting closer, at least two of the three contributing entities to our industrial environment would be 'singing from the same song sheet'. Andrew Lorenz, in his excellent article mentioned above, wrote of three instances where Board decisions had been made or criticised, purely to respond to the short- term demands of the investors. He went on to state: *'The overwhelming question raised by these developments is whether, in today's fast globalising environment, the institutions' safety-first-and-last philosophy is an anachronism that will do great damage to the future of UK plc.'*

In point of fact, the damage had already been done even then and a recovery programme is now, 10 years on, even more desperately needed. The alternative is a continuation of the economic colonisation that is already underway. Quoting Andrew Lorenz again, he referred to the investment institutions: *'Unless they raise their sights and change their philosophy they will find themselves presiding over the shrinkage of UK plc'*. With the greatest respect to Andrew Lorenz, his is a voice crying in the wilderness. The institutions are staffed by the same kind of people climbing their own corporate ladder. They are not going to put their corporate advance in jeopardy by taking unnecessary risks. The avoidance of risk is also the major reason why we do not have a robust American-style venture capital industry, also referred to by Andrew Lorenz.

Adventures in capital

The British venture capital industry is merely another industry with many self-serving employees trying to climb their own corporate ladder. The industry backs, for the most part, only near-certainties. All manner of conditions are attached, that protect their investment; so that any room for manoeuvre by the client company is restricted. Then they want their money back in two years. The so-called venture capital industry here seems to run on the basis of, 'Show us a million and we'll lend you another'. This is in marked contrast to the USA where, according to a Times Business News commentary (3 April, 1999): *'US banks and venture capital groups are more willing to lend money to new businesses and to high-tech operations.'* Indeed, the whole interest in venture capital is greater. A recent study found that American investors put an average of 6.9 % of their funds into venture capital, but UK investors venture only a minuscule 0.9 %. US venture capital groups often involve themselves in small businesses, helping with recruitment and business plans.

Most UK venture capitalists, the article continued, run a mile from management responsibility. They are increasingly reluctant to back start-ups or high-tech ventures and don't favour lending small amounts of money to entrepreneurs. Meanwhile: *'Banks remain firmly entrenched in their inflexible demand for collateral to support loans. This made sense in the days when manufacturing was the economic engine and companies had an array of machinery and factories to prove their worth. It is incongruous for the software developer whose biggest asset is the employees' knowledge and creativity.'* Quite apart from not providing sufficient capital, this British way of viewing start-ups has another dimension. Instead of attempting to grow a business on a worldwide scale in the manner of the Americans, the dream of most UK start-ups is to struggle to a point where the turnover is between, say £0.5m and £1m per annum, and then actively seek a US company to buy them out at a premium. Thus any real sense of entrepreneurialism is killed off in early life. Who knows how many potentially successful British businesses have been disposed of in this manner before they have truly proved their worth?

It is a sobering thought that the largest provider of funds to company start-ups in the UK is the Prince's Trust, a charity founded in1986 by HRH The Prince of Wales. This Trust has overseen the founding of some 37,000 businesses, started by the educationally disadvantaged and people from the ethnic minorities. The success rate is amazingly high, around 70 per cent continuing to trade past their third year. On the other hand, so many of the so-called 'business angels' in Britain are people who enjoy having their egos massaged by receiving grovelling submissions from start-up companies, but have no real intention of giving financial assistance. Thus, they not only fail to invest, but waste the considerable time of those seeking the investment, time that could have been more productively spent growing their business themselves. American venture capitalists on the other hand are more often people who have made considerable sums of money from cashing-in stock options with start-up companies that have enjoyed success, and then positively entered the venture capital business in order to enhance their wealth.

In an article written earlier than that by Lorenz, the late Stuart Steven, writing in the *Mail on Sunday* ('The Dinosaurs that are driving British business to extinction', 15 September, 1996), said: *'As long as the money men and their armies of accountants, lawyers and business consultants are in charge, the country's business base will decline catastrophically.'*

It's your career – you run it!

Because of these inhibitors, changes in the performance of UK plc. will come only from the creative end of industry, not from the top; and only by a change in the working practices and expectations of the generators of the company wealth. These 'generators' of wealth are the ideas-men and women – designers, engineers, sales and marketing people. Plus, of course, positive assistance from finance staff keeping all activities on a positive track and analysing all component parts of a company's activity in order to fine-tune its future strategy. Stewart Steven, writing in the same article, conceded: *'These people, accountants, etc., have their place – but it is in the servants' hall and not at the top table.'* He goes on to say: *'Our Japanese and German competitors know this and have always understood that in the end all that matters is the product. The man who makes the product – he is the one earning respect.'* This is definitely not the case in the UK today, nor has it been so for many, many years.

It can be misleading to categorise finance people in quite such damning terms as Mr Steven did. Finance people are as capable of running a business as anyone else, sometimes more so; but it is vital that they make the producers of the company's wealth inclusive in the management process. Financial control is an absolutely vital element of any business and good financial staff are extremely valuable, but their activities must relate to the core business; and financial management is not normally the core business of a company.

Whoever is running the company must know where the money is being spent, individual by individual, process by process – and where it is coming from product by product, customer by customer. No business will be successful without it. Every activity, every change will have a financial consequence that must be considered. No member of staff who does not acquaint himself with the financial realities will probably ever make senior management – and will eventually fail if he does make it; frankly such a person deserves to fail. Even Mr Steven's Germans and Japanese, at senior level, whatever their core profession, will certainly embrace this fact. The difference is that senior executives in overseas companies will always relate this financial analysis back to the core activity of the company, without sacrificing or losing sight of their own personal professional discipline. A financial discipline and a core skill are not, and should not be, mutually exclusive. In Britain, on the other hand, the accountants that Mr Steven refers to have been led to believe they are omniscient, above the need for non-financial skills or expertise. Conversely, many people with a core technical discipline seem almost obsessed with acquiring an ability to speak 'accountant's speak' better than the accountants. (Rarely, does one hear Gates, Dell and co. sound like partners in KPMG or PriceWaterhouse.)

Often they lose the focus of their own particular skills by so doing.

However, the increasing inability of any member of staff to depend on a long-term future with his or her company, means that the employee, particularly at the professional level, must seek to exploit his professional skills in his own area of creativity. There must be less willingness by individuals to 'buy in' to the strictures of a company bureaucracy. They must decide themselves to cease having their personal careers being 'process driven'. They should stay with their employer only for as long as it suits them and their personal goals. There is probably no better time than now for product producers to opt out of the tyranny of inadequate boards of directors, but such producers can do so only if they are educated beyond their technical limitations with a focused, more American, attitude to the ways of commerce.

The relegation zone

It is a fact that, released from an environment where their talents are undervalued, talented people will find themselves stretched and stimulated by a more demanding but better-rewarding company. It is tempting for individuals in a company to point fingers at management and their cronies in the City and hold them wholly responsible for the problem, and to expect these same entities to provide the solution. This is no more acceptable than pinning the entire blame for Britain's well-earned place in the relegation zone of industrial commerce on the unions. At whatever level, each person on a payroll is responsible for the conduct of his own professional life, and has always been so, providing he has goals that go beyond achieving a place on the bureaucratic ladder. If this calls for a change of employer, then he will, by accepting this fact, contribute to changing the system and will achieve a far greater sense of personal fulfilment. Because of the resulting increased experience, he will also be able to make a more significant contribution to a management team that shares his business or technical aspirations.

Unfortunately, many of the contributors to the current state of UK plc have little incentive to change the system, given the rewards there are for maintaining the status quo. Only if the real producers of the wealth, the product producers, say: 'Enough is enough', will a necessary change be forthcoming. Such people will have to put their own personal interests first, and not wait docilely to be recognised and rewarded.

Pressures for change

There are significant changes taking place that will make it imperative for an individual to control his own career. Since the early part of the 20th century, apart from during wartime, there have co-existed in Britain two distinct social economies; a situation which has helped to keep the 'workforce' that comprises the larger part of one of these economies very much in an ignorant and acquiescent state, entirely dependent upon the other. This situation, for historic reasons, is about to change.

At the turn of the 20th century, and to the end of the 2nd world war, there was virtually full employment. Many companies in those days provided 'cradle-to-grave' care for their employees: a working life, a social life (medical cover, sports grounds, social club, works outings, children's Christmas parties, etc.), even company housing and schools, and protection for the worker (with the ubiquitous gold watch being presented upon retirement, age 65) until the day he died, usually not long after.

At the end of the 2nd world war, the welfare state was founded, and companies started to off-load some of these extraneous benefits, which had begun to be perceived as an unnecessary cost – along with the introduction of a more 'scientific', competitive approach to management. Now, the state took up some of the slack through the national health service, state pensions, unemployment and housing benefits, the provision of cheap mass housing, free schools, etc. As a result, the dependency culture was perpetuated, the working population being cared for by one paternalistic or quasi-paternalistic body or another to such an extent that being self-dependent was and remains quite alien to most people.

Shock set in during the Thatcher decade of the 1980s. 'Globalisation' arrived with a vengeance. Two major economic recessions in ten years, combined with the devastating and repeated wave effects of the introduction of new technologies in data processing and telecommunications, put an end for ever to the cosy, pipe and slippers image of the 'working classes'. Global competition sent a biting wind through UK plc. Many companies turned to the management 'gurus', whose only advice was always to 'cut, cut, cut', and to embrace the chilly ethos of chaos through continuous 're-engineering' of work processes to meet the wildly oscillating swings of the market. Unemployment reached 4.5 million in the mid-80s, the social fabric began to crack.

By the 1990s, state provision was eroding rapidly, particularly at local government level, and will continue to do so. We have seen drastic restructuring of the health service, savage cuts in real welfare benefits, an end of cheap housing; and we are now hearing murmurings, growing in intensity, that signal the end of the state pension. We are not 'returning' in any sense to a culture of self-dependence, because few people alive today have actually known it. The generation leaving school today will actually be the first for over 100 years to learn self-dependence, and they will have to learn it the hard way; their parents cannot teach them. Workers at all levels must take on board that they really are on their own. They need to understand that if the employer, to quote Stuart Steven, believes it is: *'...admirable and clever to sack a large proportion of the workforce, save a lot of money and degrade the product'*, then the worker owes it to himself to offer no more loyalty than he himself receives.

Each employee should maintain a healthy degree of scepticism towards the paternalistic pronouncements and on a continuing basis he should make judgements as to whether it is in his personal interest to stay or move on. At the same time, of course he should recognise that his employer will have expectations of him that, while on his payroll, he should do his best to fulfil. Conversely, should this same individual become an employer, he should recognise that if he does not provide an environment where people can fulfil their personal potential then he deserved to lose them to another company that appeared to offer what they were looking for. With the changes currently taking place in the social benefit provisions, an employee needs to ensure that his own financial and health care needs are provided for, independent of his employer – a situation that will become easier as we go forward in the current millennium, because the whole structure for the provision of pensions and health care and savings will have to be re-organised. For the immediate past generation of postwar 'baby boomers', many now on the industrial scrap heap in their forties and fifties, this may not be so easy.

Maintaining the value of mobility

To provide for his own financial protection, then, and to improve his prospects of continuing mobility, it is important that each employee makes himself more valuable as he progresses through his professional life. He does this by becoming more adept at his basic skill, or by acquiring new skills. The employee then markets this new capability, either internally to the current employer, or externally to a new one. If for example, an engineer is naturally talented, he will not find it a problem to stay abreast of changes in technology and thus retain his value to his employer. If, on the other hand he perceives himself, quite realistically, to be nothing more than a journeyman, then he will find it both a struggle to stay abreast of technology and increasingly difficult to find the motivation to try. Such a person owes it to himself to add new skills in order that his value increases on a wider front. Such a person needs to recognise that he is a commercial unit, fighting to keep his place in the productive world. An engineer will eventually lose this battle if he sees the role at all times, and for all time, as one where he is compelled to attempt to push back the frontiers of technology to the exclusion of all other related activities. In other words, each person has to be ruthless with himself and recognise his own personal realities. Such self-appraisal can be painful; today, however, it is unquestionably necessary.

When the whole educational process for people in industry is biased toward instilling a feeling of elitism or 'technical snobbery', it is an immensely difficult exercise for people, so educated, to turn their back on it and seek alternative paths for their career. Nevertheless such a harsh self evaluation, followed by career moves to accommodate it, will eventually lead to a much more fulfilling professional working life. Better to use your skills to wider effect, and to make a contribution, than to attempt to stay abreast of those with more natural skills on a narrow front. Unfortunately, UK graduates do acquire a form of elitism during their studies that ill-disposes them to look kindly on what they consider to be less esoteric skills such as sales and marketing, much less practise them; again this is rarely the case with Americans employed in a technical environment. Such people are usually passionately interested in what the salespeople are doing, what are their difficulties, what were the product shortcomings, what was needed to restore the company's fortunes. They are also much more prepared to change career disciplines without any of the 'loss of face' hang-ups that preoccupy graduates in Britain.

There was once an anecdote published on the subject in a technical journal. An English engineer returning to England from working in North America was asked by a former English colleague that he had worked with before going to the States, *'What is the difference between an English engineer and an American one?'* Since both were employed in the electronics world, the returning emigre gave what he considered to be an appropriate reply. *'The English engineer would say: "I've designed the best *amplifier in the world." The American would say: "I may not have designed the best amplifier, but I've already sold ten of mine."'* This fundamentally pragmatic approach seems to underline the difference in the motivations of creative individuals from opposite sides of the Atlantic. Unfortunately to this day there is far too little signs of improvement in this basic difference of attitude.

Has the situation improved since 1997 when the former editor of *The Times*, William Rees-Mogg, under the heading 'Is Bill Gates really selling us all Ladas?' commented: *'Microsoft is thought to be charging too much for software which is still far from being user-friendly.'* This is a very lofty position to adopt when he goes on to point out that Microsoft provides the operating software for 90 per cent of all personal computers and 80 per cent of word processing. Many people, including many Americans, find Microsoft's domination not to their liking; but a company does not get to be that successful unless it is providing something the world market wants at a price it is prepared to pay. Surely, if Britain is to succeed in these knowledge-based industries the country should be learning from it and emulating it, not standing on the sidelines crying 'Foul'. Even Rees-Mogg's sympathetic view, in the same article, of the struggles of Sun Microsystems to market an alternative offering, misses the point. Sun's battle with Microsoft is not because Sun is more altruistic, but because it wants more of the market share that Microsoft has – and both of them are American. Rees-Mogg, in the same article, wryly observes: *'It is rather as though an automobile company were the sole world supplier of cars, priced them at the Mercedes level, built in obsolescence so that every owner had to buy a new one every year, and actually sold Ladas.'* Surely it must be the case that if a car manufacturer was lucky enough to be in such a position, they would do exactly as Rees-Mogg predicts.

It is up to the law to prevent such a happening if it is against the public interest, which is exactly what the US Justice Department does very effectively. In fact, Microsoft has faced massive anti-trust suits over its global monopoly of Internet access. In this regard, although Britain does have some regulators, the USA appears to be stronger than its UK counterparts. As, indeed, the pricing policy of Rees-Mogg's own paper, *The Times*, was referred to the Office of Fair Trading (OFT), who rejected calls for the policy to be referred to the Competition Commission. The executive chairman of *The Times* argued that their low-pricing policy was simply to boost market share; its circulation had doubled since the introduction of a low cost that other newspapers claimed was predatory, in other words, the paper at that time was being sold at below the cost at which it, and its competitors, could produce it in a sustained manner. Yet others have since managed to follow suit, with the result that newspapers now represent something like value for money for the readers.

One could argue that the ensuing commercial success of *The Times*, arising out of a scenario not dissimilar to Rees-Mogg's car company, provides Rees-Mogg with the security of employment that his erstwhile colleagues on other papers can only envy! By the very nature of its business, *The Times* has obsolescence built in daily, not yearly. Of course, it is unlikely that *The Times* would have engaged in such a practice before its owner, Mr Murdoch, an Australian, made the publishers aware that his primary intent was to sell more newspapers and increase market share. Economically speaking, if one were to seek two bedfellows from Rees-Mogg, Gates and Murdoch, it would almost certainly be Rees-Mogg who would be sleeping on the couch. Further to the point, if EMI had adopted some of the practices of Bill Gates, the UK might still own the lucrative and globally important industry that sprang from the invention in the 1970s by Sir Godfrey Hounsfield, of the brain and body scanner. Of course, the USA now virtually owns the industry. To quote Joseph Kennedy again, 'Business is war'.

An obsession with image

Instead of joining this competitive and more exhilarating business environment, Britain has a situation where management says, in effect: 'We'll manage, you engineer'; and where engineers say, 'We are brighter than all of you, but only with the right degree of persuasion will we impart some of our knowledge, recognising of course that you will not really understand'. This is compounded by a finance staff who, charged with preparing the company results to be presented to the outside financial community, see themselves as absolutely vital to the success of the company; quite regardless of the activities of the engineers. Unfortunately, more often than not, management also imbues the finance staff with this sense of importance; partly because it is they who can use all the considerable flexibility allowed under national accounting rules to present the company results to the best possible effect! This gives rise to the transformation, referred to earlier, of engineers, and indeed many others with important core skills, into exclusively 'numbers men' when, and if, they get on the management ladder. So many British companies, as a result, lose the plot. It is not uncommon for senior directors of companies to present the results of their area of responsibility in such terms that that area is difficult to discern; the presentation concerns itself solely with financial data. There seems to be a compulsion by these executives to air their expertise in purely financial terms even though their personal core discipline is not finance. Often no mention is made of strategy, competition, product difficulties, customer problems, staff problems, or the suggested and intended ways of dealing with these issues. This runs counter to the situation with American companies, where senior executives would be expected to show they were intimately familiar with all these details. To be so familiar, the executives typically consult with all of their direct reports. The financial staff would interpret these collected facts and present their financial projection accordingly.

This American approach gives a much more comprehensive view of the health of the business. The typically British approach does not do so and, in fact, can often lead to the numbers being ' massaged' to produce the desired result. It also means that the executive does not have to familiarise himself with all of the issues concerning his area of responsibility. It results often results in the company becoming very inward-looking at its own processes and organisation. Indeed, the only manifestation of outward looking is towards the City. American and Japanese companies are much more outward-looking, towards the markets where the potential customers are, rather than over-the-shoulder-looking at the financial institutions. This leaves them free to do what makes the money, which is selling the products. Examples are the American computer industry, and the Japanese car and motor cycle industries. However, in the case of the UK electronics and computer industries, there are some very distinct reasons for the differences in approach, quite apart from our cultural instincts. Again, these are historical.

Thank us for having you...

In the 1950s and 60s, the country held a significant position in the electronics and semiconductor industries, in the form of Ferranti (see Appendix 1), Plessey, EMI and others. ICL was a substantial computer company. Compare that with the current position where these companies are virtually invisible in worldwide terms, or at least, they are insignificant. Now the nation's political leaders express gratitude for, and provides tax incentives for, inward high-tech investment from Japan, Germany and even Korea, a country not usually noted for its expertise in this environment. On the 15 March, 1998 the *Sunday Times* Business News announced: *'Taiwan to invest £1bn in UK'* and in the ensuing article, stated: *'Labour skills and support from the British government for overseas investors make the UK a very attractive location for IT companies'*. The nation expresses pride that the ubiquitous Bill Gates, founder of Microsoft, should select Cambridge for the foundation of a computer research centre. ICL is now owned by Fujitsu, a Japanese company that was not even in the computer industry when ICL was a major player.

The fact is, the UK does not have one recognisably world-class company in the electronics or computer industries, despite the fact that thousands of UK people are employed in these industries. In fact, British engineers made a huge contribution to the founding of these industries. How has this situation arisen? Back in the 1950s and 60s, Ferranti, GEC, Racal, Marconi and others carved up the lucrative defence market with cost-plus contracts while ICL, virtually owned by the British government at the time, enjoyed single source supplier status to every government and government related organisation in the land. This situation has had many subsequent ramifications – almost all bad. The most important of these is that the companies had little knowledge, and no experience, of how to stay abreast of, much less beat, even national competition in the commercial market place. Thus when protected markets became a thing of the past these companies would be unable to compete.

Another important factor to emerge from this protected market scenario was that the financial staff in the company had no experience of analysing the effectiveness of the discrete activities in the company. As a result, there was no opportunity for management to definitively decide which activities were profitable, and which should be dispensed with, or adjusted to make them profitable. Consequently, a lot of poor strategic decisions were made. Traditionally, the finance staff were concerned with rolling up all expenses, adding the cost-plus element, and presenting the bill to the government. A cosy relationship developed between government and industry that allowed out-of-date technology to be sold on absurdly preferential terms by a state-funded industry to government, in a closed loop.

Engineering creativity was expended, extracting more mileage – and revenue – from dated technology. Opportunities were missed; while the requirements of modern warfare and leading-edge industrial operations were better-met by American and Japanese pragmatism. As a result, the UK technology industry became, in effect, no more than a professional university. In such an ivory tower, no knowledge of what was happening in the outside world was necessary – or even convenient. Remnants of this blinkered way of working are still in evidence today. Financial analysis, that could point to how the company should adjust its strategy and tactics to meet and beat the competition is still largely concerned with presenting results, using all of the flexibility available under national accountancy rules, to the investing institutions. So, a cultural lack of commercial awareness, and a captive, non-critical customer, together made a significant contribution to the current low status in the electronic and computer industries. Similar regimes, with a similar impact, existed in other capital industries: aircraft, shipbuilding, civil engineering, etc., which, forty years ago, also had a high dependence on cost-plus government business. These two factors: the cultural overtones in the way the British conducted business; together with the high dependence on government business, conditioned – and still today, to an unacceptable extent, conditions – the way in which the effectiveness of a business is to be measured; and indeed, who is to do the measuring.

On the other hand, the American defence industry, even more bloated at the time with cost-plus government contracts, does not seem to have conditioned, to the same degree, the modus operandi of their commercial counterparts. Here, the results presented to the outside world came out of the financial analysis of the internal workings of the company. This is not to say that such an exhaustive analysis leads to the automatic success of the company; both success and failure are the consequences of a number of factors, but at least the Americans usually run their companies from a detailed knowledge base. This knowledge base is usually contributed to by the wealth-generators, the designers, engineers, sales and marketing people, and general management to a far greater extent than their British counterparts. British companies, even major British companies, to a very great extent depend almost solely on their finance staff to roll-up total revenues, subtract total costs and, voilà, produce total profits – or losses. It is this 'finance-centric' mode of management that led to the late Stuart Steven making his comments referred to earlier. Back in the 60s, one of the companies mentioned above, Ferranti, became the subject of conjecture when it made substantial profits one year, and an equally substantial loss the next. To anyone working in Ferranti at the time, it should have been no surprise at all.

Not made here

One hears frequently that it is 'too expensive' to manufacture in the UK or that 'the unions have destroyed the county's manufacturing capability'... But many of the nation's imported goods are manufactured in either the United States or Japan, neither of which is a low-cost economy. It is true that there are still many items manufactured in the Far East but this is becoming less so, particularly in the capital goods arena. With the advances in manufacturing technology, cheap unskilled labour is no longer the attraction it once was. Furthermore, the cost of this labour does not stay cheap. Hong Kong is a prime example of a formerly cheap location that has lost this advantage and, as a consequence, has had to re-position itself. Provided the manufacturing activity is carried out using up-to-date technology, and with the essential scientific discipline employed in the advanced manufacturing nations, then some production in the UK is quite feasible especially when one considers the shipment costs from the Far East, and the difficulties and costs of managing Far East facilities. One has only to look at the Far East companies setting up production plants in the UK to see the truth of this, not to mention the totally different approach to industrial relations that these companies observe, which seems to bring out the best in the their labour force.

Furthermore, today's production items do not necessarily emanate from the 'dark satanic mills' of yesteryear. Indeed, many in the high-tech, soft industries require little in the way of production plants at all. Perhaps our failure to recognise the potential for ourselves, within the changes taking place, is one of the key reasons why the retail sector has become so dominant on our commercial scene. We are now truly living up to our reputation of being a nation of shopkeepers; or at least, 'shopaholics'.

PART 3

THE WAY AHEAD

5

Becoming a Team Player

If there is one thing that separates us from our foreign competitors, it is our national lack of a personal and a corporate sense of discipline. A soccer team without discipline is similarly doomed; as is the career of a tennis or golf star. Yet, to extend the sporting metaphor, all of these sports stars can express their individual flair within the rules. Industry should be no different. Industry is similarly made up of the front line team: designers, salesmen, marketing people, field engineering, people directly concerned with the market place; and the 'behind the scenes' staff, i.e., the finance, personnel, production and logistics people. Each of these members of staff can similarly express his or her own individual talent within a known structure. In fact it is often more personally stimulating to be part of a team in a company that viewed itself, and behaved, as if it is collectively fiercely pitting its will and its wits against the competition.

This section of the book will examine each of the various roles within a company and illustrate what an employer, i.e a general manager, should expect of each of them, and what contribution the general manager himself should contribute. Each person in any given discipline will typically know their own profession better than the general manager; and, to be effective, must have room to express that expertise. However, they need to be drawn into an overall company or departmental discipline by the general manager. To return to the sporting theme, a general manager should be a coach; he can educate and delegate from the touchline, but stay off the pitch! He should tell each member of staff, individually, what is expected of him when playing his part to achieve corporate goals, and then depend on him to produce results. Treated in this fashion, most staff are more likely to demonstrate their potential. However, to produce the required results, all employees need to be aware of, and draw upon the support of staff in other disciplines. No one function can, or should operate in isolation if the overall company objective is to be met. An engineer, with or without staff to manage, should make it his task to consult with marketing or sales or human resources or finance. Too often, a lack of such consultation leads to bastions of exclusivity, with no chance of a team effort.

Rejuvenating British industry

The purpose of this book is to enable readers of all business disciplines, whether sales and marketing, product design, finance or administration, to understand what makes a business succeed and how their own particular expertise can be developed to contribute towards this success. Further, in a wider context, the aim is to show how people entering industry, be they employees or employers, can make their contribution, albeit small, to the rejuvenation of British industry. At the same time, and perhaps more importantly, they should become, in their own interest, better practitioners of their chosen profession.

If the nation can shake itself free of the acceptance of the status quo, if it can look objectively at the current structure of industry, then each person can make their own assessment of the situation, and map out their own future direction. This will lead inevitably to a greater mobility of professional people. Some of these people, armed as they will be with a more rounded commercial education, will have the courage to start their own businesses with a better chance of success. Others will bring a more focused approach to their employer's business and will expect, justifiably, to be better rewarded for their personal 'bottom line' contribution. This focused approach is a euphemism for giving recognition to the fact that all activities in a business should be concentrating on making money for that business. Each individual should in effect, be asking themselves every day, *'Did I add to the profitability of my company today? Did I use all of the other resources of the company such that I could meet my personal objective of adding to the company profitability? Did I ensure that all of the other resources that are needed to assist me in my objectives are in place, focused, motivated and rewarded to assist me in my objectives?'* Only if the answer to these questions is *'Yes'*, will an individual learn what is needed to add to the profitability of his company.

Too many people adopt a 'crawling through the undergrowth' attitude. They go into their place of work, beaver away at their allotted task, and never take a bird's eye view (to mix metaphors). If each individual did take more of a bird's eye view, then that individual would recognise it to be a fact that if he or she does relate to these other disciplines, they can locate their personal activity within the context of the overall business. He or she will learn how these disciplines operate or, more to the point, how they should operate. As a result of this increased familiarity with other professions in the industry, the individual is able to decide the future direction of his career with a much wider perspective; very often it can lead to a complete career change. On the other hand, if the individual, in effect, merely asks of himself the question: 'Do I just keep my head down and assume that all these other activities are going on without my intervention or interest?', then the outcome is likely to be far different. If the individual is so skilled in his chosen profession that he is likely to stay abreast of developments, and intellectually ahead of his peers, then the consequences are unlikely to be too severe. But, if the individual is not so brilliant, then such a 'head in the sand' approach is likely to bring a career to a premature conclusion, and certainly to inhibit career advancement.

Changing our perspective

There are three well-rehearsed reasons for being in business – 'money, money, money'. In summary, every individual in business is an economic unit, first and foremost, and needs to accept this fact. He or she has no other purpose on the payroll of a commercial concern than to make that economic unit a profitable one. Even in non-profit organisations, this seemingly harsh fact holds true, though few recognise it.

It has long been a source of frustration to see American companies succeed where British ones perish. There is no difference in general intellectual terms between the British engineer and his American counterparts. Indeed, there is no inherent difference intellectually between the two in any area of commercial activity. There is a difference, however, in how they see themselves in business. Unlike his British counterpart, the American is not continuously questioning his place in industry, or in his employer's affections. He doesn't have to. His cultural heritage instils in him the knowledge that business is about two things, money and winning, and those are enough. However, what the British do not inherit as an attitude, they have shown themselves perfectly capable of learning. I would go further and say that, once they have learned it, their cultural heritage of inventiveness and creativity makes them quite capable of being world class.

Lord Marshall of British Airways, Sir Peter Bonfield, formerly Chief Executive of BT, Robb Wilmot, former Chief Executive of ICL, cut their management teeth with American companies in the States. The late Harold Geneen of ITT was born an Englishman. The chairman and CEO of the French cosmetics company, L'Oreal, is a Welshman, Lindsay Owen-Jones. Until relatively recently, Alex Trotman, a Scot, was President of the Ford Motor Company, while Brits in the Media, Harold Evans (late of *The Sunday Times*) at MacMillan, and Tina Brown (formerly of *The Tatler*) at *The New Yorker*, have succeeded brilliantly in the ferociously competitive jungle that is Manhattan.

Once this different way of looking at things is accepted, then many other things fall into place. No longer will British nationals do things because it is the 'right' or the 'fair' thing to do, from a misplaced sense of ethics; but because, economically, it is the only solution. This stated aim of the end justifying the means will horrify many people. It should not. It should horrify only if one believes that the right thing, the fair thing, the ethical thing, and the economically correct thing are mutually exclusive. They are not. It is not only possible, it is imperative, for long-term success if all those involved in a company are winners. A shareholder deserves and expects a better return on his investment than he would get investing in a bank. A customer deserves, and expects, a good quality product or service at a competitive price. Employees, at all levels, should share financially in the company's success – and, at all levels, should expect to pay some price for its failures.

The American way

As has been stated earlier, corporate discipline is the key, and it is in this area where the nation is lacking in comparison with American, Japanese and German industrial brethren. The discipline of the latter two is the more apparent and extends to almost all facets of their social and cultural lives. The discipline of the American is sometimes less visible but by no means less effective. In some respects, Americans appear informal, almost casual, in their approach. To unwary or inexperienced Europeans, this can be attractive; but it also too often leads the European to believe that the American approach to the task in hand is also casual. Nothing could be further from the truth. However, in the American way of things the corporate discipline is not an extension of his social life in the way of the Japanese and

Germans; it is more usually quite separate from it. Thus an American, hospitable to a fault in his social life, can be quite ruthless in his pursuit of business goals. This ruthlessness is not an indication of any lack of moral scruples, quite the reverse; but it is an indication of his acceptance, however grudgingly, that he is in business to make money for his employer and, hopefully, for himself. Thus the discipline that pervades most American companies at all levels and in all activities is a corporate culture that runs right through society.

There is also a very strong 'Hail to the Chief' attitude that is a quite natural part of the make-up of an American employee. The employee may not agree with the Chairman or Chief Executive, but he or she will usually obey him, however reluctantly, until he is replaced. It is not usual for American employees to practice the anarchy so prevalent in many British companies. Furthermore, the American employee, particularly in the newer industries, finds no difficulty in showing respect for those who hold management domain over him, without believing he is showing undue deference. The same is held in reverse. In most American companies, most management will talk about issues quite naturally to their reporting staff without ever being condescending or believe that they are relinquishing the respect that was their due. In UK companies, on the other hand, the culture invests in a manager the expectation that he is due a level of respect that quite transcends the issues under discussion. Furthermore, the respect did not only not have to be earned, but often is measured by how far that manager can distance himself from those below him in the organisation, often the producers of the company's wealth.

The American attitude to management is particularly useful to founders of new companies, where there is a tendency to follow the lead of the founder. Gates of Microsoft is a good example, and he is by no means the first. He is highly visible and leads from the front, with his predictions of the future of technology and the reflection of these predictions in the way he drives the company. The opinion has often been uttered, unkindly it must be said, that Microsoft people, in their devotion to Gates, are akin to the Moonies. Nevertheless, growth is more likely to come when staff feel this enthusiasm for a leader, simply because they are more likely to be pulling in the same direction.

Of course, control is an important element, and here too, the American system scores highly. Unlike his British counterparts, the American employee shows more willingness to be controlled. Of course, fear of losing one's job helps with the imposition of a corporate discipline but that is not the only reason, although it must be said that the oft-repeated view of American management as being 'hire and fire' is grossly overstated. Nevertheless, in British companies there is often near anarchy, where each member of staff believes he has a right to interpret his own priorities when deciding company objectives. The worker seems, in effect to say to himself, *'Do I really want to do that?'* and will answer his own question as he sees fit. Thus the company management has, on an almost daily basis to, prove itself worthy of the adherence by its own workforce to its stated aims, always assuming (a dangerous assumption) that the management has stated its aims. If management is invisible, it will inevitably be subject to scepticism, cynicism, and even ridicule on the shop floor.

At a recent management seminar, the audience was addressed by an American female executive working for a major British telecommunications company. She had previously worked for a similar telecommunications company in America. She set out to explain to the seminar her perceptions of managing British and American staff in the two companies on different sides of the Atlantic. She chose to do so in military parlance. *'When I worked in the US, I could gather my departmental staff together and say: "We're going to take that hill on Tuesday. Go away and report to me tomorrow on how we can meet our objective." Accordingly, they would do just that. My experience in England is that if I gave the same directions to my UK staff, not only did they not re-appear as instructed, so that I had to go find them, but when I did find them their response, after 24 hours of consideration, was – why that particular hill – and why Tuesday?'*

Understanding how the parts fit together

Only by understanding how the various parts of the business fit together can employees hope to understand the specific expectations management will have of their own part of the operation. Too often employees are not properly briefed about their interface with other functions, sometimes with disastrous results. The design department may find that 'marketing' will devise a world-beating product and expect the designers to make the dream come true. But the brief has been expressed in only the vaguest terms and the marketing concept may be incomprehensible to those who are expected to bring the concept to market. The result can be a product that completely misses the mark. More serious in company terms is that, often, board level management will, in their own interest, be telling the investment community about this world-beating product, with only the vaguest idea of how the concept is to be turned into reality – while the responsible engineer has even less of an idea. Again, responsibility for this does not lie solely with management. Very often the staff enjoy making their own decisions autonomously, and without regard for the impact of so doing on the rest of the company. There is an inherent attitude that says, in effect, *'As long as they do their job and let me get on with mine, I don't care'*; yet they expect to be taken care of by the very people they disparage.

Sometimes, this is born of sheer bloody-mindedness that British industrial culture often instils in individuals towards management, any management. Sometimes the individual feels that, if he seeks clarification, he will be judged harshly and not be rewarded with his place on the management ladder; or, he will not get recognition and the consequent favourable pay review. As has been said earlier, if an individual is working for a company with an ill-defined structure, with muddled objectives and a lack of proper consultation with its workforce, and he sees no changes coming in this way of working, then he owes it to himself to seek alternative employment. Conversely, for an individual in management, a disciplined structure is vital, in order to monitor and measure the effectiveness of individuals within it.

The following chapters in this section are intended to give a full perspective of the way different functions inter-relate, and to show readers in each particular function how they fit into the business as a whole.

Taking control of your career

An interesting anecdote told by a former Chief Executive at a management training session is appropriate here. A valued young member of the technical staff left the company headed up by the speaker. The company had been through an extensive period of putting three companies together to form one. At just about the time the merger was completed, the company embarked on another acquisition; and the young engineer, quite understandably, felt he could not stand yet another protracted period of amalgamation and so left to join another major British company in the same industry. When the speaking Chief Executive eventually heard that the young engineer had gone, he requested his home telephone number from the personnel department and he telephoned the young man to thank him for his help with all that had been achieved with the original merger. He wished the young engineer well in his new career, and then told him that he genuinely hoped that he would be happy and fulfilled in his new job; but that if he was not, he hoped the young man would not let his pride stand in the way of his returning. The young engineer returned after just 10 days. He had found that, as a technical professional in his new company, he was totally buried in a bureaucracy where his personal creativity could find no home. He had no sense of being invited to make a recognised contribution to the company's progress.

The important conclusion to be drawn here is that by leaving the original merged three companies' employment, and then by returning he, at least, was taking control of his own career. Furthermore, he was interested in achieving some form of job satisfaction and personal fulfilment. There was a further twist to the story of this particular young man. He apparently moved on some time later to become a successful technical salesman. The speaker was demonstrating that each individual must take charge of his own career.

Given the amount of time and energy devoted to a career or job, it is crucial for everyone to have as much control and fulfilment as possible. Unless an individual is in control of his own career at all stages, then that control must, by definition, be in the hands of another person or organisation to such an extent that, at some stage, the individual will never be able to be in control, and then will ultimately live a life of suppressed fear and apprehension and subservience. It is but a short step to becoming totally resentful towards the person or organisation to whom control has been relinquished, and who might one day exercise that control by taking away the livelihood of the individual.

It is not uncommon for people to work for one company for some twenty or twenty five years. If in that time he has not developed or added to his skill set within that company he is liable to find himself not only redundant but virtually unemployable by any other employer; he has become institutionalised. Often such an individual will be too terrified to even apply for a job elsewhere for fear that even if, in the unlikely event, he was to be offered a job, he would not be able to fit into a new corporate culture – and he would probably be correct. This is not to say that everyone in a given professional environment should aspire to management. But there should be a consciousness of the dangers of conducting a career on a very narrow front for too long. Such an individual has effectively lost control of his own career and by so doing has invited redundancy.

Since all people in industry will work in one discipline or another, much of the rest of the book will concern itself with addressing people in each discipline and to point out some issues they need to consider to be more effective in their task. The aim is not to teach such people 'how to suck eggs' because they will already be earning a living in one of the selected disciplines and, as a result will and should, know more of that discipline than can be expounded here. However, it has very often the case that very few people approach, or practise, their discipline with the instinct or the focus or the training that underlines the fact that every decision made, or conclusion drawn, will have an impact on the financial well-being of the company. Furthermore, the extent to which an individual's efforts contribute to the effectiveness of others employed in the same arena, or indeed, the extent to which other people affect the effectiveness of the individual, is still not sufficiently understood or appreciated.

The following chapters analyse the role, the contribution and the relative importance of a variety of staff and management positions.

6

The Designer

The word 'designer' is used rather than, say, electronics designer or mechanical designer, because most of the points put forward are true of the designer of any type of product, and not just the specialist. It's also important to remove the intellectual categorisation, and the elitism that a designer receives when he is defined by his particular speciality. Electronics designer – very clever; computer designer – even cleverer; mechanical designer – well, maybe; shampoo bottle designer – definitely not. Yet all of these are designing an item that needs to sell. All of these people need to design something that will attract the attention of the potential buyer more than that of a competitor's product.

There is no question that the shampoo bottle designer knows this. He must know consumer trends. He must use research to know consumer colour preferences, the size and shape of bottle that is acceptable, the price range. He must consider the ease of use by the consumer, and whether that can be accommodated by a manufacturing and filling technique that will still produce an acceptable gross margin in a market place where margins are already perilously thin. He needs to know about packaging and recycling legislation because it can dictate his choice of materials and weight. He has to consider the type of cap, and the size and positioning of the area that will carry the label, as there are tooling costs and technical implications that again, will dictate the limitations of his design. And he needs to achieve good 'standout' on the supermarket shelf, where his bottle is battling against all manner of creatively-designed competitors. The design must be safe in children's hands, and not likely to leak during its transportation or its shelf life – either at the store, or in the home.

The designer would not dream of embarking on such a project unless he was armed with all of this information and more. The cost of manufacturing a new design is enormous. His employer cannot afford mistakes. He would expect to obtain this information from his market research people; who would, in turn, have liaised with the marketing department and the retail outlets before defining the brief to the designer.

It is quite possible that the problems and issues facing a shampoo bottle designer have been over-simplified but common sense and observation says that some attention to the issues as outlined will almost certainly have to be given. The shampoo bottle example has been outlined to draw parallels with designers engaged in more technical products and to question whether they are concerned as much as they should be with design issues beyond functionality. Once again it is valid to point out differences on the two sides of the Atlantic and there is a marked difference of approach to the task in hand. Of course, companies on both sides of the Atlantic can get it wrong. A notorious case in America during the 1960s was the Ford Edsel. Using the vast market research at their disposal, with great panache the Ford Corporation created and marketed the Edsel, predicted to outsell all other automobiles. It turned out to be a complete dog ... Nonetheless there is a willingness, in fact a corporate demand, for the American designer in industry to work with, and take direction from, the marketing staff; who, in turn, would be close to the market-place and its trends, and knowledgeable of the competition. The approach of UK technical designers is usually quite the reverse, and the culpability for this does not lie exclusively with the designer.

Often, there is insufficient direction given to the designer, sometimes, but not always, due to an exaggerated respect for his intellectual brilliance. More often it is just that management has just not clearly laid down from where the designer should take his direction. Nor does management insist that, having told him by whom he should be directed, he should then take direction from no-one else. That direction should come only from marketing if it exists, or from senior management if it does not. This of course assumes that not only is marketing doing its job correctly but more importantly it assumes that marketing knows what its job is, and how to carry it out. For a country renowned for conceiving and designing brilliant products, only to see them exploited by companies in other countries, this is a very dangerous assumption indeed.

There is later in the book a chapter dedicated to the extremely important role of marketing It is a peculiarly British phenomenon, however, that the majority of engineering companies still do not have a marketing function, and see no need for one. In many companies, even those who would have a

The Designer

marketing department, it is too often the case that technical designers take their direction from salesmen, intent on winning an order from a current prospective customer. Or the design merely satisfies the intellectual aspirations of the designer himself with almost no collaboration with other disciplines whatsoever. It is regrettably not flippant to suggest that Managing Directors might give direction to engineering designers immediately after a good business lunch with a long-standing customer. Perhaps most frightening has been where the engineering design people have been working under the direction of a major customer, not only without collaboration with the rest of the company, but without even a guarantee from the customer that he will, or can, buy the end result!

There are many other such instances of a lack of corporate discipline leading to dire consequences for the company. Unfortunately all of the events recounted here have happened and are not as rare as they should be. Furthermore, such occurrences are not restricted to small companies where perhaps such work practices are understandable, given the pressures to stay afloat, but in multi-million pound turnover companies where such practices are inevitably, and eventually, disastrous. It is not uncommon for marketing staff to promote and allow to be sold, via the sales force, products that the design engineers had yet to design. The problems thus arising are often compounded by the fact that the design engineers have produced some other products that marketing were totally unaware of, and these products were also being sold through the same sales force...

It is vital that a designer be given clear, unequivocal direction and directives, based on sound marketing strategies. To not do so, or to continually 'move the goal posts', for the designer, can have dire consequences; not to mention the state of continual frustration in which the designer spends his working life. Often such behaviour arises from no more than mutual personal animosity and power play between the directors of marketing and engineering! Such antipathy exists from time to time in all large companies worldwide, and companies worldwide suffer for it. But the total non-existence (or non-observation) of internal corporate discipline is far more in evidence with British companies than with overseas counterparts; the word 'empowerment' which was first introduced to encourage people to think for themselves within a corporate structure has been interpreted with such licence, and allowed to be interpreted thus, that anarchy is the result.

A lack of corporate discipline can only be the result of indiscipline by individuals. But by the same token individual indiscipline can only occur where there is no corporate discipline to constrain it. This discipline theme will be returned to again and again throughout this book because it is the one issue that lies beneath the national inability to bring the results of creativity to market. In a television interview, a former Chief Executive of Granada Television, speaking of the creators of television shows, said: 'Unless the creative people work within disciplined parameters, the results of their efforts are not viable, but if you define the parameters within which the creators are to work and then give them the freedom to do so, the results can be quite breathtaking.'

This is equally true of capital goods design. The designer's role should be pivotal, not secondary. Now, it may be that our designer, in the absence of any other form of direction, needs to define his own parameters, his own discipline. He owes it to his own sense of satisfaction to establish the defining criteria he will work to. It is beyond doubt that if a designer knows his product is competitively successful and is selling well his personal satisfaction will increase enormously, not to mention his productivity. On the other hand, if a designer beavers away in a laboratory or development centre, and he sees no evidence of his having made a recognisable contribution, nor indeed even knows if his contribution is recognised at all, then his job enthusiasm commensurably reduces and likewise his productivity will decrease. So how can a designer define his own parameters?

We must assume that the designer knows how to design his product from a functional standpoint, but that is less than half the task. In reality, he is not paid to conduct his work as if his employer is merely a professional extension of his university and he can indulge his own creative whims. Sadly though there are many working regimes, even in large companies, where the designer could be forgiven for thinking that was the case. If he accepts the economic role in a constructive manner, he might actually get to enjoy the fact. The author of this book was once acquainted with a company where the Director of Engineering decided to hold an Engineering Day. The intention was to bring all of his design engineers together in one place to swap their individual experiences. The need to do this arose from the fact that, as a result of a number of mergers and acquisitions, the Director had several geographically-dispersed engineering centres, and the design engineers in each had never met, and did not know how their individual efforts inter-related, nor how their combined efforts were being used, to produce compliance with a company strategy. In fact they didn't know the strategy, or that one existed, simply because management, including the engineering management, since the acquisitions, had been too deeply involved in formulating a viable strategy.

While this formulation of strategy was taking place, management could not too readily take the risk of distracting staff from their day-to-day activities. Obviously, they were not starting from a clean sheet. Although they had taken a long hard look at industry trends, the competition, and their own resources in order to determine a workable profitable strategy, the fact remains that they had, to coin a phrase, to 'pay the rent'. In other words, the company had to maintain an on-going revenue stream whilst producing a cohesive family of products and services in observance of their chosen strategy. The company's current activities had to continue alongside the gradual introduction of, and the eventual total dominance by, that strategy.

This meant that some design engineers were going to have to continue to expend further effort on, and enhance the capability of, existing products, while other designers worked on bringing the new exciting product releases to launch status. It seemed to the Engineering Director that this would never be achieved unless all of the engineers could understand how the strategy had been devised, what it was, and what part each engineer was to play in its realisation; hence the Engineering Day. Now, it is quite normal for those designers working on new products to be seen as the stars of the company and those working on existing products to be the journeymen. This often gives rise to preening by one group and resentment from the other. The purpose of the Engineering Day was to create one team out of these geographically dispersed designers working on different strands of the company's overall plan. A country hotel was rented and all design engineers attended. The Sales Director, the Marketing Director, and the Engineering Director made presentations to the assembled design engineers. The purpose was to acquaint the designers, who worked for the Engineering Director, with the overall company strategy; and to show them that, while they played a part in its implementation, unless they 'bought into it', it could not be implemented. They were the key personnel to bring this strategy to fruition. Finally, they were told where the input of each designer into the strategy formulation process would contribute to the final result.

Of course, it was also pointed out that cost and time scales had to be met if we were to successfully implement the strategy. An additional purpose of the presentations was to show that those working on existing products, far from being the less glamorous, were, in fact, the very people who, by their ingenuity with ageing products, were actually keeping the company afloat with day-to-day revenues. What is more, they were actually funding the efforts of those bringing the new products to market, products that were yet to produce a penny of revenue. It became clear to them that all had a key role to play in the company's future. Designers could directly relate their efforts, and their importance, to the future of the company. At this Engineering Day, they were indirectly receiving a lesson in the commercial aspects of the overall business. Awards were given to selected designers for outstanding initiative, or voluntary contribution beyond the demands of normal company duty. The final day of the meeting was given over to recreation events in a manner normally only accorded to the sales staff after a sales meeting.

Now the designers knew where they fitted into the overall scheme of things, they could see how valued and valuable they were, and the company showed its recognition in a way that the designers had never experienced before, but which was really enjoyed and appreciated. Team building was underway. However there is a danger that such an event will be received by the attendees with cynicism and scepticism simply because it has not been attempted before. Yet why should it be? The entertainment business, with its Oscars and Emmys, does it all the time with no objection from participants or observers. The cost to the company of an event of this nature, relative to the payback produced in terms of motivation and productivity, is negligible. There seems little point spending considerable sums of money on external public relations and advertising, extolling the company's services and products, if you are dependant on a neglected and demoralised workforce to produce those services and products.

Integrating areas of knowledge

The event described is just one example of how a company can contribute to the knowledge of the individual designer and how he fits in the overall scheme of things, but the process must be ongoing; not just a one-off, discrete event, appearing as if the management is just seeking gratitude. However, the designer must relate back the knowledge gained about an overall company discipline into his own personal professional behaviour. Even if his employer does not see fit to inform him then, in his own career protection interests, he needs to see his personal role in a wider context. He

The Designer

should establish himself, either by examining the outside market, through the reading of technical journals, trade newspapers etc., or by consulting with his own sales and/or marketing people, just what product, or to be more specific what product features, he is to produce in order for the company to be competitive. He should ascertain what is the sale price of the competitive offering. Hopefully, the design engineer will have access to marketing people who will tell him what should be the sales price of the new product if it is to be successful in the market place. If there are no marketing people, he should use the sales people or, as a last resort, outside researchers or consultants to find out. If he has access to neither, then he must concern himself with the marketing of his product in the same manner as our erstwhile shampoo bottle designer.

The designer must consider all the marketing issues if he is to be fully effective. This is not to do someone else's job, but to improve his own performance. Yet all too often, when consulted on the subject of marketing, the technical professional will become self-effacing and protest that he has no knowledge of those things, as if he has always kept his eyes and ears firmly shut while out shopping with his wife, reading the ads in a magazine or traipsing around innumerable trade fairs. For too many British company executives, marketing is still a Black Art, at best a particularly lowbrow form of show business, better left to those without higher intellectual aspirations.

So, there are the key questions to be asked – and answered. Can the cost of designing the product guarantee a saleable price at a satisfactory margin? If not, what design adjustments and feature sacrifices can be made? Is the product easy to manufacture? Are the components being contemplated, the most cost effective, or have the most recent components, and by inference the most expensive, been used unnecessarily merely to satisfy some intellectual whim deep in the breast of the designer? A product designed to carry out a specific function with little or no idea of its required features, essential or optional, or of the cost constraints imposed by the market place, is quite futile and will eventually lead to grief of one kind or another. Further if there is no process external to the designer himself to provide him with that information, or with information regarding all the other concurrent activities associated with bringing that product to market readiness, then he must come down from his ivory tower and provide it for himself. At least by this means he is acting in a disciplined, professional manner that must benefit his own career, either with his current employer or with another. It is not the mark of a good design engineer to design a product to carry out a certain function without regard to a variety of constraints, and then to be completely disinterested in the fact that someone else has to manufacture it, and someone else has to sell it, while yet others support it and maintain it after it has been sold.

Cost of sales

The days when an engineer could just design, and management could just add up the costs of so-doing and then add a percentage mark-up before sale are, to all intents and purposes, over. A relatively unsophisticated form of financial control will determine the gross margin that the company can tolerate with the product range in general, or needed from a new product in particular. This, in turn, determines the allowable cost to bring the new product to market. The designer should know what this figure is to be. It is quite possible, almost certain in fact, that all of the features requested by marketing or sales or determined by his own investigation of market forces, cannot be achieved within the cost constraints so imposed. It is at this stage that all of the combined ingenuity in the company should come into play. What features can be sacrificed? If we include these features instead of sacrificing them is there a market for a product sold at a higher price? When must the product be ready for launch if (a) there is still to be a market for the product and (b) our current product range is to hold up until the release of this new product? Of course, if the sales of existing products have fallen away from their hitherto steady level before the new product sales have reached the same level then there will inevitably be a dip in company revenues, the consequences of which must be considered.

Once again, the designer must be prepared, having taken all factors into consideration, to give a realistic launch date and stick to it. By the same token, he can hardly be held accountable for a launch date artificially prepared by marketing or management in order to meet some demands, either internal or external, being made on them. It is not uncommon for design engineers to be castigated by sales people and customers and the press for not delivering a product, the launch date of which they had no part in determining. However, it is equally true that often, when this responsibility is given to the designers themselves, they are pleased; but they are less pleased when it is pointed out that, along with the opportunity to determine their own dates and realisable design aims, came the responsibility of performing to these committed criteria. Of course, when committing to launch dates, designers will invariably attempt to 'sandbag', a name given to the device of building extra time and money into the budgeting process to ensure that deadlines are comfortably met but the leeway for this is limited simply because 'market forces' will constrain it.

As part of the regular review programme, design engineers should be asked about the manufacturability and maintainability of the product. Situations too commonly occur where each product delivered to a customer has either been modified at the customer's request to such an extent that each product is unique, or the product range is so complex in its manufacture, with little or no thought given to its maintenance in the field, that post-delivery support is beyond the capabilities of local field service personnel. Thus the downtime is excessive and the cost of maintenance is prohibitive. The author recalls a hospital installation of telecommunications equipment where downtime could not be tolerated for obvious reasons, and a similar telecommunications system installed in a foreign exchange bank, where downtime meant transaction losses to the customers, of millions of pounds, and a threat to the job of the man who had selected the equipment.

It may be of value to detail the case of the hospital referred to above, which had bought its equipment from a very small company, designing and manufacturing switches for telecommunications networks. The switches had found their main market in hospitals in various health authorities throughout the UK. Logically, the functionality of the products should have been similar across the whole market; but in the event, each authority had asked their area sales representative for modifications to the core product. The salesman had put pressure on the management to accede to the customer's request. Consequently, each of the said switches was virtually custom built. In principle, there is nothing wrong with this approach, as long as the modifications are well documented and priced accordingly, and all the ramifications of post-sales support have been considered and accounted for, and properly costed. However, when a company is small, it cannot appear to quibble when it is desperate for an order. As a result, none of the sensible measures for commercial self-protection were taken. Whenever there was a fault, the design engineers had to go on-site to cure the problem. No-one had pointed out to the customer the problems that might ensue from incorporating extensive variations from the standard product. Understandably, there was little forgiveness from the customer for all the subsequent downtime of the equipment, even though he, the customer, had been allowed unwittingly to contribute to the problem.

Another inevitable outcome of not examining, comprehensively, all of the relevant issues at the time of embarking on the product development programme, was that no time scales could be relied upon. Design engineers were spending so much time in the field fixing unserviceable existing equipment, that no reliance could be put on the amount of time they had to spare for original design activities. Furthermore, it had not occurred to the designers to build the product in such a manner that enabled replacement parts to be installed by the customer or that diagnostic measures could have been incorporated in the product such that the customer could more easily define the problem. For a company of its size, vast expense in the form of travel and hotels and loss of development time was being incurred unnecessarily. It was hardly surprising that the company was teetering on the verge of bankruptcy, despite near-heroic attempts by the management to keep it afloat.

Strangely enough, even while the company's very survival was at stake, many of those involved resisted the changes and disciplines we put in place to save it. They enjoyed 'riding the fire engine'... The salesmen resented their loss of freedom and ability to direct the company in their own financial interest; the design engineers enjoyed the frequent all-expenses-paid trips away from home... Only the original founders, still with the company, recognised the danger. It was a classic case where the founders, designers themselves, had shown resourcefulness by finding a niche market for a niche product and had managed to exploit their initial success. However, being bright technically was not sufficient qualification to run, much less control, the business as it grew. Their finance man was an accountant who could see where the problems lay but felt powerless to correct them – possibly because he was never asked.

This is another lesson to be learned by design engineers and budding businessmen whose fundamental skill is that of designer. It is one thing to disparage financial people and the undue influence they sometimes hold over a business, but quite another to under-estimate their value to that business. Their activity should form the core of any and every part of the disciplined process I have referred to many times. Any design engineer or businessman who does not exert financial control over every aspect of his endeavours or his business, is heading, inevitably, for disaster. Too often the phrase, 'You have to speculate to accumulate' and it is usually uttered by someone with little business experience, who wishes to spend someone

The Designer

else's money, usually that of their employer, and is rarely the person to be held accountable for the consequences. The reality is that the expenditure on a project and realistic targeted revenues should be worked out in detail before the project is embarked upon, and then all activity needs to be accommodated within that planned expenditure if there is to be any eventual profit margin.

The actual expenditure needs to be monitored on an on-going basis. If the small company in the parable had done this, the management and the designers would have been aware that the cost of modifications to the basic design could not be undertaken without a commensurate increase in the eventual cost of the product. Several courses of action can ensue from this early study. The easiest and most straightforward, is to persuade the customer that his requested enhancements have an incremental cost out of all proportion to the benefits he will derive from their inclusion. This is not always easy in a competitive situation. The next is to attempt to limit the customer to the changes which can be incorporated with least incremental cost and, equally important, least impact on the cost of any post-sales support that may be called for. Another approach is to persuade the customer that he does not need all the modifications at the outset and they can be included at a later date after the initial equipment has been installed.

Whatever the outcome of such negotiating, it is imperative that all forms of control of expenditure, whether it be materials, labour, capital equipment, overhead, post-sales support, sales commissions or travel and accommodation must be accounted for, and all levels of staff controlled. In the case recounted here, the engineer founders had never before employed, much less controlled, a sales force. As a result, the salesmen virtually devised their own commission plan such that they were drawing an income the company could not afford, and which bore no relationship to any increased profitability for the company. If a commission plan is drawn up to reflect the order value, without that order value reflecting a pre-set pricing structure, then it is obvious that the salesman will not be averse to allowing the customer to add every conceivable extra and modification, without any regard to its impact on the profitability of the company. In fact, it is far from being beyond the bounds of possibility for the salesman himself to persuade the customer to request the changes to the equipment to increase the overall revenue value of the order – and enhance his personal commission.

Thus this example company, which truly existed, staffed by very keen, very bright, very dedicated and very honest people, was rapidly going broke.

The proprietors of the company did not consult the working designers to weigh up the options, technical and financial. Conversely, the designers just responded to demands without question or challenge. They did not have enough commercial education to explore the commercial consequences of responding to ad hoc demands for changes to equipment design. Although the core product had been designed by the company's designers the end product sold to the customers had been, in effect, designed by the customers and the salesmen, each of whom had absolutely no regard for the long-term health of the company.

Another actual example is one of a company that was supplying computer printer networks around customers' premises. In many ways, the methods employed at the time were a technological breakthrough and the company was successful and employed many people – too many. Put crudely, the company's recruitment policy was run on what can be termed the 'Fred's busy' method. 'Fred looks busy, so we recruit Charlie. Fred and Charlie look busy so we recruit Bill. Fred, Charlie and Bill look busy so we recruit...', and so on. (More thoughts on the subject of recruitment and recruitment timing are given in chapter 10). All of this recruitment was done for the very best of reasons – to keep the customers happy. As a result, everyone was busy; the company was growing, the customers were happy – but insufficient attention was being paid to the ticking time bomb. The company was introducing a technological breakthrough, and there were difficulties. More and more resources were being thrown at the problems, regardless of cost; the company went out of business because it did not sufficiently appreciate that every additional member of staff had to be paid for by an incremental increase in gross margin of the product or service equal to the salary of the new member of staff – and that's just to enable the company to stand still. So a company based, exclusively, on the design of a clever technological breakthrough, was brought down as the result of a lack of attention to the harsh commercial realities.

Quite apart from the general concepts of marketing and company cost control, as outlined above, every design engineer should, in his own interest, confront these issues with his own specific task. If the costs of a product, by the time it is ready for market, render that product non-competitive, either by cost or features, then all involved are at risk. Frankly the view, commonly held, that: 'I am a clever designer, and if this doesn't work, the company will give me something else to do' is a highly dangerous, self-deluding position. Maybe the justice of the situation would suggest nothing wrong with the attitude, but justice often has little or no effect on the financial realities. The attitude is one from which great amusement is often drawn – from ostriches. Regrettably, it is a position all too often adopted by many in industry.

Designers as accomplices in their own demise

It is would be worthwhile to illustrate the point by recounting a situation of a company whose financial state was parlous and whose design team was misused to disguise this fact. Again it involves a company engaged in the manufacture of telecommunications equipment but the lessons to be drawn could equally apply to many other companies employing designers. In this case there was a substantial engineering team involved in designing and developing a new telecommunications product. The commitment of resources to such a programme is always high risk for several reasons. The direction of the telecommunications industry has always been difficult to predict, not only because of the rapid changes in technology, but also because not so long ago the national and international carriers, the PTTs, as they are called (BT in the UK) had enormous influence. Seldom could a non-PTT commercial company in the industry lead the way technologically. It was nearly always compelled to attempt to reflect the industrial trends, determined by the PTTs, by launching products as soon as possible after the trend has been established.

British companies had a particular problem here, because new trends were and still are usually initiated in the United States, and therefore Britain is often in the position of playing catch-up. As far as launching new products is concerned, the telecommunications industry is different from say, the computer industry. If the computer industry introduces a new popular concept, then there is little restriction to its success, other than market acceptance; witness the almost instant success of the PC manufacturers such as Apple Computers and software designers like Microsoft, for instance. Products into the telecommunications arena, on the other hand, will often have to contend with restrictive practices by national governments protecting their home-grown PTT. Alternatively, the PTT may be dependent, for its near future, on the maintenance of a particular tariff structure that the new proposed product would adversely impact.

As a consequence of these considerations and many others, to embark on a new product development is a very costly venture – and there is no guarantee of success. If the market predicted for the product, predicted at the outset of the development, has moved or disappeared by the time of launch, there is no payback of monies spent. Companies have been ruined for getting such things wrong. The telecommunications company referred to here was a case in point. Their total employee number comprised a large percentage of design engineers. These people were very competent but the company for a variety of reasons, mostly managerial, had lost its way. In order to stave off a take-over – an exercise in which they were to be unsuccesful – the board of the company needed to make a significant announcement. To this end it announced the imminent launch of a new 'flagship' product that was promoted by the marketing department as being state-of-the-art. The design team was established, a new building was occupied, and the design process started.

After the take-over, it quickly became clear to the new management, that sadly, at no time had the previous board consulted with the design team to establish if the product concept was viable. It is probable that they received an input from marketing staff with no engineering consultation. The design team was not asked for its views on the product launch dates being published to the outside world. The dates bore no relation to reality, but were issued simply to sustain the book value; i.e., the share price, of the company. To maintain this subterfuge, many engineers worked long hours to produce a demonstration mock-up of the finished product, to be displayed at the leading industrial trade exhibition. Thus the trade were deliberately misled. In fact, there were no funds available for the very sophisticated design and test equipment that the team would need to bring the actual product to market. Perhaps most damaging of all, even though there was a design team in place, and working, there were absolutely no plans for marketing or selling the product if, and when, it was ever ready for launch. There was no discipline in place that recognised that this was the future flagship product of the company and that, if it was to succeed, every one in the company had to support the endeavour.

People of all professional disciplines in the company, including some in the design team itself, held their own views on the likelihood of the product's success. Furthermore, they followed their personal instincts, in terms of the contribution they were prepared to make towards its eventual success, an unacceptable position for them to adopt. Such people are drawing their salaries dishonestly when they accept money from the company to do a job they are not prepared to do, whatever their misgivings. Of course, all participants in a project should be able to question the wisdom

The Designer

of a project by way of normal managerial communications. By the same token, management should tell staff why they have chosen a particular course of action.

Once the decision is made, then all people engaged on the project – and taking salary whilst doing so – owe it to the management to fully support the project. It's a symptom of the anarchy referred to earlier that British professional staff assume that they can be judged by different criteria to those in the non-professional ranks. It is somehow considered acceptable for the designers or sales people, etc., to say, in effect: 'I cannot, or will not, do my job because management are going in the wrong direction' or, 'I cannot do my job because the product is not equal to that of the competition, either in price or performance or quality or features'. At the same time, it is assumed by these people that they should continue to be employed and paid while refusing, for whatever reason, to do the job they were employed to do. Rarely are the same attitudes adopted by the non-professional staff, probably because they assume, and rightly, that they would have been given short shrift.

It is yet another example of the lack of commercial realism that is so often part of the character of the British professional. Somehow the professional status is interpreted as bringing with it a view that the individual is no longer an economic unit on the payroll, but is, and should be, a free spirit with freedom of thought. Nothing could be further from the truth. A professional not doing the job he is being paid to do, whatever the difficulties, is merely a more expensive economic unit – and one the company can do without. At the same time, a professional is in an invidious position when instructed to compromise standards and produce, in an unrealistic time, an inferior product which he believes is not in the company's or the customer's interests to release.

To interject, it is an unfortunate fact that often, management offers no consultation to its staff, or a means of providing answers to reasonable questions. Perhaps the company has a history of entering projects that are ill-conceived, and its financial history proves it. Under these circumstances, if he cannot affect the situation by a direct confrontation, the more professional employee, the one who really is interested in personal fulfilment, and obviously the one who has greater job mobility, owes it to himself to consider his long-term future with the company.

To return to the subject company, it became clear to the new management team, after some time into the development of the new 'flagship' product that there was, at least an eighteen month disconnect between the product launch dates that had been given by the previous board to the outside world, and the realistic date by which the product could actually be made ready for launch. Furthermore, the product specification was not finalised, its eventual market ill-defined, and the costs of bringing the product to market were unknown. Here again, is a classic case of people buried in the language of the technology, conceiving a product whose only justification for being developed is that it is different from any other, and would be deemed to be 'very clever'. The board did not appear to have questioned the efficacy of the product. Apparently their major, almost their sole, concern was with relations with the investment community. They certainly had not concerned themselves with embracing all of the disciplines that would have to play a key role in making a success of the product, or even in ensuring that there would be a product at all. There is absolutely no question that any product that has a ' two-years-plus ' gestation time, and which is trying to create a new market for itself, has a far from certain future in the telecommunications industry.

Of course, with the commitment to the product that had already been made, and the public utterances that had accompanied that commitment, it was not possible for the new management team to abandon the project without serious consequences. Once the gap between aspiration and reality was known the first task was to attempt to retrieve the situation and turn the project into the success it was predicted to be. Is there a market? Is this product likely to reflect an industry trend at the time of the predicted product launch date? Can the projected development costs be justified, in the light of knowledge gained as a result of a somewhat late examination of the market? All these questions, and more, needed to be answered – and they were being asked after the train had left the station. But now questions were being asked by the new management team of the people who would ultimately be responsible for bringing the product to market: the design engineers, who should have been enquiring of the earlier lack of reality. They knew that the launch dates given by the board were unrealistic. They knew that the project they were working on was going to be too late to catch the market – always assuming there was a market. Here were very bright people who knew they were being misled, who knew that the market was being misled, yet who seemed oblivious to the danger – or chose to ignore it. Their employment had lasted through some terrible times that had led to the imminent take-over. They were extremely critical of the management that ostensibly led

The Designer

them – and yet they had not sought answers to very fundamental questions that would, and did, affect the future of every one of them.

Of course, to suggest that these people should not give their loyalty to the management while they are on the payroll, runs counter to my earlier arguments about company discipline and potential anarchy. Nevertheless, not to raise questions, and express real concerns, via normal management channels, about issues in which all were going to be deeply affected is tantamount to lemming-like professional suicide. Why were these people prepared to be managed and to be kept so totally in the dark? It is difficult to escape the conclusion that it is the blinkered ignorance that arises from an excessively deferential management system.

In his book *The State We're In*, Will Hutton says: *'The presumption is simply that workers will do what they are told, and have no rights of redress, or even channels through which they can make suggestions of better working practices. They are meant to be impotent, and it is assumed that they have nothing to contribute to workplace organisation'*. Now it is obvious from the context in which Hutton expresses this view, that his 'worker' is the artisan. Such a person, because of educational limitations, does not always enjoy mobility and has less opportunity to reject the messages that management hands down. Such an excuse should not be acceptable for his more professional colleagues.

Unfortunately the professional worker, the graduate, often accepts, with no justification whatever, exactly the same constraints as his less educated colleague. This inevitably leads to an intellect being developed to a level determined by others. It leads to talented people not exploring the extent to which they could develop themselves, surrendering their power to control their lives and careers to 'them' – the management. This, almost instinctive, cultural belief that: *'Them upstairs knows what's best for us'*, is a major reason why the country does not produce entrepreneurs of the type seen so often in the USA and elsewhere. Professional employees retreat into a form of intellectual snobbery that enables them to surround themselves with a warm glow of intellectual self-delusion. It is difficult to disagree totally with Will Hutton's observations about industrial relations in the United Kingdom, but too many people, some from a relatively senior position, acquiesce in the process.

The conditioning is so pronounced and entrenched that it is extremely difficult it for a technically qualified individual to shake off the 'technical snobbery' that is instilled in him as part of his education; sales, marketing and management are avenues closed to him as a result. American technical staff suffer from these inhibitions to a much lesser extent, indeed they see moving on to these other disciplines as a natural career progression; this leaves the young to deal with the purely technical issues. It is indeed very difficult in the UK to shake off years of conditioning, both educational and industrial, but it must be done if an individual is to realise the potential of his talents. What is more, with industrial globalisation, there was never an easier, nor a more pressing time to do it, than now. The blind reliance on sticking forever with one employer, the assumption that the employer has a genuine concern for the employee, is less credible now than it ever was. More and more, the individual has to take charge of his own future. The motivation for doing so does not always spring from courage – it just as often springs from fear. It doesn't matter which, the result can be the same.

It is dangerous to avoid an examination of where one's personal effort is leading. Remember the expression, 'Life is not a rehearsal'! Time spent, however enjoyably, on a project going nowhere, or in a company going nowhere, is self-indulgence few can afford in today's harsh commercial reality. Self-indulgence is also an apt word for those never moving on from a favourite project in a quest to produce the perfect product. In the words of the American designer mentioned earlier, 'It's not perfect – but it sells'. It's the difference between commercial survival and commercial oblivion.

To continue with the new flagship product saga, whilst the design team were being acquainted with the realities, the new Engineering Director and Financial Director needed to establish the financial viability of the whole project. The design engineers themselves needed to give their assessment of a realistic launch date; how would that be affected by a reduction of product features to accelerate the launch process? There was little time for 'sandbagging' the time predicted to develop the product up to launch date. If there was any such 'fat' in the development time the overall company plans would be adversely affected and the introduction of such a contingency would be self-defeating. Now, for the first time, the design engineers were being meaningfully consulted on some of the business realities of the project with which their future was very much concerned. The positive change in the attitude and morale of the designers to this consultation, albeit belated, was manifest. Even the responsibility that this level of involvement brought about was accepted willingly. However, it had to be pointed out that such involvement, previously denied them, carried a responsibility and this too, was accepted willingly.

Of course, with so much of company time, money and effort being expended on an unannounced product whose launch date was at least a year out, the deliberations now underway had to include an examination of the status of other products in the range. These were going to be called upon to sustain the company revenues in the interim. Some of these products had been long established, so the possibility of enhancing their capability in order to increase their sales or extend the product lifespan was explored. Were there any other new products under development that are nearer to launch date? Could these programmes be accelerated? Would there a better return on investment if some of the engineering design effort being expended on the new flagship product was switched to these other products under development and nearer their launch date?

While all of these deliberations were going on the costs of abandoning the whole new flagship product project now had to be assessed whatever the risks that posed to the outside perception of the company. This ill-conceived and ill-managed product could not be allowed to bury the company. It just could not be a 'sacred cow'. A very bright team of people had had their activities determined, and their professional futures were being affected, by a process they were not involved in, and did not even know was happening. Nevertheless, in this new regime of designer involvement, all discussions now taking place were product discussions, technical discussions, marketing and sales discussions, discussions regarding the status of the market and the competition. All of these discussions would have a financial outcome. The costs and the aspirations would have to be adjusted to match the realities of a highly competitive market place. Any product programme of a highly innovative nature, that assumes a market readiness at some point in the future, without regard to the costs or time scales of getting to that point, is like trying to construct a building by putting the roof on first.

So what can a member of the design team do in order to be comfortable that all relevant issues have been addressed, issues that affect his, or her, job satisfaction and job future? There are few companies that can disguise from their staff some of the signs that the company is ill-disciplined, lacking in direction, and not matching the competition in the market place. There are fewer still that forbid anyone from asking relevant questions of colleagues or peers. Such questions can, of course, include querying the whole future technical direction of the company, and it would be a rare company where there was not number of differences of opinion among its technical staff regarding this particular issue. However, if a member of the technical staff feels so strongly that the company is going in a direction not in accord with his or her own views, then there is only one course open. The individual must leave, either willingly or unwillingly.

To stay and unilaterally follow a course different from that decided by management is usually unworkable, unless there has been a severe examination of motives. If it is merely motivated by a desire to 'do one's thing', regardless of the impact on the company's fortunes, it is likely to be disruptive and counter-productive. Sometimes if the motive is the correct one, then a technical renegade approach works on occasions. One such occasion is chronicled in a book called *The Soul of a New Machine* by Tracy Kidder. This book, a true story, describes how a team of very committed and dedicated design engineers brought a completely new computer to market readiness in rapid time. They did it for an American computer company called Data General (since acquired by EMC^2), that had in the 1970s enjoyed the kind of growth since enjoyed by Microsoft. That growth was threatened by the launch of a competitor's computer, breaking new technological ground. The Data General team, despite enormous tensions and disputes inside the company, produced the competitive offering in record time to save the company. However there were three key issues that made the anarchy work. First, there was the unique atmosphere that existed at the time in Data General. Secondly, Tom West, the American renegade design engineer featured in the true story, was not motivated by self-regard, out to prove management wrong. He was determined to put his company out in front in the race against the competition. Finally, his efforts did not disrupt the existing direction chosen by the company management – they complemented it. It is interesting to quote Kidder at one point in the book: *'Executives might make the final decisions about what would be produced, but design engineers would provide most of the ideas for new products. After all, design engineers were the people who really knew the state of the art and who were therefore best equipped to prophesy changes in it'.* How many British companies use this approach to their product development plans, where young enthusiastic designers, involved in the business issues, have their state-of-the-art knowledge harnessed in a collective fashion to positively determine the company's future direction and profitability?

Assuming that the designer is comfortable with the overall direction of the company, there are still many legitimate questions to be asked. What is the competition expected to be at the time of product launch? What are their strengths and weaknesses? What is the best estimate of the sales price of the

The Designer

product? At least the designer should assure himself that someone has asked, and received answers, to these questions. What is the minimum gross margin that the company can live with? This is the difference between the predicted, or the actual, selling costs, and the direct costs; i.e., costs of materials, production labour, transportation, etc., of making the product ready for sale.

The establishment of a gross margin figure is crucial because from this gross profit is deducted all of the other costs, R&D, marketing, selling, administration and overhead, that will establish the net profit of the product and its contribution to the overall profitability of the company. The gross margin figure is also, ultimately, the measure of the effectiveness of the design engineering that went into the product, and the market acceptability of the product.

In summary, from an engineering standpoint, the designer should be concerned with measuring his own effectiveness, by using criteria beyond whether the device he is working on fulfils the function, or functions, for which it was designed. If he is an employee, he should also make himself aware of the criteria by which his employer will judge his effectiveness. None of the design engineers had the remotest idea of such issues in the case of the new flagship product recounted above. To correct this, many meetings were conducted by the new management team, and the design engineers were appraised of the realities. They were left in no doubt that control of costs incurred bringing the product to market readiness was their responsibility, not the finance department's. If all the other departmental activities associated with launching the product were geared to the predicted launch date, then that date had to be met. A new product brought to market has to have an impact. All related activities have to come together on the predicted launch date for that impact to happen. The alternative is disaster, where the product isn't launched – it's drifted away from its moorings (see Appendix 3).

But it is rare in UK companies for design engineers to have knowledge of related activities simply because of the elitist, protected, environment in which they work. The shortcomings of the knowledge of the designers went beyond those relating to the product features, benefits and costs. The wider issues of sales, marketing, promotion and aesthetic appearance (if appropriate) were totally unknown to them. This lack of knowledge was not restricted to this particular product at this particular time. The designers had little or no knowledge of the wider issues generally. More worrying was that it did not seem to occur to the designers that they should acquaint themselves with these wider issues or that, if they did so, they then would be much more effective performing their own particular tasks.

By acquainting himself with the overall context in which he is performing his allotted task, the design engineer or engineering manager, in effect, becomes a businessman on a payroll. It enables him to manage himself as such, and judge the effectiveness of all those working around him. In summary, he has gone a long way to learning and practising the rudiments of management that does not always entail the management of others, but improves his capability to manage himself. Furthermore a design engineer who has acquainted himself with these associated issues can, if appropriate, demand improvements to the manner in which they are implemented. If his motives are honest ones when demanding these improvements, then the improvements will minimise the danger of the designer wasting both his own time and that of his employer. No-one, least of all the employer, can object to such a worthwhile motive.

7

The Marketer

'Marketing is too important to leave to marketing.'

Beware the person who claims the title of 'marketing something-or-other' in a technical or industrial environment. Does he or she really understand the task, or is he merely a person who has proved inadequate as a technician, or considers himself to be too brilliant to remain one, and is too fearful, or too pretentious to be in sales? Marketing is often seen as, and allowed to be, by non-vigilant management, the quiet haven from the demands to perform placed on designers and salesmen and others. Sometimes, marketing is used by management as a slot in which to fit people they deem suitable for management, regardless of whether there is anything really meaningful, or contributory, for them to do. Thus, the marketing department often swells the headcount, boosts the unproductive ranks and calls endless, fruitless meetings in order to justify its existence, a further waste of productive time. All of the above is a denial of the true importance of marketing.

Marketing should be the driving force of the whole company. It should be staffed by very bright people, well organised with no overlap of duties and they should be prevented from overloading the field force of the company with more and more initiatives, to a point of diminishing returns. It is marketing that has made the Japanese and the Germans the success they are in capital goods, the Italians and French in fashion, the Americans in everything from movies to hamburgers. Conversely, poor marketing has contributed significantly to the demise of Britain's own motor car industry, motor cycle industry, computer industry, etc., etc., etc. Some commentators and industry observers would contend that it is poor investment, poor quality and poor service, together with low investment in manufacturing has led to the demise of British industry. But such issues of investment, quality and service all arise fundamentally from poor marketing, or from insufficient attention given to marketing by company management. This, in turn, is because, as has been said earlier, the British as a rule are too concerned with their own internal company problems and pay little or no attention to the needs of the market. Although marketing has been referred to as a science it is, in a wider sense, merely the multi-faceted presentation of the company, its products and its people to the market. Everyone on the payroll should be involved, design staff in particular. It was Bill Hewlett, of Hewlett Packard fame, who coined the phrase, *'marketing is too important to leave to marketing'*.

It is very difficult to quantify the effectiveness of marketing and marketing people. Sales people can be measured by performance against their sales target. Manufacturing effectiveness can be measured by production figures or quality assurance figures, inventory turns and many other quantifiable criteria. Marketing, on the other hand, is not only difficult to measure, but if there is tangible success in the company, someone else will almost inevitably claim credit. By the same token, if there is a disaster, no prizes for guessing where the finger is usually pointed. Many times in a company the accusation will be made that marketing people either do nothing at all, or what they do is not worth doing. Notwithstanding these uncomfortable truths, it is a fact that marketing deserve, on occasions, to be held accountable for company shortcomings. Too often, people in marketing in engineering companies have sought and found what they believe to be a role where they can be admired, but away from those roles where a lack of performance is more readily identifiable.

If marketing enjoys the key role that it should in any successful company, then it should not be reluctant to adopt a high profile in that company providing, of course, that their motive for doing so is beyond reproach. The role of marketing is to ensure that the company's capabilities, be they manifested as a range of products, or a range of services, or both, is presented both internally and externally, in such a fashion as to maximise profitable sales. To be effective in this role means to take the lead in producing a concerted effort from all the disciplines in the company. Because of this, it is not so necessary to be technically clever as to be logistically well organised. If the latter springs from a base of being technically bright, so much the better, but it is not a pre-requisite. An eye for detail, on the other hand, is essential.

Good marketing people have multiple personalities. They need to have

The Marketer

an eye to the outside world to assess and understand market trends. This knowledge, together with an understanding of the capabilities of the company as a whole, and of the individuals in it, will enable a good marketing man to conceive of a product, or a process, or a service, that will increase sales or market share. However, without being dismissive of the value of such far sightedness, it is often the easiest part of the whole exercise. You will see below, where details of an actual product introduction are given, that the vision of what a company needs, or can do, to improve its performance, is of little value unless that same marketing person is prepared to work through all of the minutiae of every activity, both within and outside the company, to bring that vision to fruition. Only then does the original idea stand any chance of success. An idea can sometimes be the result of a few seconds inspiration, but depending on the size and history of the company, that idea might take a year of quite tedious work, before it becomes a profitable reality. If the company can't afford a year, then a more practical idea is called for. Remember, at all times, 'the rent has to be paid'.

Too often, so-called marketing people believe, quite sincerely, that as long as they have an idea a minute, they should be basking in the admiration of all to whom they relate. Equally often the majority of such ideas have a very short fruitless life. It calls for tremendous self-discipline – that word again – to be excited, and to excite others, with an idea, and then effectively drop from view to become an administrator implementing all of the necessary detail; hence the allusion above to multiple personalities. Only by being so, can marketing select a profitable role for the company and its products.

At the same time, it is equally important that marketing people keep a tight control over their knowledge. It is too easy for marketing to map out a role, and a series of activities for the company, merely to display their own cleverness. Again this is danger particularly prevalent in British companies. The author recalls one occasion in particular, where a so-called marketing man, technically very bright, made a presentation of 45 minutes' duration, to the company's worldwide senior management. The subject he selected was an in-depth analysis of some American features of the industry that the company was in. The presentation was informative and educational, and showed that he knew his subject extremely well. Nevertheless, it had to be pointed out to him, with some force I might add, in view of the time that the audience had wasted listening to him, that his dissertation had not added, nor would ever add, 'one nickel to the bottom line of the company'. It was sheer self-indulgence, displaying his knowledge to no particular purpose, as far as his employer was concerned. If marketing people study technology in isolation, rather than its acceptability in the market place, and its relevance to the company, then the company will almost inevitably overreach itself – or, to use an American expression 'just spin its wheels'.

This national disregard for market realities in favour of technical brilliance so often leads companies astray commercially. The result is that the company's ambitions cannot be matched by its capabilities. It has been said many times that one of the most successful marketing companies of modern times, IBM, never led the market, but it was always a very close second. From this position IBM was invincible for many years. It's has often been said that 'a pioneer is a guy with an arrow in his back'.

Of late, there has been some improvement in British marketing of capital goods, but it's often merely mechanical. Lessons in marketing, degrees in marketing are available and, of course valuable, but unless real disciplined thinking – that word again – is applied to the task, the results are doomed to failure. It is analogous to a belief that, by taking golf lessons and learning how to correctly hold the club have the shoulders square, and the head down when hitting the ball it will bring about a transformation into Tiger Woods. In UK companies too many marketing people are pre- occupied with impressing management and peers of their own brilliance and spend too little time in the detailed work necessary to bring a selected product or service in a profitable manner.

Marketing is a science, allied to a judgement and implemented with a discipline, but ultimately it can have only one objective – to increase profitable revenue. A good design engineer may make a good marketing person, a less gifted engineer may make a good marketing person, a non-engineer may make a good marketing person. However, it is my belief that a design engineer, not necessarily endowed with technical brilliance, can often bring more to the task than those with no technical skills at all. This is providing he is prepared to subjugate his technical knowledge to the new task in hand. He cannot allow himself, nor should he be allowed, the indulgence of saying, in effect 'I'm doing this marketing job but I want all to understand that I am, in reality, a clever engineer at heart.' This was the basic problem with the man, referred to above, that gave his worthless presentation to senior management. For a good marketing person, a whole new range of skills is called for, for which his technical knowledge could, and should, be used only to form a valuable backdrop.

The Marketer

Marketing is multi-dimensional and every dimension must be considered and dealt with. Remember our shampoo bottle designer? A product can be designed to be of beautiful appearance, to be sold at an acceptable price and exquisitely presented to the market, but if it is of poor quality it will eventually fail. Witness the Jaguar car of the 1980s. It used to be said in the USA that if you bought one Jaguar you needed a second one at the same time to provide spares for the one being driven. During this same period, Mercedes and BMW made reliability a cornerstone of their marketing and, in this luxury end of the car market, made inroads into the Jaguar market share as a result; Jaguar is now owned by Ford. At the lower end of the market, the reliability of Japanese cars, together with their marketing skills, effectively killed off the remainder of the British car industry. It is therefore essential that the marketing staff make inputs to the manufacturing regime to ensure that quality is accorded its due regard. If poor investment, poor training, low workforce morale and motivation have given rise to poor quality then it is for marketing to bring this fact and its consequences to the attention of management. This is part of the minutiae referred to earlier.

The work practice where each professional discipline works independently of all other is largely responsible in British organisations for the problems experienced in bringing products to market. If each person, at a professional level, gives no regard to other related professional activities, then that person deserves to be professionally vulnerable. By the same token, if management have not played their crucial role in ensuring that all elements of the company infrastructure are 'singing from the same hymn sheet' then they, too, deserve to be replaced.

Product presentation is another key marketing issue. In this regard, it is legitimate to draw parallels with the motor industry. Offer one price with all of the 'sexy' features included, and the likelihood is that the car will not gain market share. Offer a basic price and make all extra features easy to add either at the outset, or later, at a commensurably higher price, and the customer will not only select the features he can afford, but is likely to reach for many of the features he might not need but which look very desirable. The selection and pricing of these features should ultimately be the responsibility of marketing. Nevertheless, on such issues, the designer and marketing personnel should automatically be working in concert. Unfortunately this is more often the case with American companies than with British ones. In the USA, there is an almost cultural acceptance of the fact that, 'when we're all done, we have to sell this stuff'.

Both the designer and marketing have a responsibility to deduce the cost/benefit of every feature. Every feature adds to the complexity of the product and there needs to be a ruthlessness when culling, at the design stage, features for which the demand is limited, where the cost is high and where the launch date of the overall product will be delayed because of undue development time. Again there is an attitude with British engineers whereby for all their technical skills they do not want to 'expose the product to the risk of sale', but prefer to design it to death. An American working in Britain once described the process by which a product had been exposed to this endless design process as suffering from 'widget blight', a phrase that seemed to stick with the design engineers. Subsequently, they all consciously worked to avoid having this description applied to their particular product. Remember the comparison given earlier, between the American designer and his British counterpart. Lately, there has been in circulation on the Internet, an 'engineer's joke' that precisely makes the point. 'Normal people believe, if it ain't broke don't fix it. Engineers believe, if it ain't broke it doesn't have enough features yet.'

Market driven or marketing driven?

Another true account is that of a team of design engineers in a small company working on an enhancement of an existing product that had been moderately successful. As the development stage was nearing completion, this small company received, from a very large company, an invitation to tender for a product very close to the specification of the enhanced product. The tender was submitted and an intense sales campaign followed. The prospective customer put the small company and its competitors under intense scrutiny on every front; the order to be won was to be worth millions of pounds and would almost certainly guarantee the company's future. The prospective customer was made fully aware of the stage of development that the company had reached. Nevertheless, the product so fitted the customer requirements that the small company won the business. Initially everyone, including the customer, was delighted.

Unfortunately, shortly after deliveries began, some of the inadequacy of the development time began to manifest itself and the customer, not surprisingly, put the entire company under even more intense pressure. At one stage during this pressure, the head of development expressed his reservations: 'We should not have sold the product prematurely – we needed more time to improve the feature set and more testing time before we released the product'. But it was pointed point out that, had the company not released the product for sale, the order would have been lost to a competitor. If that had happened, his entire development team would have been at risk as far as their employment was concerned because the future success of the product without this order, not to mention the future of the company itself, would obviously have been less predictable. The company desperately needed to recoup its considerable development expense as rapidly as possible. This window of opportunity would not wait or come again. There are no silver medals. In the event, all the problems were subsequently fixed and the customer was still taking the product many years later.

In a previous section of this book the opinions of Mr William Rees-Mogg, former editor of *The Times*, regarding Microsoft have been examined. It is precisely because the company needs to recoup its development costs as soon as possible, and because all high-tech products carry 'bugs' that are only revealed in the field, that these reputations for sharp practice are gained. (Of course, from the user's end it can look as though the companies such as Microsoft are using the rest of their customers in an extended beta trial... at the customer's considerable expense.) There is another reason. It would be perfectly reasonable to argue that if a car manufacturer was to release a product, knowing there were serious design problems to be fixed after deliveries began, there would be a furore, and rightly so. However, a major problem for developers in the high-tech world is that manufacturers cannot stay abreast of the demands made by the marketplace. As soon as a customer or number of customers, acquire a capability for a given function they put pressure on the suppliers for the next stage of the process; extra capability or higher speed? Fail to meet these demands and it's not too long before the customers are telling their supplier of the shortcomings of the product.

Building bridges

Another actual instance of a member of the marketing staff making a very common mistake concerns another medium sized company; again although the instance concerns a telecommunications company, the facts could apply to any company concerned with bringing products to market. This marketing man perceived a gap in the company's product line that needed to be filled. To support this perception, the results of his market analysis were presented to the company senior management, including his own director of marketing. His conclusion was that the company needed a 'bridge'. It is sufficient for this explanation to know that a 'bridge' is a piece of telecommunications equipment that has no in-built intelligence, no software. All the senior management at the presentation agreed, a 'bridge' in the product line was a definite asset. It was also agreed that there were no in-house resources to develop one, nor was it a good idea from a cost/benefit point of view for the company to develop its own 'bridge'; it was agreed that they would seek a 'bridge' from an outside source. The marketing man duly received the go-ahead he had sought, and permission was given to search the market for a suitable device. He found his source, an American manufacturer, and the company duly signed a distributor agreement with the manufacturer's president.

The process that had been gone through by the marketing man was routine for new product introduction. However, two years later, the same marketing man came to make a similar presentation to senior management, but this time it was for a 'router'. Again it is sufficient for this explanation of events to know that a 'router' is a 'bridge' with intelligence; that is, with software built-in. Once again, the marketing man convinced the same management that a 'router' was necessary to fill a gap in the product line; once again the senior management gave its approval. On this occasion however the company finance director happened to attend the presentation. He it was who pointed out that the president of the 'bridge' supplying company had complained to him that during the previous two years, that is since the 'bridges' agreement had been signed, none had been sold. Thus it was that two years after an agreement had been signed, the marketing man, apart from finding a technically sound product to fill what he considered to be the 'bridge' shortcoming in the product line, had done nothing whatever to bring it to market. He had not established that any of the sales resource was available to him. As a consequence, he had done nothing to ensure, by means of incentives and commission, that he would gain the attention of the sales force; not surprisingly they ignored his product. There was no promotion of the product, either within, or outside the company. No one in the company was educated about the product. No one in the field support force received any education on how to maintain and support the product in the field. No one in the finance department was consulted about selling price, to determine whether the company, which was obviously likely to make less margin on a bought-in product than one that might have been developed in-house was going to make an acceptable margin.

So, a product had been included in the company portfolio by a so-called marketing man, whose sole evaluation criterion for the acceptance of the product was its technical functionality. Of more importance to the overall scheme of things was that an entire management team not only allowed this process to take place once, but were prepared to allow it to happen again when the results of the first exercise were plain for all to see. They too were so mesmerised by technology that they had overlooked the only purpose the company had – to conduct profitable business. Furthermore, it was now obvious that the 'bridge' product that had been presented as so necessary for the continued survival and increased profitability of the company was not so vital after all.

All these conclusions are quite apart from the obvious one of questioning whether the company could afford a member of staff, glorifying in the title of marketing manager (not to mention the part played by his erstwhile boss, the director of marketing), who wastes scarce company resources, time and money bringing products into the company that do not sell. In this particular case, the man responsible had obviously felt that his responsibility ended when he brought the product into the company. Metaphorically speaking, he lobbed the product over the wall into that space within the company where, he presumed, it was someone else's problem.

Product introduction

The case study above is by no means unique, nor is it confined to small start-up companies with little experience. Similar situations occur in large companies engaged in product development. Many such companies have a long history and have been in business long enough to have learned from their mistakes, and corrected them. It is also too often the case in large companies where marketing staff have presented business plans for a new product introduction. The plans, as presented, have been immaculate in their compilation, but they usually contained a fatal flaw – the plan started from the desired profit required and worked back to the revenue that would be necessary to give rise to the required profit after costs had been taken into account. Fine, as long as the market being relied upon to comply with the plan does exactly that. Unfortunately, potential customers are rarely so accommodating. So, the dates given in the plan, predicting when revenues will begin, are usually wildly optimistic and do not reflect reality.

If the top line, the revenue line, does not reflect reality, then the bottom line never will. Sound obvious? It should be, but such plans are not always put forward by people with experience or knowledge of the realities of the market place. Often if they get their plan accepted they are deemed, especially by themselves, to have done their job. In the best-ordered companies there is a uniform process to be completed before a new product can be approved and the considerable expense of so doing incurred. This process should consult all that are likely to be involved in the journey of the product from concept to launch. By this means, most of the difficulties and hurdles that will be encountered should be revealed. Of course, the larger the company, the longer the process; but whatever the size of the company, time spent at this stage bringing some uniformity to product introduction (see Appendix 3), will minimise disaster later and should, at least, make easier the recovery from a plan going astray. For a newly conceived product to reach the point of being successfully marketed there is a critical path to follow. Designers, marketing people, manufacturing, finance, post-sales support and sales people should all be consulted and their views incorporated in the product launch plan.

Unfortunately it needs to be recognised that for a multitude of reasons, not everyone consulted on such a project will have the company's interest at heart. As a rule, the bigger the company, the more will this be the case. Furthermore, the bigger the company, the more difficult it is to know the reasons behind any particular input. It is essential that individual inputs are signed off in order that people recognise their own accountability. To gather these signatures as part of a cohesive product introduction process is a key role for marketing personnel if the product is to have any chance of success. In summary, any launch plan has to be implemented such that it is sensitive to any non-compliance by individuals or departments.

SWOT – of and to the company

A SWOT (strengths, weaknesses, opportunities, threats) analysis provides the platform to examine the company's internal structure and processes, as well as the ability of the company and its staff to attack the market and to withstand any onslaught by the competition. It is imperative that such an analysis is exhaustive and comprehensive. It must not be an exercise in self-

The Marketer

delusion; nor must it be used to provide an excuse for defeatism. Finally, it should not provide a forum for an endless debate. A company is a commercial concern – or should be. It is not a debating society. All professional staff should, in effect, be intellectually involved in carrying out a SWOT analysis of their particular part of the whole process.

Marketing does not always involve bringing a product or service to market. One major British company decided to introduce a different method of trading; this method had to complement its existing method. Though practised widely elsewhere this method was totally alien to the company. The Chairman, quite rightly, decided that the company had to adopt this form of trading or see its market share diminish. The issues are probably best explored through another hypothetical motor industry analogy. Supposing Ford motors had always sold its vehicles directly to the end user, the car owner. Sales expenses per car are, as a result, high. Post-sales service is inefficient and expensive. Customers are demanding extra services that Ford find difficult to rapidly respond to. Other car companies have responded to this phenomenon by using dealers. Ford now decides, in the interests of its own survival, to do the same. But Ford, in our example, has a history of doing business in one way, and now needs to change. There are several hurdles to overcome, not least of which is a company culture steeped in its historical way of doing business. Employees of the company will resist change for all manner of reasons. Dealers have to be persuaded to take Ford cars, as opposed to those of the competition. A completely new operational and financial and marketing infrastructure has to be created – and the company has thousands of employees, not to mention existing customers, worldwide. The decision has been forced on the company by market pressures. All it has to do now is change. But a company, like an ocean-going liner, cannot change direction at the flick of a switch.

The scenario above is fictional, but many large companies are faced with this reality. Companies like the new privatised utilities, especially those like BT, under threat all the time from American giants making inroads in their traditional market, or the BBC, under threat from satellite and cable commercial companies. The company whose story is recounted here was a British computer company with a thirty-year history. It had always sold its machines, usually large ones, to end users, to banks, to building societies, to government departments, to large commercial concerns. Then, a completely new threat appeared on the horizon.

The software industry was emerging, and customers were attracted to, and demanding, their products. What's more, these products were often mounted on smaller computers produced by American competitors. Thus these products, software and hardware, were invading the company's customer base. Traditional sources of revenue were turning elsewhere to satisfy their needs. There were many companies in the market place, dedicated to generating software for the company's computer products but the company itself had not hitherto sought to harness this activity in its own interest. Thus the company was missing out on a substantial source of revenue even though it had provided the basic source of income for these software companies, the computer itself. The company wanted, and needed to provide a channel to its customer base for these software companies, many of which had been formed by former members of the company's staff. By providing this channel, the company could prevent the erosion of its customer base, and hopefully by doing so realise some extra company revenue.

It is not appropriate, or particularly productive, to detail the entire process that was undertaken. Nevertheless, it is interesting to note that, to meet this new trading objective, the marketing initiative alone took a full year to put into practice. To begin, a small team of six people sat in a large room and brainstormed. All the 'what ifs?' were examined? There were some 30,000 employees worldwide, divided into a number of discrete companies, each responsible for their own P&L. Few of them were going to take kindly to what they would perceive to be 'head office interference', unless it could be shown to be in their financial interest. Undoubtedly, the exercise would be easier with a company with a recognisable worldwide discipline, but the small team had to operate in the company world-wide as it was, not how they would wish it to be. So this small team wrote, on paper flip charts, as many of the issues to be confronted that they could think of. The walls were of the room were literally covered with the completed flip charts. It became a massive exercise. Every thought the team had and recorded led to another half dozen, and each of those led to a further half dozen, and so on. But because of the importance of the task, the issues could not be ducked. The team were also acutely aware that every issue recorded meant a task to fulfil; the task ahead grew to gargantuan proportions.

Also underlying the team's efforts was the implied threat from the staff around the world, 'If you are going to change things, you'd better be right'. Senior management would view the team as a threat to their autonomy, regardless of what the Chairman wanted. The team would have to prove they were going to be beneficial. Sales people would see a possible erosion of their commission. A complementary commission plan would have to be introduced that would reward sales equally, whether they sold under the existing end-user regime, or under the new third party regime that was being devised.

Having been founded and staffed mostly by former employees, the software companies had a cosy arrangement with staff still employed by the company; they had become accustomed to being introduced for free into the company installed base. Quite frankly, they viewed the company as a huge milch cow from which they could all feed for nothing. Why should they accede to these new ideas, where they would have to pay a fee for introducing them to the same customers where hitherto they had paid nothing? The team would have to prove that, hitherto, these software companies were dependent on only those sales people with whom they had a personal cosy relationship; this was likely to be a relatively small number, whereas under the new proposed regime they would be formally introduced to a worldwide customer base by a worldwide sales force of 750 people. Few software companies, at that time, had any dedicated sales capability of their own.

But if the computer company implemented the new scheme and introduced these third parties into its customer base, then the customers would inevitably hold the company responsible for the performance of the third party company and its products. Standards would have to be set for the product before it could be taken into the computer company portfolio; standards of quality, of documentation, of support. A list of existing customers, prepared to give testimony for the product needed to be compiled

Supposing some of the software wanted or needed by the computer company was mounted on equipment made by its competitors? Incentives would have to be offered to the software companies to migrate the software to the company machines. Isn't it likely that the software companies, in order to avoid the fee for using the computer company sales force, would contend that they had already found the opportunity and had not used the company sales people at all? Further, it is more than possible that there would be some measure of collusion with the company's own sales people, such that a reduced fee would be paid to the salesperson, but a fee in excess of the commission that the salesman would earn legitimately. A method of registration would be needed that would accommodate this possibility.

The above is just a flavour of the issues the team had to confront, but it is by no means comprehensive. It should, however, illustrate the types of disciplines involved if any new marketing initiative is to be successful. Because what the team were planning to introduce, represented a fundamental change in the way the computer company was going to trade. There was not one department worldwide that was going to remain unaffected one way or another. Over the course of the next year or so, it was sometimes difficult to maintain a high level of morale within the small team, simply because a good deal of the work was just sheer tedium. It was difficult to sustain for the team to sustain their original excitement with this new marketing idea. Nevertheless, when the team was acutely aware that when they started to promulgate this particular initiative to their colleagues worldwide, to the existing customer base, to the industry press, it was realised that they would be subjected to intense scrutiny, borne of cynicism, scepticism and resistance to change. They would have to withstand severe questioning and prove that whatever objection was raised, it had already been thought of it and provision made for it. The team's morale, when they went through this ordeal unscathed, was at an all-time high. Perhaps it is worthwhile reminding the reader once more that the programme partially recounted here did not involve a company product or service at all, but merely a difference in the way the company wanted to present itself to the market place. Nonetheless, from a marketing standpoint it was as crucial as if it were a product or service that was the subject of the exercise.

Another illustration of how a company can be damaged by the lack of attention to detail is the true story of a product introduction. Although the story is a long one, it is a good illustration of how catastrophic a relatively simple oversight can be.

The company concerned is an American company, again in computers. Since its early days the company had rarely put a foot wrong, and had enjoyed spectacular growth from a standing start. To explain the point, it is useful once again to draw on a motor car industry analogy; it is well known that car companies do not make all of the components that make up the finished product. A car company may use, say, carburettors from a specialist carburettor company. When it does so, it will inevitably place a mass quantity order on the carburettor company, and be given a special price for so doing. Now, if the car company decides to make its own, less expensive carburettor, it will need to cancel its order with the carburettor company. The financial ramifications of such a move by the car company are far-reaching – and they are not confined to the car company.

The Marketer

The issues for a computer company are similar. In the case recounted here, the computer company was using disk-drive storage devices from a specialist third party company. In order to improve margins, the computer company decided to design, manufacture and sell its own disk storage units. These were, of course, much less expensive than those being bought in from the specialist company. At the time of the introduction of its own disk storage units, the computer company had many outstanding orders for its computer systems, which incorporated disk drives from the specialist company. The computer company was incorporating its new storage units in all computer systems in the future, and it also persuaded all customers with existing orders to change to the newer, cheaper units. However, the computer company was faced with a massive bill-back from the specialist disc storage company. This bill-back would be the difference between the price of those units of which the computer company had actually taken delivery, and the heavily discounted price of the units that the computer company had previously predicted it would need, and which it had placed forward orders for, and was now cancelling. Of course, the specialist company would have also placed orders on component companies, and it would similarly be faced with bill-back charges for cancelled orders – and so on, down the line.

The computer company has a dilemma. It is now selling lower-priced systems as a result of its lower-priced disk storage systems, but it has a very substantial bill-back to pay. It's an immutable fact that no matter what the reason the only source of any bill to be paid is the ultimate customer; there is no alternative. The computer company can either spread the bill-back over all of its disk storage devices, built in-house, or it can pass on the bill-back to those customers who ordered systems incorporating devices from the specialist company. The computer company decided to do the latter. Since the customers would, because of the new low price devices they were taking, still be paying less for their systems, even with the bill-back, this did not seem unreasonable. Why pass on a share of a 'bill back' to customers who had no existing outstanding orders? So what went wrong? All of the computer company's thought processes for marketing its new disc-drives were sound. Customers would be getting less expensive computer systems, even if they were subjected to a part of the 'bill back', the computer company was making better margins. Everybody should have been happy (except. of course, for the specialist company).

The problem was that the computer company did not explain its reasoning to the sales force – or to anyone else involved in contact with the customer. The customer's attitude was: 'You persuade me to cancel my current disk drive orders, and to re-order for your new device – and when I do so, you present me with a bill-back?' Around the world, staff concerned with customer contact found themselves confronted by angry customers, without any information with which to refute the accusations of 'sharp practice'. Over and over again, explanations had to be given that the ultimate deal for the customer was a better one, and that it would be better still when the bill-back had been totally redeemed. Customer relations took a long time to recover; many customers continued forever after to entertain a feeling that the company was not to be trusted. A fairly classic case of marketing overlooking a vital 'what if?'... If staff are not fully educated about the intentions and plans and decisions of the company, it is hardly surprising if the staff fall back on the old maxim: 'I'm sorry, I don't know – I'm just doing what I'm told'. It's the one statement guaranteed to infuriate loyal customers.

Responsibility cannot be delegated

'The buck stops here.' This slogan, so the story has it, used to be displayed on the desk of the late President Truman. Many people in industry need such a message on their desk, not so much to inform their subordinates, but to remind themselves of where responsibility actually lies. The reason this piece of advice is interjected is simple. If any marketing initiative is to succeed, then authorisation for that initiative must come from where the 'buck' stops. There must be a structure in place that recognises and accepts that authority and responsibility.

In these days of management by 'fad', there is a danger that, because of increased empowerment to staff, subordinates can be given too much power without the experience to use it wisely. In these circumstances, the dilemma arises where the person who is carrying the buck has little or no real control over his area of responsibility; yet still takes the rap when plans and initiatives do not work out as intended. This is not to suggest that those in authority should rule by pronouncement; that brings its own problems. Nevertheless, it is crucial that for any new initiative to work, there must be points at which its progress can be measured and monitored by those who have the responsibility, or those charged with reporting to him. But that responsibility must be accepted. It is inexcusable for a manager to allow,

The Marketer

either by neglect or commission, a subordinate to exercise, without question, his initiative, and then deny responsibility for the outcome.

A case in point is that of Xerox's ill-fated attempt in 1969 to diversify away from its traditional product offering and into computers; to do this Xerox Corporation acquired a computer manufacturing company. Xerox at that time was an enormously powerful company, with a worldwide monopoly on the sale and distribution of photostatic copiers and duplicators. On the horizon, however, was looming the day when this monopoly would lose its patent protection and other competitors, mostly Japanese, would enter the market; hence, Xerox's protection strategy to diversify into computers. In all of the countries of Europe, the American parent company was represented by Rank Xerox. All of the Rank Xerox companies were formidable companies in their own right. The heads of these companies were, accordingly, very powerful executives. This meant that, whatever strategic decision was made corporately, in the long-term interest of the company, the local CEOs often had their own view of whether or not to recognise it. By the same token, some executives, including many senior ones in the USA., did not agree with this new departure, or see the need for it. Thus, the biggest hurdle to overcome for the new fledgling computer company in the Xerox nest was not the other computer companies with whom it was competing in the expanding global market, but the powerful interests at very senior level in the traditional Xerox copier/duplicator organisation.

This worldwide management perceived this new venture as a threat and set out to ensure that it did not succeed. Xerox pulled out of the computer business five years later, at a cost of millions of dollars. As a strange postscript to this tale, some time later, Xerox used a different route to re-enter the computer business, because changing technology in its core copier/duplicator business demanded that it did so. Thus, a very necessary initiative, introduced at the most senior level of a company, for the very sound reason of protecting the long-term future of the company, foundered because the management structure militated against its success. A classic case of where the ultimate responsibility for the success of an initiative did not rest with the people who, for very sound motives, had made a strategic corporate decision.

A similar example is ICL, at the time a major British computer company. As part of its product offering, the company sold printers made by a Japanese company, Ricoh. It was thought that, since the company sold a number of these printers in the UK as part of its computer systems, it could take on the national distributorship of these printers as stand-alone items. By doing so, the quantity of printers sold would go up; therefore, because this would lift the company's quantity discount price, the price per printer would decrease, creating a resultant decrease in the cost of computer systems because they now incorporated lower cost printers. The logic seemed faultless. Ricoh were delighted to have such a large company as its distributor. A new agreement was signed between ICL and Ricoh, giving reduced prices to ICL, based on the predicted quantities ICL would sell worldwide, both as stand-alone items as a function of its distribution agreement, and incorporated in computer systems.

However, the arrangement did not go as planned. Firstly, ICL had no discipline that ensured only Ricoh printers would be incorporated in computer systems sold world-wide; there was thus a proliferation of different printers in such systems. Secondly, as in Xerox, the company had absolutely no experience of the distribution of fast moving commodity items such as dot matrix printers. Indeed, it had no experience of distribution marketing at all. Thus the proliferation of a variety of printers within the ICL customer base continued, and there was no way of imposing the decisions made on high. ICL did not come near to selling the quantities predicted, and negotiated, with Ricoh. Therefore, they had bought some printers at a price lower than Ricoh's discount structure allowed.

At that time, British Telecom, for reasons that were never really clear, was in printer buying mode. They could not resist the bulk price being offered by ICL, and many were purchased. Unfortunately, BT didn't use them to the extent planned at the time of purchase either, and so they re-sold them back on to the market to anyone who would have them. The price was virtually a 'dump' price. Ricoh were even more upset. Since ICL entered this whole scenario as a means of buying lower-cost printers for its computer systems, the amount of time, effort, thought, commitment and resource allocated to this new distribution channel had been minimal; three very junior people, selling at a discount to a small number of dealers. The performance was abysmal. In fact, many of those dealers were selling, at lower margin, back into the ICL customer base – so that ICL, instead of selling lower cost printers to their customers had, in effect, set up their own competitive sales channel. The amount of upper-echelon management time given to this activity, whose turnover, relative to that of the company as a whole, was microscopic, was grossly out of proportion to its value. The operation eventually foundered. Another example of where an initiative has not been thought through; where the initiative does not properly sit with the company structure or historical culture; where inappropriate initiatives can, without financial justification, distract a major company from its main task. However, if senior corporate management had been able to impose its decisions; or, to be more precise, have its decisions, by agreement, promulgated throughout the organisation, then the resultant chaos need never have ensued to the extent that it did.

With the examples given above, it is not whether the ideas themselves are, or are not, worthwhile, that should be of prime concern. It is that no idea will succeed, if that idea can be destroyed because of the innate anarchy of an organisation, even at the highest levels. If everyone on the staff can not only make their own judgement on an idea agreed by their management, at whatever level, but can undermine the implementation of that idea, not always for the best of motives, then the idea is doomed. Companies can survive under this form of laissez-faire management – many do – but they will never achieve their full potential. Unless there is an enforceable recognition of where the buck stops, then most initiatives, be they for a new product, or a new process or a diversification of the core business, will fail – and it's likely to be a very expensive failure for the company. Marketing people would do well to bear this in mind. It might be worthwhile at this stage to recall that, for all of the adulation and esteem heaped upon him by the nation, a national icon and military hero of the United States, General Douglas MacArthur, needed reminding where the buck stopped – President Truman fired him!

All companies, in all industries, must be aware of their image when introducing a new product or a new service or a change of trading conditions. But to concentrate on image as an end in itself, to the neglect of substance, is to court unforeseen problems. The correct image will arise only if real, detailed effort is expended on the substance of the project under consideration. Failure to do so will result in the company acquiring an unnecessarily bad reputation. The temptation to start a hare running as a means of improving the company's image without examining, and dealing with, all of the associated issues of substance, must be resisted. This is particularly true today, when media hype and the sound-bite culture have taken such a strong hold. Industry is in real danger of not knowing where image ends and reality begins. Trendy, eye-catching slogans extolling a company's products and services can return to haunt a company – and sometimes be very expensive – if the slogan is not backed up by substance in performance.

It may be illustrative here to touch briefly on another situation where a major change had not been fully thought through, with severe problems ensuing. Although the situation is not an industrial one, it illustrates the point very well. In 1999, the British government announced a change in the method of income tax collection. There was, for the first time, to be a method of self-assessment. Self-assessment of income tax has been in place in Canada, to name one country, for over forty years. The British government introduced it hurriedly, with deadline dates for self-assessed tax returns to be submitted. Fines were going to be imposed on those who were non-compliant. This was a totally new experience for thousands of working, and retired, citizens. The previous method of submitting tax returns had existed for many, many years As a consequence, many people were confused by this new methodology, not least because the forms were complicated and confusing, the Inland Revenue staff themselves appeared not to understand them, and many people were left feeling frustrated and angry, but powerless to do anything. The introduction of this new method gave rise to a burgeoning tax consultant industry. A good illustrative example of insufficient thought being given to an initiative already practiced in other countries that was going to affect thousands. In other words, a sound idea poorly marketed.

Look before you leap

Examples have been given here of initiatives that should be within the remit of marketing. The examples given are by no means comprehensive. The purpose of recounting these examples is to provoke thought, or to be more precise to prevent action until there has been thought. Too often British industry and commerce, particularly of late, has tried to throw off its image of conservatism by rushing into a flurry of activity. There are countless other examples where the 'front end' marketing promotion of new products, services or offers is not backed up when a potential customer seeks to take advantage of the offer. This is not confined to the British but Americans, although by no means infallible, are less likely to make the same mistake for two reasons. First, Americans in industry, generally speaking, have a multi-disciplinary approach to the market; and secondly, marketing people do enjoy a higher profile and are therefore less likely to find forgiveness for the ensuing problems. Although they are valued in the States, it is also recognised that they are very much 'in the kitchen' and that is where the heat is. It is unlikely that they will acquire a reputation for what they are, only for what they do. To repeat an oft-used expression, 'Don't confuse activity with capability'.

A proper send-off

From time to time, a company needs a shot in the arm. One sure way of producing this is to have the company give the market a shot in the arm... Witness the announcement of a long-heralded new car model, such as the new VW 'Beetle', a new wonder-drug, the success of 'Red Nose Day', or the anticipation afforded Apple or Microsoft prior to any of their major product announcements. But such events seldom happen in British industry with anywhere near the same sense of excitement.

All of the events referred to are launches of one kind or another. If a company or organisation has spent months preparing a new product or process for the market, then it is imperative that that product has an impact in that market, and a launch is the appropriate way to achieve the maximum impact. Otherwise the product has not been launched – it's merely drifted from its moorings. The very word 'launch' is appropriate, with its nautical connotations. When the liners QE2, or United States or Canberra were first launched, people queued to sail in them. At the time of launch, months and months of work has gone into the building of the ship, and the planning of the launch. As the date of the launch draws near, there is a heightened tension, an increasing air of expectation, to be shared by staff and public alike. This is no time to be self-effacing and diffident. All of the effort, all of the disappointments on the way, all of the hurdles overcome should culminate in this big event! In general, the Americans are far more willing to shout from the rooftops. However abhorrent the British find this manifestation of the American way of doing things, the fact remains that it sells the products of their commercial activity. The British seem less reluctant to emulate the Americans when it comes to launching cars or fashion or pop music albums; but for industry in general, there is a retreat behind the more dignified, technically elitist approach to the market. A great opportunity is thus missed, as the PR agency is told, yet again: 'Oh, we don't want to say anything about that just yet...'

Although the nation's instinct is to understate its achievements in technology, it is very often the case that when exposed to the American way of announcing products and services, the British technologists enjoy it just as much as their American counterparts. This is particularly so if the technologists themselves are given due recognition for the part they play in bringing the new product to fruition.

It is strange how Britain that can be as triumphalist as any nation when launching a ship or a new aeroplane can seem almost diffident about other products. It's considered to be very 'American' to launch a product with a bit of pizzazz. Yet the British can launch a product with some excitement and in a way that engages the attention of the staff without cynicism.

In yet another true example, a British company was launching a product that had a multitude of capabilities; a product 'chameleon', in fact. With this concept no doubt in the Creative Director's mind, a short sound and video presentation about a chameleon was commissioned, to be shown in an hotel suite rented for the purpose The music evoked the jungle, the chameleon was filmed in the jungle, the darkened presentation room was gradually filled with smoke from a dry ice machine. All this was played out while the staff filed into the room. The staff were intrigued, a little apprehensive and not a little amused – but it was a break from the routine. A formal presentation followed, when all of the features and prices of the product were announced to the staff. Thus they could feel part of the finished result, they could see their own contribution. The original design engineers were identified and presented with mementoes. Each department was given a poster showing a chameleon, for displaying on office walls. Thus all staff felt an affinity with the product and all had enjoyed the fun. It instilled some excitement into an otherwise fairly tedious working existence. Just as important, because they were the first to see the finished result, their importance was recognised. It is always the case that staff dislike learning what is happening within their company by first reading about it in the press.

SWOT – of and to the product

Earlier there is reference to the dangers of an idea-a-minute. Even if all of the proper thought processes have been gone through to avoid the usual pitfalls of bringing new products to market, there is still the danger of a lack of product planning. Some companies, to avoid the dangers of a lack of planning, make the person or people responsible for planning a totally separate department from marketing. However, more often than not, there

The Marketer

will be no member or members of staff responsible for this activity, known specifically as 'product planning'. Yet to not have such an activity is very dangerous; in fact the role is so important that the position in the organisation and the title given to the person carrying out the task, or the head of the department of product planning in the event of there being more than one person, should reflect the importance of the role; by this means, no-one on the payroll could refuse to co-operate. Secondly, to be effective, it was necessary for product planning people to work outside of the traditional organisational interplay between design, marketing, sales, etc and indeed finance.

So what is so significant about product planning? In most organisations concerned with bringing products to market there are likely to be a number of engineering teams working on different product development programmes. Accordingly there are likely to be marketing people working with these teams to bring the products to market. But with a specific product planning role in place it is possible, to coin a phrase, 'to know where the money is going – and where it is coming from'. Product planning is therefore partly a technical role, partly a marketing function, each of which would have a financial impact. Therefore the Product Planning Director can bring a technical dimension to a task that, if carried out by a more traditionally financially-oriented individual, is likely to be devoid of a certain amount of realism. One vital role therefore is to ensure that the financial realities are not obscured by the normal dialogue that would take place between the marketing staff and the financial staff, particularly when the marketing staff are likely to be 'promoting' the cause of their particular product.

It is important that the task of the planning person, or people, is not to expose the engineers engaging in some subterfuge; in fact engineers will typically welcome the results of his findings. Typically, too often, engineers do not relate their individual efforts to the contribution they may or may not be making to the company's cost structure or profitability. They are usually unaware aware that a good deal of their effort is being expended on tasks that produce little revenue, or that commensurably too little effort is being expended on products that are likely to provide the company with its 'rent money'. Left to their own devices they are likely to work on, or aspire to work on, what interested them, or what they considered to be glamour products. To work on such products carried kudos. To not do so is to be thought of as working in the hinterland. Without a specific product-planning role neither the engineers nor their associated marketing people will typically make the vital connection between their individual efforts, and the company's ultimate financial performance. It is not the role of the financial staff to make this vital connection because that would necessitate them involving themselves in a technical role beyond their remit or capability. The planning people will therefore ensure that the engineering effort is properly directed in order to provide maximum effectiveness.

Setting the spending targets

Inevitably, the company's budget, or year-end revenue forecast, is, or should be, directly linked to the effort being undertaken by all involved to achieve that result. Sound simple? Sound obvious? The statement of the objective is simplicity itself; that the desired result cannot be achieved unless the co-ordinated, focused, requisite effort is expended should be abundantly obvious. Unfortunately, it is too often the case that the compilation of a budget and the company activity are totally unrelated, except in only the vague terms. Although certainly not exclusively so, this is truer with British companies – and not only small ones. The formulation of a budget is, in reality, an intellectual exercise by various levels of subordinate management, the only purpose of which is to get it signed off by senior management. Senior management, in turn, need to get it signed off by the board, and the board need to get their year end forecasts believed by the City. All these various entities, assisted by the entire financial staff, revel in the whole exercise. All manner of people work long hours, secure in the knowledge that so much effort must, by definition, be in a sound cause. Everyone's happy? Well, no!

Whether this document eventually represents a realistic view of the financial goalposts is often irrelevant to the game in hand. To coin a phrase, 'The numbers are cranked and re-cranked until we get to the target numbers we first thought of'. It is in this process that proper plans get overlooked, capital investment gets trimmed, time scales for realisation of project completion get shortened, sales of dying products suddenly, for no tangible reason, acquire a new lease of life – the list is endless. The budget is no longer a realistic blueprint for company performance, it's not even a wish list – it's more like a prayer... Once accepted, it is largely ignored and everyone goes back to the day-to-day tasks they were working on before 'budget time' came along and interrupted their cosy reverie.

This is where product planning is crucial. When did we plan for a current product or range of products to go into decline? Perhaps, to put that same point more accurately, when are such products going to go into decline, whether planned or not? Has the decline already started? If so, and work is still being carried out on the product, is this work going to sustain the revenue any longer – is it going to add to the revenue? If the work currently being undertaken is not going to sustain or increase planned revenue, can the work be terminated? What would be the effect of such termination? Sometimes this whole process can be very painful to engineers. They enjoy working on a particular product. It's their baby. But it is absolutely essential that a degree of objective external control is brought to bear on the actual engineering activity; one role of product planning

Tracking the product cycle

Any product has to be conceived, it has a gestation period, it is launched, hopefully it produces revenue for the planned period, and then it goes into decline. This process, in the best-ordered companies, is a formal one, constantly monitored to establish that the process, prior to launch is, or is not, on track. If it is, then other complementary marketing activities are called in at various stages of the process leading up to launch.

If the process is not on track, because of an engineering design problem – after all, design is not done by rote – what contingencies can be called into play? If the launch is delayed, revenues from that product will inevitably also be delayed. For how long, giving rise to what revenue shortfall? Can the company recover? How? By extending the life of existing products, perhaps. How? Add in some additional features to extend product life? Perhaps the market has changed during the life of the product; the product, and the company would maybe benefit from the introduction of some 'mid-life kickers' into the product. Would the effort necessary to produce these extra revenues really generate an acceptable gross margin, or should this effort be put into the new product in order to recover from its predicted late launch? Perhaps the nature of the work is such that more effort is not the answer, because the problem is not effort-related, it's an insuperable technical problem to which a solution has to be found.

If there is a delay in the launch of a new product, and the predicted ramp-up of revenues from that launch are, as a consequence, delayed – and if no contingencies are brought into play – then there will inevitably be a dip in actual revenues. Unfortunately, unless action is taken, there is no automatic compensating dip in costs... It is in grappling with these realities, and taking the measures to cope with them, that the product planning activity comes into play, whether that activity is in marketing or independent of it. Ultimately, the choice of options, weighing all the consequences on company performance and customer acceptance and market position, is a marketing responsibility but product planning should play a key role in the choice-making process.

SWOT – of and to the market

All of the 'what ifs?' surrounding the impact on the company of a new initiative have been studied. All of the details of the new product, or service, or process have been analysed, and the opportunities and dangers assessed. Time scales for introduction are known. The company is ready to go. But is the profile of the market as it is today known accurately, never mind what it will look like at the time of the introduction of this new initiative? In many respects, this is the most difficult part of the whole process, if only because of the gestation period of any new initiative. It is also at this point when whoever is ultimately responsible needs to be most on their guard. Everybody purports to be an expert on the state of the market. Few people are called to account a year or so later, if the market was unkind enough not to fit the profile predicted for it a year or so earlier.

A variety of inputs can help in the determination of the market. Many commentators use grandiloquent language to speak of the speed with which today's technology becomes obsolete; in reality however the market seldom moves as rapidly as much of the hype would suggest. Even in the high-tech world, renowned for its speed of change, many companies in the industry derive their major source of revenues from product lines long in the tooth. Enhancements are added to keep the product as current as possible but the core product goes on. There are many reasons for this. Customers cannot, overnight, write off investments in equipment. Even though the market has moved on to some degree, and technology has progressed, a customer company has to commit at some stage to a level of technology and stay with it for a number of years, the longer the better, commensurate with maintaining competitiveness in their own area of commerce. The customer company then looks to their supplier to ensure that, as far as possible, they (the customer) haven't 'walked the plank'.

Therefore, marketing needs to build in as many contingencies as possible into the marketing plan. The product or service or process needs to be capable of being updated or upgraded in a number of different directions, determined by changes in market conditions. As an example, witness Microsoft's Windows 95, Windows 98, Windows 2000 and Windows XP. Sometimes, these changes will be necessitated even during the gestation period of the initiative. This is not as difficult as it sounds. Occasionally, changes in market conditions are revolutionary; but usually, evolution is the order of the day. It is also important for marketing to remember that the market is that germane to the company specifically. It is pointless to indulge in 'blue skying', attempting to meet the perceived demands of a market 'out there' while ignoring or even neglecting the company's installed customer base.

Very large customer companies will often spend enormous sums of money to bring a new technology to market in their own commercial interest; it is surprising therefore to find out that more often than not, this source of ongoing revenue to the supplier is overlooked by that supplier. If this installed technology continues to be upgraded, then the installed base provides a relatively inexpensive source of additional revenue to the supplier. Thus a fraction of the sums being spent on new product development can produce very substantial revenues, at very little sales cost, from this captive customer base. Of course, the engineers want to work on new technology, and are often allowed to do so regardless of the impact on company income. In an ideal world, the products considered to be the stars of the company should always be the ones that are producing revenues, the ones ' paying the rent ', and not the ones that might emerge in due time. It is imperative that there is a balance maintained between attention to such current products and those not yet launched.

Marketing and selling – the link

There is a sales force or sales capability. A person, or people, charged with finding prospective customers and converting them into actual customers. As a rule of thumb, it is reasonable, in the capital goods arena, to expect a salesman to convert one third of his prospective customers into actual customers. The salesman on a company payroll is usually paid with a base salary and a commission. The proportion between these two elements can vary depending upon company policy or market pressures, particularly if, in a growing market, there is a scarcity of salesmen.

It should be the responsibility of marketing to ensure that the new product or service gets the attention of the salesmen. Salesmen (and, for that matter, anyone else) will, by nature take the line of least resistance to achieve success. If he is correctly managed and rewarded, the salesman's performance is judged by his bottom line contribution to the company. He is not going to put that, and possibly his career, at risk by expending a great deal of energy on bringing a new product to market unless he is specifically rewarded, financially or otherwise, for so doing. The actual activities of selling and sales management is covered later, but suffice it to say here that the new marketing initiative must be reflected in the sales force's compensation if it is to succeed. Therefore, marketing must study, and have an input to, the sales commission plan.

Marketing must also be satisfied that there are appropriate controls and disciplines in place to ensure adherence to the marketing plan for the new product. In the words of the Americans, marketing must ensure that the salesmen will obey the first rule of selling: 'Sell what's in the book'. If there is no advantage to the salesman in selling the new product, and he's under no competitive pressures for it, and the market is not demanding it, then he will ignore it – the product is thus stillborn!

The salesman is not employed to be a marketing man. He will almost certainly have an opinion, usually a cynical one, of the company's marketing efforts – as will everyone else not actually employed in marketing. Instead, he needs to be focused on his allotted role – to sell 'what's in the book', i.e. the sales manual. Marketing must ensure that there is a proper balance, in getting the salesman's attention, between current products in the sales manual and new ones just going in. There is little point having a salesman pursue opportunities for a new product, if the revenue from doing so merely replaces revenue from a current product with much sales life still in it. On the other hand, it is not in the company's interest to have a salesman dedicate himself to pursuing opportunities for current products, if analysis shows the sales for such products to be in decline. Add these considerations to the undeniable fact that there is a finite limit to the amount of goods or services any salesman can sell, and subsequent attention to his reward package – indeed, the size of the sales force itself – will have a marked impact on whether or not a company's aspirations are to be met.

Post-sales – a pivotal role

An area of considerable neglect by marketing people, when all of the marketing issues have been dealt with and the product or service is to be launched onto an unsuspecting market place, is the staff in the field who have to deal with the customer, be they customer support staff or dealer's staff. Companies ignore these entities at their peril.

This, as the Americans are wont to say, is 'where the rubber hits the road'... Just look at the history of the automobile industry. Many once-famous names have passed into history because of terrible after-sales service: poor distribution of service capability; poor or expensive spare parts availability; ill-educated, ill-trained post-sales staff with poor customer relations attitude; an unwillingness to sort out endemic mechanical problems at their own expense... Above all, a product with a poor record of reliability, leading to excessive downtime and consequent lack of availability to the customer. Yet, how many executives employed in the marketing of industrial products ever think about their own company and performance in those terms?

Again, in a British environment I have found this indifference more prevalent and it seems, in part, to stem from the prevailing cultural attitudes. The British professional tends to be more interested in the intellectual stimulus arising from the marketing activity, than he is with customer needs. Even meeting the customer is considered a chore. This also extends to there being an instinctive feeling that those responsible for looking after the customer at the sharp end, the sales and after-sales service staff, are, in some ways, inferior beings to those responsible for bringing the product to the market in the first place. But the way in which such matters are handled can make or break a company. As has been said earlier, there is little point extolling the virtues of the company's products and services by means of expensive and elaborate advertising and PR campaigns, if the people responsible for dealing with the customer in the market are neglected or poorly trained and, most importantly, treated with disdain by their professional colleagues and management. Treated with respect, these people can see the company through some very difficult times.

Service with an electronic smile

In these days of vastly improved manufacturing techniques and telecommunications technology, reliability of all forms of capital equipment and 'soft' products, has improved; and, in parallel, so has the ability to support a customer from a remote location, either by telephone or email. This does not lessen the need, within the context of financial prudence, for carefully thought-through after-sales service. On the contrary, without the cooling hand of a live human being to mop the customer's fevered brow, the need to be concerned with post-sales support is more essential than ever and a failure to recognise this is damaging, both to the company's reputation and to its bottom line. It is vital that recognition to the importance of such issues is included at the time of product design. In these days of internet selling where the customer and supplier are physically remote from each other and post-sales support is by telephone call-centre, it is this post-sales support that is often the determining factor by which a customer judges his supplier.

Marketing must ensure that this has been taken care of. In the case of capital equipment, features that ensure that the maximum support can be given remotely, without the physical presence of a field support person, must offer rapid return to serviceability, and in a cost-effective manner. Ideally this would entail replacement of parts by the customer himself, to the maximum extent possible, resulting in rapid return to 'up time', both logistically and psychologically. Perhaps it is less expensive to consider returning all equipment to the source of manufacture? Remember, the customer is only concerned with restoration of his equipment to working order, and often his job will depend on how quickly this happens. Should the equipment be of a nature that field personnel are necessary, it is vital that they are valued people, that they are well trained, with rapid access to necessary spare parts and back-up supervisory support. It is not unusual to find situations where all of the product issues are taken care of, but where the field support personnel are largely neglected, while others in the company were more valued and fêted. The resulting lack of morale within a force frequently called upon to spend many hours of their leisure time trying to keep the customer happy cost the company dear.

An actual situation where this was manifest concerned the British subsidiary of a large American company employing a force of 120 field personnel who were expressing frustration and this was obviously reflected in their working practices. Discontent was being freely expressed and morale was sinking fast. Unable to get to the root of the problem, but suspecting all the usual grouses about salaries, cars and working hours, etc., the UK general manager invited the entire team, except those on customer

The Marketer

call, to an hotel at Heathrow. On hearing of the intentions of the general manager, his American employers became apprehensive. They were concerned that the discontent of a few, given this environment, would spread to the many. A very real concern and one the general manager shared, but something fairly drastic had to be done if the situation was to be improved. Since he was ultimately responsible, he felt he had to take the initiative.

Because he wanted the attendees to feel they could express their problems freely, their line managers were asked not to attend. He told the attendees of this decision, but made it clear that any criticism of the absent management had to be constructive and mature. He could not ask management to stay away and then have them be the subject of a free-for-all complaining session. The only other management person in the room was the Director of Human Resources; this was necessary because of Britain's sensitive industrial employment laws. All attendees were told by the general manager that he would deal with any question relating to the company, and their employment and value in it. The question and answer session lasted from 10 a.m. until 4.30 p.m. The fundamental problem, when it was eventually revealed, came as a totally unexpected surprise. Due to its phenomenal success in the market, the company was growing at a rate of 40 per cent per annum. As a result, the product support infrastructure was lagging behind. Inadequate training for new products, extremely poor supply of spare parts, the introduction of new products at a rate that these field people couldn't handle led to customers expressing dissatisfaction.

The field personnel were dealing with these issues, and many others on an almost daily basis, resulting in long working hours in very stressful circumstances. They felt distinctly under-valued and unappreciated. They told the general manager that there was a complete lack of information from their employer about the products and services being sold to the customers that they were responsible for supporting. Because of the rapidly changing nature of these goods and services, problems arose, usually at the time of delivery to the customer. In the euphoria of this spectacular growth in revenues, no one had thought to tell the field support people what to expect from the customers, and how to deal with it. No one told them when to expect things to improve or how they would improve – or even that they would improve. They had to suffer the full brunt of any customer discontent that was being expressed

Their feelings were justified. All of the people in other areas of the company were so busy that too little attention had been given to the point at which severe problems were being encountered. The company was so euphoric with its sales success that too little attention had been paid to rumblings of discontent from the field; it now had to be dealt with. First the attendees were told why the company was in this position. None of these explanations were fudged. All of the attendees were adult – the whole meeting would have been undermined by any attempt to be less than candid.

Apologies, sincerely meant, for the lack of attention to their very real concerns were given. Remedies were thrashed out in the meeting or, where that was not possible, time scales for devising solutions were given. The attendees themselves were asked for suggested remedies, both short- and long-term. Any attendee who felt, after the commitments were implemented, that management had ducked the issue could raise it again, either personally or in the company of his colleagues. Another similar meeting was held three months later but on this second occasion, the meeting was informal and used as a 'thank you' session to the field service personnel. Valuable lessons had been learned, not the least of which was that the company had grossly under-estimated their staff by believing that they had motives other than the desire to do a good job for their employer.

All of the fears that the meeting would be one of with mutual abuse and recrimination proved unfounded. The staff wanted it to be understood that they were doing a difficult job under very trying circumstances. They wanted to hear that these trying times would be eased at some time in the future, and they wanted these assurances to be given without meaningless platitudes. They wanted job satisfaction by being able to look after their customers properly. Most of all, they wanted to be treated as adults, not patronised as unthinking rebels who could be placated with a few paternalistic utterances. Unfortunately this open communication between the managers and those managed is all too rare yet the benefits of doing so can be enormous.

Made in the USA

A common expression used by Americans is, 'The Americans put their pants on one leg at a time, like everybody else'. This is pointing out that Americans can be just as fallible in business as any other national. They are equally capable of making wrong decisions from all the data available. Many American companies fail, many new initiatives die on the vine. However, they are nowhere near as likely as their British counterparts to fail as a result of a lack of focus on the issues that lead to success. Their activities are more likely to be conditioned by their view of the market, than by the constraints imposed on them by their own company's internal processes. The description above of actual events and situations is not intended to be a definitive, or comprehensive guide to marketing. There are countless books in libraries and bookshelves to give that. The intention here is to encourage the use of thought processes that take into account the real world and are not conditioned by custom and practice. It is also to encourage the reader to 'think outside the box', to think freely, unbounded by a formulaic approach. Marketing must be the guiding spirit of an overall, ruthless company strategy to gain market share.

Many readers of this book will imagine that their company does not permit this necessary freedom of thought. That the company is too set in its ways, and their path through it too far determined by a tradition of selfishness and immovable, illogical structures: 'The way we do things'... Despite the foregoing criticism of much of British industrial methods, it is still rare for a company to completely stifle all attempts to show personal initiative. Companies are made up of people and there is always room to move away from practising tasks in some pre-determined historical manner; such excuses are offered usually as justification for practising lethargy. It is your job and you must go at it with a sense of purpose, in a comprehensive, studied, disciplined manner and with a firm idea of what you are attempting to achieve. It is a very rare employer who would object to this, provided it produces results, and is not simply an elaborate show of self-aggrandisement. Just for a moment, take your eye off the next rung of the management ladder and do something useful

8

The Salesman

A professional like any other

One often hears the statement, 'I could never be a salesman'; yet the same statement has a number of different meanings. The most common meaning is that somehow, all salesmen are people lacking in the moral fibre so enjoyed by the rest of society. Another meaning is that all salesmen are shallow characters, with a ready line in off-colour jokes – and who would want to be part of that? Yet another meaning is that a salesman, to be successful, has to have a particular stereotypical personality, perhaps a relentlessly positive attitude, and few people believe they have this personality, or would dare to admit it if they did.

As a result, it is unquestionably true that the career of salesman is attractive to a great number of people who fit one, or all, of the above somewhat undesirable characteristics. Unfortunately these stereotypical characteristics tend to disguise the fact when the task of selling is done properly, it is as much a profession as any other. This is particularly true in the capital goods arena. This not to place those engaged in such selling on a higher moral plane relative to others engaged in selling, but simply because a salesman in the capital goods arena is usually persuading a prospective customer to make a considerable investment that requires a significant act of faith in the salesman's company and its products. Furthermore, the selling cycle is likely to be longer and hence, any flaws in the integrity of the salesman will be more readily exposed.

There is unquestionably a difference in attitude towards a salesman on the two sides of the Atlantic. Americans have a completely different attitude to selling and salesmen, and are far less likely than the British to avoid selling as a career for fear of the contempt or disdain of their peers;

The Salesman

university graduates in the US are far less likely to see selling as an unworthy occupation than their UK counterparts. Of course, even in the States, a salesman is likely to be the target of humour, and even of criticism, but there is more recognition that the salesman is in the front line as far as the company's interface to the market is concerned. He is a recognisable, identifiable, key part of the company's workforce. In Britain, however, even though the reluctance to enter a selling career has greatly diminished over the past thirty years, the salesperson is still considered to be part of a totally separate entity called 'the sales force'; a stigma akin, perhaps, to that of being 'in service'... Perhaps that is why sales people tend to adopt any job title that will distance them from the 'boot room'; they look to be called 'marketing representative', 'technical representative' and so on.

Generally, the sales 'rep' is thought to have no concern for the company, or its reputation or standing in the market place; but is merely focused on his commission and perks. Whilst this charge can be substantiated on occasions, it is difficult to separate cause and effect. Because they are often considered to be 'irresponsible cowboys', it should come as no surprise if sales people act accordingly. One major British company had a Sales and Marketing Director who, when questioned about his attitude towards the salesmen protested, 'I'm not the company's leading salesman'. Yet his business card said that that was exactly what he was. His income was directly related to their performance. Yet he considered it a social stigma to be associated with the very people he was paid to lead and motivate! His attitude inevitably permeated his peer group. It can hardly be surprising if his staff did not feel valued. If they are not valued, then it is easy to see why they do not behave professionally. More to the point, unless they are managed and rewarded in such a manner as to militate against them behaving irresponsibly, the company will inevitably reap the reward of its own attitudes.

Compare the attitude, outlined above, concerning a British company and its Sales & Marketing Director, with that of an American senior executive assisting a UK salesman with a prospective sale in a real situation. The salesman was attempting to close an order with a British government organisation for equipment worth £1m to the salesman's company. The company's research and development headquarters was in Los Angeles. As part of their deliberations, the prospective customer decided to make a one-day visit to his company's HQ in Los Angeles; the customer delegation was to be about ten strong. The salesman left for LA some three days before the customer delegation arrived. His task during those three days was to brief various development engineers and executives, and tell them what the visitors wanted to hear regarding the future direction of our products and the company; all of these US colleagues made themselves available to him because he had asked them to; of course this meant taking time out from their normal work, Of course, for their part they all needed to be assured that the salesman was fully cognisant of the relevant issues and was in with a real chance of closing the business back in the UK. But as far as they were concerned, for these three days up to and including the day of the visit, on this specific project, they, including the very senior executive, a Vice President of the company, worked for the salesman. The Vice President met the delegation, answered all their questions and then entertained them to lunch. Between the question and answer session and lunch he sought the salesman's opinion on his Q & A performance relative to the brief the salesman had given him; he needed to know if any 'fine tuning' was necessary. He then held discussions over lunch, following the briefing to the letter. His contribution to a successful sales campaign was invaluable. Compare this attitude to the British Sales and Marketing Director referred to above; and it is not untypical. It is worth repeating here that too often British management too often measures its own effectiveness by how much managerial distance they can put between themselves and those working at the 'coalface'.

Sometimes this distance manifests itself with the 'meetings syndrome'; with tongue firmly in cheek it can be said that it is surprising that there is not a professional Institution of Meetings Engineers. It is quite incredible how often management is totally out of bounds to the rest of the organisation because they are in an almost endless round of meetings. The salesman in the case related above went on record as saying he had learned a very valuable lesson that he was never to forget in a subsequent successful career that led to his becoming a Chief Executive. He made a personal policy decision that any salesman needing his help to close a sale would get that help in any location, and at any time he needed; he would never be 'in a meeting' to a salesman or his manager. Meetings never brought business through the door. However, the reasons for calling on this type of help, with this degree of urgency, had to be sound.

This parable is not a plea to 'love thy salesman', but it is a suggestion to have a different view of their worth in a company. By so doing, a company will have much better market intelligence, they will be better represented and, because the salesmen are 'part of the family', so to speak, then the

The Salesman

whole company can attack the market in unison. Furthermore, such a change in attitude will attract a more professional type of person into selling. It is unfortunately a fact that even today a selling career is one that carries a stigma and as a result too few really good people are attracted to it. By the same token many people who could have a fulfilling career in selling will stay too long in the more 'respectable' end of the business, such as engineering design, where they may be competing for professional survival with more naturally gifted individuals. The competition in the pure engineering sense might be just too fierce from colleagues who are truly brilliant, with outstanding qualifications. Facing up to this reality might just point the way to a different but equally rewarding way of earning a living.

It does not have to be ambition that moves one to consider a move to another aspect of the industry. It might just be a realisation by the individual that he has other attributes in his personal armoury to bear and he has to use them if he is to avoid being overshadowed by the talent around him. Quite apart from the talent of his own generation there is always the threat of the talent of those of subsequent generations who will inevitably be more technically up to date and, by virtue of their youth, less expensive to employ. This returns to the point made throughout this book that individuals must always seek to add to their skill set if they are to retain their place in the fiercely competitive world; this will often entail moving outside of one's core capability. This will become more and more the case, particularly as the advance of technology makes some careers, once thought of as a 'job for life', seem less certain. Even if a chosen profession is not at risk, it is inevitable that the manner of its practice will change. All of this indicates that there is little room for complacency anywhere.

So what is the role of a salesman; a simple question? Surprisingly too few salesman really know the answer. Is it to represent the company? Is it to advise the customer? To do what? Again, it is more illustrative to relate a selling situation that actually occurred. A salesman was bidding to sell a complex computer system to a prospective customer. The computer part of the package was a mid-range machine. Unfortunately, the price of the proposed system was, in the salesman's opinion, too expensive to fit the customer's budget. As things stood, the salesman was not going to win the order.

As part of an attempt to assist the salesman to win, his manager asked him: *'Could a lower range (and therefore less expensive) machine do the job?'* The salesman's response was, *'Oh no, I could never bid that, it will not perform anywhere near as well as the machine I am currently bidding'*; which, of course, did not answer the question. This was pointed out by his manager who went on to suggest that the salesman re-think his current bid; the salesman was very reluctant to do so and said, *'After all, we are consultants to the industry, aren't we?'*

'No we are not,' said the manager, *'We are salesmen. Our job is to get our equipment out of our factory and into the customer's premises as quickly as possible – and his money out of his bank and into ours as quickly as possible – and we do not have any other purpose. If we provide advice as part of the exercise of fulfilling our prime purpose, that is part of the cost of sale – but it is secondary to our main aim'.*

This may seem ruthless, but such ruthlessness is employed in successful businesses on a daily basis, and the higher the stakes, the greater the need to stay focused on the main aim. The cost of failure can be catastrophic. For salesmen it has to be severe. In general they are better paid, their pay being directly related to endeavour and success. The rewards of success are often high, the 'fun' side of the business is often directed at them, they enjoy expense account living and they are subject to less day-to-day management control than their colleagues in other disciplines.

As always, there is a price to be paid. It is not possible to put a salesman's excuses in the bank He is rewarded to sell a company's goods and services. If he does not do so then he is just a cost burden the company can do without. Sound harsh? Any other person on the payroll not performing the function he is paid to do would receive little sympathy, and his job would be at risk. The unsuccessful salesman has to be viewed in the same way. All too often businessmen, some very senior in very substantial businesses, seem to believe that salespeople should be judged by a different set of criteria than the rest of the staff. It is believed that if the salesman does not sell, it is the fault of marketing or manufacturing or engineering. Even if this is the case, a salesman who cannot sell his company's products is still a cost burden the company cannot afford.

A one-man business

A salesman should be a one-man business on a payroll. He draws his base salary and his training and his products from his employer. Therefore his salary determines what he sells and how much he is expected to sell, at what price, in accordance with what terms and conditions and company

The Salesman

constraints may exist. To earn the incentive part of his income, he manages his business any way he chooses as long as he meets all of the criteria imposed by his employer. If he meets these criteria by taking one customer out to lunch every day that is his decision (although, of course, this may result in a territory change the following year). If he pursues one major opportunity, because he is convinced he can make his target that way, as opposed to pursuing many smaller opportunities, that is his prerogative; decisions such as these are made by entrepreneurs every day, so a salesman is given a better opportunity than most to learn some of the fundamentals of running a business.

Like all entrepreneurs, a salesman cannot afford to waste his time. He must plan, every day, where to spend it to maximum effect. Maximum effect means concentrating on those opportunities where he is most likely to successfully win business. There is a very vulgar expression, which emanates out of the USA, suggesting that some salesmen, unless they are monitored closely, are more likely to find somewhere quiet to visit the washroom. The burden and stress of finding business is just too much effort and, in any case, they can manage their lives on a base salary, and a bit of commission from long-term customers (they provide the 'washroom'), so why bust a gut? For a salesman to have this attitude is one thing, for a company to allow this attitude to prevail is quite another.

Just as he would if he was in business for himself, he must mentally examine all the 'what ifs?' He must think with a wider perspective when pursuing a particular piece of business. **Think what might happen, then work to make it happen or work to prevent it happening. Thinking after it has happened is too late.**

A very common mistake made by salesmen is to misread the signs. They become very close to prospective customers, or to existing customers who intend to order more equipment. A smile here, a willingness to lunch there, an after-hours drink in a nearby bar, a game of squash, are often signs to a salesman of that he is about to be successful closing the sale he is pursuing. Any objective examination of the sales activity, or any seeking of true buying signs will reveal a much more barren picture than the salesman truly wants to believe from his friendly contacts with the prospective customer. All salesmen need to understand that being friendly with a customer is not at all the same thing as believing he is a friend. A salesman should never forget the true basis of the relationship. By the same token, the customer cannot afford to allow friendship to cloud his professional judgement. He has his own pressures to contend with, and satisfy. The salesman should ascertain what these are and attempt to satisfy them.

A salesman should always compile his forecast in as objective a manner as possible. It is his way of conducting himself as the one-man business on a payroll; if he were a self-dependent businessman providing for himself, his only source of income he would have to be this objective. Such an objective forecast should tell him where he should be expending his effort. He learns how to detect, and dismiss, questionable opportunities. Just as importantly, it prevents self-delusion. Using such objective criteria invariably shows that the chances of winning a particular order are considerably less than when that forecast is allowed to be based on a salesman's gut feel; it corrects any self delusion that there is no further work to done to win the order.

The forecast should depend on two elements, the percentage chance of there being business to be closed at all, and the chance of that business being won by the particular salesman. For example, if the prospective customer has not requested a formal quotation, then that is one indication that there might not be business to be won. If the prospective customer has not yet negotiated internally for funds to be allocated to this particular piece of business, then that too is another negative sign. If there are three competitors for a particular piece of business, then, by definition, the chances of any salesman winning that business cannot be more than 25 per cent. The salesman would be wise to think in these terms. It makes for a much more realistic assessment of the work still to be done to win.

Describing a salesman's task in terms outlined above is to concentrate on those aspects that contribute salesman's behaviour as a professional, as a businessman; in other words, where he wishes to be taken seriously. Where he is making, and recognised for making, a valuable contribution to his employer's business, and to his own career prospects. Where he knows his task, and the capability of the company and the competence of his non-sales colleagues in it. He does not have to be a manufactured personality to be successful. In general, if a salesman behaves professionally, he will be treated accordingly.

The sales manager

When a salesman changes to being a sales manager, he is taking on a role distinctly different from that of a salesman. A salesman is very akin to being an entrepreneur, but with his efforts tied in very closely with a single employer. He is something of a free spirit working under constraints. The sales manager, on the other hand, has completely relinquished the free spirit element of the selling task, and has allied himself totally to the company and its aspirations. It is highly likely that he has been promoted from the ranks of the sales force. As has often been said, he may not have been the most successful of the sales force, but he may have been deemed to better represent the company at a managerial level, or to have those mysterious 'management attributes' which other managers prefer to believe they, exclusively as a caste, possess. He may indeed have been the most professional salesman. But will he make a professional manager?

Many salesmen find great difficulty making the transition from salesman to sales manager, particularly if the promotion has been made internally. 'Poacher turned gamekeeper' is an accusation often levelled at the man who has accepted this first rung up a management ladder. Such an accusation is levelled, simply to lessen the resolve of the new man to professionally manage his former colleagues. He must not be intimidated. The easiest, most straightforward way to deal with this is to recognise within himself that he is now being called upon to do a totally different task. He should now manage his colleagues the way he wished he himself, and they, had been managed.

First, the new sales manager will hopefully recognise the valuable contribution made to the business by professional salespeople. Nevertheless, that contribution must be monitored and measured and judged in no less severe terms than any other member of the staff. The salesman, or salesmen, are on the company payroll, and it is inexcusable to treat them as if they are prima donnas, allowed to behave irresponsibly towards the company simply because they are expected, purely as a result of being salesmen, to submit to no form of control or supervision. This can lead to a state of collective, rebellious indiscipline which must be stamped on firmly as it very often leads to salesmen unconsciously 'rubbishing' the company and its products, even to prospective customers. At the same time, a sales manager must be fair to his sales force. All too often sales forces, in various countries, achieve less than their maximum effectiveness, simply because the manager has been less than even-handed with his people; perversely this is sometimes the fault of the employer who often offers rewards for managers without really thinking through all the consequences.

The allocation of prime geographical territories, or named lucrative accounts to particular salesman is a very common method of creating discontent. To award such territories or accounts to favoured salesmen as soon as they have been relinquished by the incumbent indicates a decided lack of control. It inevitably results in new incoming salesmen feeling that the cards are stacked against them. Rather like raising a family of children, if one is to achieve maximum success, it is vital that there be no favourites.

It is essential that once put in place such management controls are adhered to with fairness and resolve. The controls should be clear and unambiguous and not liable to misinterpretation; the sales manager should be able to stand any amount of inquisition by any salesman and show that he has been scrupulously even-handed towards the whole sales team. Only thus can he ensure that all of the sales force put their maximum endeavours into the task at hand without distractions. To keep up the morale and motivation of a sales force, within the context of overall company performance, is of paramount importance.

One illustrative true occasion was when a sales manager was adding new salesmen to a small sales force; it was obvious that some territory had to be relinquished by each of the existing salesmen. Inevitably, with the sacrifice of some territory, some potential business being pursued within that territory would also have to be relinquished; never a popular move. There is a maxim in successful, sales-orientated companies, 'Two things you can be sure of – your quota gets bigger and your territory gets smaller'. When salesmen are fighting for territory or accounts, no prisoners are taken. On this occasion, the sales manager had spent many hours alone, examining the current business levels of each salesman; he had examined their forecasts. Examined how much business had already been gained from each piece of territory or each account. The sales manager used a detailed map and coloured pins to show the location of each piece of business gained, and business being pursued, together with the location of each salesman's home.

After much deliberation he re-allocated the business within the region. Several issues had to be considered by the sales manager if the pursuit of current opportunities was not to be disrupted. He needed to maximise, for each salesman, the benefit of the business that the salesman had already gained in the territory he was relinquishing. He needed to ensure that the salesman gained personally as much as was possible from the prospective business he had located in that territory, and was currently pursuing. The sales manager needed to reduce to the minimum, the travel time that would be necessary for the salesman to get to his new territory. Finally, the sales manager had to generate a hand-over plan. In other words, each salesman

The Salesman

would need time to complete the business that he was pursuing at the time of the new territory allocation. This meant that each salesman should be allowed some time to enter the territory he was relinquishing, in order to close prior opportunities.

The sales manager introduced a 'hand-over' rule. Each salesman could go into his old territory for up to 60 days from the start date of the new territory allocation. If during that time he closed the prior opportunities, then the commission for that sale would be totally his. For the succeeding 60 days, he could still go into his former territory, but he would share any commission resulting from his efforts on a 50/50 basis with the new salesman to whom he had relinquished the territory. Throughout this whole exercise the sales manager was acutely aware that his decisions were going to affect the short-term livelihood of every member of my staff. But he also knew that, given the amount of time and effort he had put into the exercise, he had produced the best result he could, judged from any objective standpoint. But there's the rub. Salesmen are rarely objective when discussing territory allocation. Paranoia in a salesman is usually raised to an art form. The sales manager knew that no matter how carefully or logically he did this task, there was going to be some upset. An American army general is quoted as saying: 'If you are not prepared to inflict some pain occasionally, you shouldn't be in the job'.

However, the sales manager was perfectly prepared to discuss his reasoning in detail to any salesman that wished to challenge the reasoning behind the territory re-allocation. By this means, they could, at least, see that there was no element of favouritism or lack of serious thought. Most of the sales force accepted the decision with a certain sense of inevitability. One person in particular chose to do otherwise. He entered the manager's office in a state of apoplectic fury. This is not something that, in any other profession, one would normally be expected to allow. With a sales force however, given the pressure that salesmen are under, and given the fact that salesman must display more aggression than most, some licence in behaviour must be given. It also has to be recognised that salesmen, by their very nature will use any emotional device to win their argument. However, it is important that the sales manager does not collapse under such an assault. The issues have been thought through thoroughly, a decision has been made which can stand considerable interrogation and examination. There is no reason to submit to pressure. But anyone should be entitled to question the reasoning that had resulted in a major change to the way he was to earn his living, if only to prevent a grievance being nurtured.

The salesman in this instance was pursuing, in an area of London, a major order, the biggest of his entire career. Consequently, he was under enormous pressure. He was also responsible for a rural territory that, as a result of pursuing this large order, he had, understandably, neglected.

Strangely though, for all kinds of emotional reasons, salesmen become quite attached to territories. They know the terrain, they know the way business is conducted there, they will have formed relationships with people in the territory. But in this instance the salesman had overlooked the fact that there was business to be done there and because of his neglect the company was denied that business; remember the sales manager has a duty to maximise the company's business and this must always transcend his obligation to maximise a salesman's income. Given the choice between relinquishing the major account he was pursuing, or changing his current rural territory for another, elsewhere in the region, there was no contest as far as his personal income was concerned. The salesman, however, saw things differently. He accused the sales manager of being unfair, and of taking away a lucrative territory, even though the sales manager had proved conclusively that this was not the case. The salesman was just not going to listen to reason. Eventually, the sales manager submitted to the salesman's demands. The salesman was satisfied.

But as the salesman turned to leave the manager's office, the manager mentioned calmly that, since the salesman had elected to keep the rural territory and relinquish the London one, he should now prepare to hand over, in accordance with the hand-over rules, the major London opportunity he was pursuing, to the new man in that territory. The salesman was totally stunned. He thought that he could 'cherry pick' his way around the region, and that his display of uncontrolled anger would see him through. He wanted it all. He wanted to retain the rural territory where he had been neglecting opportunities and at the same time retain his very major opportunity in another territory altogether. The sales manager was left with no option but to point out that to accede to the salesman's demands would have worked against the interests of his sales colleagues. The sales manager had awarded the salesman with that part of the existing region from which he was likely to gain most business. If the salesman wanted to conduct his business on some other basis, the sales manager had indicated a willingness to accommodate him as far as possible, just as long as he made his quota at the end of the fiscal year; of course this meant he would have to make quota

The Salesman

from his rural territory, a territory he had neglected. A split-second's reflection changed his mind, and, albeit reluctantly, he accepted the new territory as originally planned.

This true account has been recounted for a number of reasons. Firstly, to point out that salesmen should be managed just as any other member of staff, fairly but firmly; and on the principle that, for the sales manager, ultimately the company's interests have to come first. Secondly, to assert that salesmen are entitled to have as much thought given to the conduct of their area of responsibility as others, more if the company is to benefit fully. But thirdly, because the incident related here had an interesting effect on the salesman in question. In subsequent years, he went into sales management himself, and eventually became a Managing Director. He was to meet his former sales manager several years later, whereupon he told him that the confrontation that they had had many years earlier had left an indelible impression on him that, in the exercise of his own management responsibilities, he had never forgotten

Another crucial part of the task of sales management is the interrogation of a salesman's forecast. The integrity of that forecast and its closeness to the budget, set at the beginning of the year, will greatly affect the company's fortunes, short-and long-term. By the very nature of his task, a salesman must be optimistic. It is also true to say that if a salesman manages to persuade his management that the forecast is a true reflection of his business outlook, and it is satisfactory, then he stays alive and well, on the payroll, until the next forecast review. If that forecast is not vigorously scrutinised and actions taken, predicated on its ready acceptance, and it transpires that the forecast was not accurate, then the company has suffered – and, of course a non-performing salesman has stayed alive.

It has been outlined above how a salesman should compile a forecast, in order to professionally conduct his business. But how should the forecast be interrogated? Typically too little time is given to this exercise, particularly in smaller entrepreneurial companies. But perversely it is in such small companies that interrogation of the sales outlook is imperative. Of course, if the interrogation of a forecast is not being carried out by someone with a personal history of selling and/or sales management, the task is just that more difficult, but not impossible. If the forecast is made up of a number of objective criteria, as suggested earlier, then each of those criteria can be tracked on a month by month basis throughout the sales campaign, in the case of a specific opportunity. Under these conditions, it is just not acceptable for a salesman to report no progress on a given prospective sale. Either the chances of closing a sale have gone up or they have gone down. The number of competitors has reduced or increased. The closing date has moved out, or is now predicted to be earlier. Funding has reduced or increased. The salesman wants management help or technical expertise...

All of these questions, and more, need to be asked; an effective method of getting answers to these questions is to individually interrogate each salesman once a month. The meeting is not primarily to call the salesman to account so much as an offer to bring another opinion to the task. The objective should be to help win business. Usually, the salesman will welcome such a meeting. He will feel less isolated, more a part of a team. Each prospect can be discussed, and the best way of going forward decided. Any other help that the salesman feels is needed, and who might best provide that help, can also be discussed. At the end of such a meeting, it should be clear between the salesman and his manager who was going to carry out which action. A review date for a month hence should be set. This is a process that any manager, with or without direct selling experience, can set in motion. What is very dangerous, in any business, is to allow the sales force to be a law unto itself. It is wise to view salespeople with a high degree of suspicion, not because they are intrinsically less honest than any other staff, but because salesmen, for the sake of their own self-motivation, are often self-deluding. Secondly, because the consequences of planning and running a business based on the unexpurgated version of a salesman's view of the world can be dire!

Planned rewards

The commission plan is a valuable tool for the company to use, to induce the salesman to do the company's bidding. Sound obvious? Most salesmen in the capital equipment arena have a commission element in their total remuneration package. This total remuneration is usually made up in some proportion of base salary to commission, say 70/30 or 60/40. When added to his cost of employment, a salesman can be an expensive resource. Cost of transportation, car or car allowance, travel expenses, hotel and lodging, acceptable business expenses, etc., etc. Is he worth it? It is important that a company knows the answer to this question. Many companies simply do not know how many items a salesman must sell at the gross margin of the company's goods and services before the company breaks even on the 'raw

The Salesman

cost' of the salesman; i.e., before he has sold anything at all to produce a profit on his employment. It is just assumed that the company has to have salesmen, at a salary the salesmen believe they have a right to, regardless of whether the company can afford it or not. Remember, the company is a business, not an employment agency. Any salesman may be employed on the payroll for a considerable part of the financial year, during which he is no more than a cost burden. Does his sales achievement in Month 12 justify the cost of his employment in Months 1-11?

Given that he cannot live if you pay him entirely in arrears, the total projected remuneration of a sales person should be directly linked to the total amount of the company's goods and services it is necessary for him to sell to produce an acceptable profit. Often salesmen believe, and many companies inadvertently collude in this, that his total income is what he should expect to be paid, regardless of the quality of his performance. Another frequent error, commission is sometimes paid to salesmen who merely 'service' the business, in other words, who perform a perfunctory job involving little selling. This may justify a fixed salary, on the grounds that it keeps the business ticking over; it is a form of 'merchandising' which a modestly intelligent van driver could probably do equally well. Commission should be linked to effort, not to the mere perpetuation of existing business. Such 'salesmen' have their territory and they know the people in it very well; remember the 'washroom' syndrome mentioned earlier. A few calls a week, a chat with a friendly customer of long years' standing, a regular order collected, then it's off home or to the golf course or the pub.

Why do companies continue to pay inflated incomes to people who bring in business, that frankly they would get if they sent the office cleaner to collect it? This is a common failure of many companies, both large and small, who have allowed themselves to be intimidated by salesmen's demands and expectations. It is an expense burden few companies should allow themselves to bear. The larger the sales force, the more attention that needs to be given to the sales force's remuneration. It is vital to remember that the salesman's task is to sell, not to take orders from captive customers. The commission plan needs to reflect this.

If it is necessary to employ a sales force, then just bear in mind that new business is required, of a type determined by the company. It is imperative that, without formal permission from the company to do otherwise, the salesman sells the company's goods and services in a form acceptable to the company. It is disastrous if a salesman is allowed, without consultation, to sell modified, or different, versions of the company's product line or an extension of the company's services. This is an area where the British tendency to indulge in lax corporate discipline really produces dire consequences. By the very nature of their task, salesmen are employed to be businessmen. In many companies, this leads to a situation where salesmen really believe they are employed to run their business, and hence the company, the way they believe it should be run. Very often, the lack of control over their activities merely serves to confirm their view of their task. But it should never be forgotten that a salesman is employed, and paid, to do what a company wants done, in the way the company wants it done – or, at least, that ought to be the case.

Apart from the monitoring of the activity of each salesman, the formulation of the commission plan should play a key role in how a sales force performs. If a salesman sells the goods and services that the company wants sold, in the manner, and at the price it wants them sold, then the salesman should be well paid, relative to his reward for not fulfilling these expectations. For example, if a new customer is defined as a customer with whom the company has never done business before or, at least for a prior acceptable period, say two years, then business from such a customer should attract a higher commission rate than that paid for business from an existing customer. Sometimes, just the gaining of a new customer attracts a 'new account' bonus. It may be that certain items in the company's portfolio of goods and services, produce a higher gross margin than others, and it is on these that the company wants the salesmen to concentrate their efforts. Again, this can be achieved by the application of differing commission rates. The commission plan should ensure that a salesman is well rewarded if he really is selling, in the true sense of that word, and less well paid if he is coasting, or 'order taking' as it is sometimes called. Too much order taking by a particular salesman should call his employment with the company into question.

As well as the mechanics of the compilation of the commission plan, a few other issues must be borne in mind. If a salesman is making his sales target, then the commission paid to him must be affordable. There is little point rewarding a salesman for the selling of a particular product or service, if that commission erodes the gross margin on that product to an unacceptable level. Secondly, a great deal of thought needs to be given to the wording of a commission plan before its issuance, particularly in these days of very sensitive industrial relations law. A commission plan must be unambiguous and not prone to interpretation. The plan should be written and compiled, such that a salesman will examine it thoroughly to determine how he will maximise his income. However, salesmen will also pore over every 'full stop and comma' of a plan in order to persuade the company that the company did not make themselves sufficiently clear and that they, the salesmen, are entitled to the benefit of the doubt. On the BBC Today programme (12/10/2005), an executive of Onetel was responding to accusations from BT that Onetel salesmen were mis-selling; his defence was that if the salesmen were being less than ethical in their efforts, it was not out of order with the precise wording of their instructions issued by the company as part of their commission plan. In the mind of most salesmen there is no such thing as the 'spirit' of a commission plan!

Sales order processing – the last line of defence

There is another aspect of control of the sales activity quite separate from the control of salesmen and the duties of sales managers. Since, in most companies, salesmen, by the nature of their task, are away from the company's offices, it is vital that they have clear instructions that define their task. Furthermore, it is equally vital that someone in the order administration office is charged with the task of ensuring that these instructions are adhered to – to the letter. The salesman must know that this person has the authority to determine what is, and what is not acceptable as an order on the company. To not make this clear is to see the company committed to orders it may not be able to fulfil, or on which it will lose considerable money. Whether the company is small where orders are likely to be accepted by an office administrator or the company is large and there is a substantial order-processing department, all involved should know the rules. Of course, with very large companies, order acceptability should be a key part of the company's data processing environment. All orders ought, under these circumstances, to pass through a 'gating' process that allows, or denies, the acceptance of an order.

Whether the salesman carries his instructions by computer or sales manual, they need to be comprehensive. He should be in no doubt about Terms and Conditions acceptable to the company. Payment terms must be equally explicit. Thirty days net extended by a salesman, without permission, to 120 days net, can be the difference between loss and profit, particularly if poor credit control allows the customer to extend this by another number of days. Equipment pricing must be clear and unambiguous. Discount structures, if appropriate, must similarly be strictly enforced. But the salesman in the field, i.e away from the office, must be armed with all this information if he is to behave in the company's best interest. The sales manual, in whatever form it takes, should be the 'Holy Bible', and no-one should be able to work outside it. When the manual needs to be updated to accommodate a new product, or service, or a change to the company's previous way of doing business, the update information should be circulated to the entire sale force at exactly the same time. The information telling the sales force how to update the manual should allow no room for error in its implementation; the sales force should incorporate these updates on given incorporation date. The order processing system should be adjusted to accommodate the changes at the same time so that there is no discontinuity between orders being entered to be processed and the processing system.

9

The Financial Controller

The financial controller must control the finances

This sounds such an obvious concept, that it might be difficult to accept such a sub-heading to a chapter. Yet it is beyond doubt that there are many people carrying the title financial controller who do not control the finances; and many Financial Directors who do not direct the finances.

Many finance people, often at director or controller level, see their task as 'adding up the score'. Many others see their task as presenting financial data to the management, and only to the management, in the way that is most acceptable, regardless of the facts. It is not unusual for finance people, without any deliberate attempt to mislead, to use all of the flexibility permitted under national accountancy rules to such an extent that the figures bear little relationship to the true condition of the company. To be fair to such people, they are sometimes uncomfortable when stretching to the limit, the flexibility of presentation allowed. They will, on occasions, seek the advice and approval of the company's external auditors, to see if this financial device or that one will be deemed compliant within the financial regulations. Of course, this permissible financial sleight-of-hand is not always performed at the instigation of the financial people themselves, but more often by order of the management; who seek, and sometimes direct that they receive, a report more praiseworthy than reality might indicate. The discomfort of the financial people is thus often silenced.

To present the company's performance in the best possible light is of course quite legitimate. To distort that presentation to the point where the company's performance as related is distinctly misleading is in no one's interest, least of all that of the company itself. The views of the late Stuart Steven of the *Mail on Sunday*, on accountants are quoted earlier in this book.

Given some of the manipulation of company figures by some financial people and the use to which this manipulation is put by some boards of directors it is not difficult to understand what gives rise to the sentiments expressed by Mr Steven. However, to accept those views without qualification would be wrong, and unfair to the very competent financial people that are employed across the nation. In most cases financial people can only work within the parameters laid down by their management.

This being the case, it is difficult for finance controllers and directors to withstand what can become enormous pressure from a board also under pressure to concentrate on financial manipulation, to the exclusion of a concern with the integrity of the figures or the need to represent the true position of a company with regard to the market. This pressure is not unique to British industry as is evidenced by Worldcom and Enron in the USA and Parmalet, currently under investigation in Italy. Nevertheless, the industrial environment in the UK where senior finance people tend to be so ensconced with management that they are cut off from the realities of the market does tend to make the manipulation of the figures an end in itself; it is this divorce from reality that Stuart Steven referred to.

But if a good financial controller is encouraged, and indeed directed, by his management to report scrupulously on the true state of the company, in order that the management can decide on the options open to it, then all will benefit. For, in simple terms, there is money coming into the company, and money going out. What happens in between those two simple events can bring about the success or failure of the company. Because of this simple truth, a good financial director, properly directed and allowed to contribute, is 'worth his weight in gold'. Unfortunately, because of the cachet of wisdom accorded to finance people in British industry – far more than is the case in the USA – it has over the past few years, been very common for senior management at CEO and General Manager level to turn their back on their native skills, be it as engineers or sales people or marketing or production, and present themselves instead as financial wizards. They seem totally submerged in the jargon. Undoubtedly it is almost a demand in the City that CEOs use 'accountant-speak' to explain the state of the company; it is this again that part explains Stuart Steven's objections.

One obvious disadvantage of this apparent skill shift is that it is just not possible to give adequate time to all of the intricacies of the financial structure of the company and, at the same time, give sufficient time to all of the other company activities, not to mention the overall direction of the

The Financial Controller

company. Unfortunately many CEOs undertake this skill shift precisely because it is a form of escape from the need to determine company direction and strategy. Any reasonably intelligent person can add up, but it requires a totally different skill to have a vision of where the company can go, and to put in place an infrastructure to fulfil the vision.

It is beyond question that all professional disciplines should use the finance resource of the company to assist them with their task. From the manufacturing director's standpoint, what are the costs of manufacturing each item in the projected company portfolio? Do these costs make their appropriate contribution to the product gross margin? If they do not, can we sacrifice this product and increase the proposed production run on another item? Again, what are the possible financial consequences? How can obsolete equipment be written off? Could a 'fire sale' be held? These, and many others, are the questions, here expressed very simply, that the production man can ask of the true financial controller.

Conversely, it should be possible for the financial controller to be the initiator of an examination of the production costs, because his own analysis shows that costs are running ahead of budget, or sales of a line item reveal that production costs can no longer be justified. Similarly, if an examination of engineering costs reveals that a product has not reached a particular stage of its planned development between concept and launch, then it should be the task of the finance controller to bring this to the attention of first, the engineering management, and then the company management. Adjustments can then be made to the engineering activity and perhaps, if necessary, to the overall company cost structure and even the company strategy.

Each product has an associated cost – a development cost, a launch cost, a sales cost and a marketing cost. Each of these costs can be further broken down. By the same token, each product will have a monthly projected sales volume and an associated cost of sale, by salesman, by region, by country. All of these criteria should be known to the financial controller/director. In many companies, because there is no directive to produce to these criteria, the facts are not known, and the company merely rolls up all the revenues, from whatever source, and subtracts the total costs to determine whether the company is in profit or loss. This is unforgivable, but such practice is by no means restricted to small companies. Too often, people in the finance sector of industrial companies (and indeed the same is true in other businesses) beaver away at their spreadsheets, isolated from the mainstream activities of the company. Other areas of the company's activity know the finance people ae there, they know they are considered important, but they have not the remotest idea how the activities of the financial community relate to their own. Sometimes, the converse is true. The finance people themselves have no real feeling for how their activities have any meaningful impact on the company's relationship to the market. Yet the financial regime should permeate every part of the company, to such an extent that no product should get beyond concept stage without the financial implications of every stage from concept to launch being understood and recorded. Similarly, no staff should be recruited, or indeed made redundant, no new production line established, no new buildings leased or purchased, no commission plan issued without consultation with, and the very detailed involvement of, the financial staff.

Not the be-all and end-all

To make the compilation of financial data as important as indicated here is by no means a guarantee of company success. Nor is it the core activity of the company, as some students are led to believe. If this were the case, all companies with a strict, meticulous financial regime would be, by definition, successful. They aren't. Many American companies analyse their financial performance exhaustively but still fail in business. The gathering of financial data is not of itself the determining factor of a company's fortunes, because this data has to be used wisely, and with judgement. Nevertheless, to not know, in detail, the income to, and cost of, each discrete part of the business – to be flying blind, in other words – should be unforgivable. No Chief Executive can properly direct a company without sound financial advice and data. It is only by having a good financial reporting regime, one with integrity, that the senior management of the company can effectively concentrate on the company's overall direction. It is this reporting regime that will reveal weaknesses in the company's initial strategy and will also point up how adjustments to this chosen strategy can be made to produce better results. The same reporting regime should be used to determine personal time and attention allocation by senior management between the various company activities, and between the company and its customers. Thus the financial reporting system is vital, not only for reporting the health of the company to the outside world but also for directing the internal day-to-day management of the company – but it must have integrity.

The Financial Controller

If he is performing well, a good financial director will be viewed as fearsome by his colleagues. One British company had a financial controller who kept the company on the rails so well while the CEO was meeting other members of his management team, or visiting offices and customers, around the world, that he became known as the 'financial rottweiler'. If necessary he would inform the CEO of a problem the moment the problem became evident, such that the CEO could make any decisions or adjustments necessary – and he could make them regardless of where he was in the world. It has to be said that many members of staff around the world were terrified of this particular financial controller. He had set up such a detailed reporting regime that any variance from the submitted plan was instantly identifiable, and he was not shy in pointing out the variances. However, this definitely had the effect of making every element of the company ensure that their particular activity was financially viable. It is worth reiterating here that every activity in the company has a financial implication, every activity is financially measurable and able to be monitored. The company is, or should be, about money first and foremost. That alone should put the financial staff at the heart of the company; but they, in turn, should see their role as contributing positively to the company's success. They should be helping their colleagues to be successful in their endeavours, not standing on the sidelines attempting to demonstrate their own cleverness or indispensability.

10

The Human Resources Manager

The term 'Human Resources' has replaced the humbler 'Personnel' as a management prefix throughout much of British industry, mostly within those companies operating in or envious of a market dominated by the Americans. Other companies still use Personnel; but over the years, whatever its title, this area of a company's activity has become thoroughly unpopular with the staff, and very often, is treated as a Siberian outpost by the rest of the management. Even where the department has been viewed as lying outside the management mainstream, Personnel Managers and Directors have been allowed by default to wield enormous power over the staff, not always wisely, and certainly not always in the interests of the company. Many crimes can be laid at their door. It could be argued, for instance, that they have helped to perpetuate, and indeed have even accentuated, the classical 'them' and 'us' set of values that has divided British industry for decades. In the recent past, some companies, realising the dangers of this, have dispensed with the human resources department altogether; this often makes matters worse. It is not a cliché to say that the most important asset in a company is the staff; it is a fact. Therefore it is vital that there is an entity in the company dedicated to the activity of looking after the company's most important asset. This function should not be entrusted to an impersonal, external agency. But there needs to be a re-assessment of the role. The people in the department must be in the mainstream of a company's business. They must be much more than people processors, preening themselves on the fringes of management, wielding power without responsibility.

Many times one hears the quote, 'Americans are hire and fire' and, in some respects, there is an element of truth in the phrase. Someone's performance doesn't measure up, their face doesn't fit, a disagreement, a political manoeuvre, a staff cutback or a temporary loss of business. All of these reasons, and many others, can give rise to a dismissal in American companies. But all these reasons can, and often do, prevail in British companies. So what's the difference? American companies often offer platitudes about the value of their staff but beyond that there really is little attempt to disguise the fact that employees are valuable only as economic units; they are, as a result, recruited and dismissed generally in accord with the company's fortunes. So, when a person is to be dismissed, he is called before the boss and fired, and then sent to the human resources department to have the dismissal processed. In many major British companies, on the other hand, there is a tendency to dispense platitudes to cover the staff in a form of quasi-paternalism, borne of the nation's cultural history. This gives rise to a false sense of security by the staff. Then when there is a need to dismiss the 'kitchen maid', so to speak, management cannot summon up the courage to do the deed themselves, so they send the 'maid' along to the 'butler'; i.e. the HR department, to do the deed. This has led to enormous power being unjustifiably wielded by HR managers; it also means that the HR department is often despised as the tool of management rather than key to the personal development of staff. Of course, there are human resource departments in American companies, and they can be, and often are, very influential. However, in general, they act on behalf of, and under the very close supervision of, whichever department has responsibility for the member of staff being recruited or dismissed.

Another major difference between UK and US companies as far as the treatment of staff is concerned is when there is to be a major re-organisation. Usually with American companies whenever there is a major re-organisation, every member of staff knows where they fit into the new scheme of things. Typically this would be communicated by the human resources department but they would be known to be only the messengers not the originators. In British companies on the other hand it is by no means unusual for a re-organisation to be undertaken at board level and not even middle management would know of their new role. The staff would find out some time later by a process of 'trickle down'. There have been notorious occasions when employees have first learned of their redundancies on the local radio morning news. Unfortunately this again would lead to the personnel or HR department unjustifiably falling into disrepute in the eyes of the staff. This is not to state that American companies care more for their employees in any emotional sense of the word; but there is an understanding that to disregard the staff is to unsettle them or de-motivate them – which has a distinct, and sometimes long-lasting effect on business performance. So in American companies on such occasions the human resources department will usually instigate the formal, 'right way' of informing all staff so that disruption to the business is minimised. Unfortunately in British industry such a formal process is rarely used and human resources are not involved in the process at all, leading to the 'trickle down' mentioned earlier; thus a resource that could be used to ensure minimum disruption to the day-to-day business is not used at all and staff morale is unnecessarily undermined.

So, the solution is not to dispense with personnel departments, but to bring them closer to the mainstream of the business. The Personnel Director should advise top management of the implications for personnel of every decision and plan under consideration. They should be abreast, on an ongoing basis, of all the changes in employment legislation, and know the implications of such for the future of the company. They should feel that they have sufficient stature in the management hierarchy to be able to speak up for personnel concerns, or to advise (and expect to be heeded) on the best way of breaking announcements affecting staff. Like PR people, they may have difficulty in quantifying these activities; but if there is a case to be made that such activities will have a direct impact on the bottom line, then it should be made, if possible, in financial terms. Finally, they should liaise more closely with line management, to gain a proper understanding of what qualities are really required from job applicants. If staff know that the human resources staff have this position of influence, and it works to their benefit on occasions, then the HR people can also carry sometimes unpalatable messages in the other direction. In other words, staff can be treated as adults and not as 'below stairs' servants.

If human resources/personnel have this position in the company hierarchy then a good deal of straightforward administration work can be delegated to the HR department, freeing up management to concentrate on the main activity of the company. It is quite incredible but by no means unusual, that the board of a company, or its executive management team, will spend hours of a management meeting discussing the company car policy, or pensions policy. The research into such issues, and the resultant recommendations, including the affordability of such recommendations, arising out of discussions with finance, ought to be brought to the attention of management for little more than a final interrogation and approval, or adjustment; all the preparatory work can be done in advance by the HR manager. By the same token, if HR management are aware, because they have been intimately involved in its compilation at budget time, of the business profile the company is trying to achieve, then HR are in the best position to devise an appropriate commission plan. This particular suggestion will horrify many people, but it in reality they are the best people for the task, providing they are competent for the task. They know what is permissible under employment legislation. Their experience in writing employment contracts means that they are better able than most, to write unambiguous plans. Because of their neutrality, they are in the best position to objectively attempt to reflect the wishes of the management by orchestrating the activities of the sales force, via the commission plan.

For this, it is obviously vital that management have been quite explicit to the personnel people about what it is they are attempting to achieve; a worthwhile exercise in itself. The personnel staff can continuously monitor the effectiveness of a plan, independently of the sales force and the sales management. They can administer the plan and adjudicate in disputes between salespeople and their management. This means that with each successive year, there is ongoing concentrated experience being gained on a crucial area of the company's activity. Thus, each year they can weigh up the various options that will determine the degree of complexity that is advisable before the plan becomes too complex for it to be practically workable. Just like other disciplines, human resource people should know their task better than anyone else and, within normal corporate disciplines, they should be allowed the room, and the responsibility, to do the job properly. As someone once said, 'There's little point in keeping a dog and barking yourself'.

A good Human Resources Director should be the keeper of the company's recruitment policy. He, or whoever is nominated to be responsible for the human resources activity if the company is not big enough to afford an HR director, should be acutely aware of the consequences of recruiting new staff. He should relate all planned recruitment to the budget and company performance, planned and actual. Whenever it is proposed to recruit a new member of staff, the Human Resources Director should be sufficiently commercially competent, and enjoy a senior enough managerial position to ask the question: 'Is the company going to benefit from an increase in revenues such that the resulting profit will at least pay salary and costs of employment?' The phasing of recruitment of staff at all levels is crucially important. Many of the redundancies seen in industry at all levels over the years might have been avoided if management had avoided the 'Fred's busy' recruitment policy in the first place. What does the 'Fred's busy' syndrome mean? Too often staff are recruited simply because a current member of staff is deemed busy. As a result someone is recruited to help him regardless of the financial consequences. Once someone is recruited to help 'Fred', say Charlie, someone is then recruited to help 'Charlie', and so on. All recruitment should only take place within the context of financial prudence. Recruiting people in the third quarter of a financial year has to be particularly scrutinised because the recruits will undoubtedly impact the bottom line when there may be insufficient time to bring about a revenue recovery to cover the incremental cost. It is undoubtedly true that a particularly gifted new employee can have an immediate impact on departmental and company results. Nevertheless, all people in a position to recruit staff, or to influence recruitment, should give real thought to the timing of personnel recruitment. This is particularly true when recruiting salesmen. The costs are immediate but the sales people recruited are unlikely to be substantially productive for at least six months.

One final but crucial word on the subject of staff recruitment. Remember that, at whatever level of management, staff reporting directly to you are crucial to your success, and can equally be instrumental in your downfall, either accidentally or deliberately. It is therefore vital that you recruit them personally, and judge them personally regarding their suitability to the task you want them to carry out. Of course, you take advice from HR, who can acquire the c.v. of the applicant, get references, give remuneration guidelines, perhaps compile a shortlist of candidates, but the eventual judgement call should be yours. Do not, because that is the way the company has always worked, allow personnel to take over this crucial part of your work.

Furthermore, see the task through to the point where the new member of staff walks through your door on induction day. It is all too common for management to do the initial interview, and then pass the candidate along the hall for personnel to process him. Very often, personnel staff, wielding the power they have acquired over the years, will see it as their duty to get the man on the company payroll at the lowest possible cost. If that is not in line with what he had been led to expect, either from the job advertisement or the recruitment consultant, or from his initial interview with you, then the personnel staff have succeeded in de-motivating him before he has even got his feet under the desk.

11

The Production Manager

When all the design has been completed, when the product has been launched, when the marketing programme has been devised, when the sales force has been trained, then we'll tell production that they can go ahead to produce the product...

It is a sad fact of our industrial heritage that the person ultimately responsible for making and getting the goods out through the door to the customer enjoys almost the lowest esteemed position in the company hierarchy. It is as if Production bears unto itself the stigma attached to that almost pejorative expression, 'the workers'– grease monkeys in suits... Given this historical attitude to the production end of the business, it is hardly surprising that Britain has a reputation for unreliable products and shoddy workmanship, second to none in the Western industrial world. It has been largely responsible for the demise of all of the nation's major industries. It springs, once again, from the 'islands of exclusivity' concept that still demarcates the separate individual disciplines within a company. In the USA and Japan, where such these social attitudes matter less in industry, there have been tremendous strides in production techniques. The British rather lofty attitude to the whole process of manufacturing still renders industry incapable of applying due analytical thought to it; it is quite definitely the poor relation in the whole business of bringing products to market. Yet a crucial financial area of any business is the time spent and the expenditure on people and materials between the concept of a product, and its delivery.

This traditional view of production workers and production management has led to a more serious problem. When budgets are being formulated at the beginning of a new fiscal year, it is tempting to defer major investments in the production area. Budgets are always a time of prioritising investments and expenditure, and production often suffers the same fate as public relations when expenditure cuts are contemplated. Management often shirks the vital investments that are necessary if the company's products are to be acceptable in the long term. The current machinery works, the products are still being shipped and the advertising is still running – so why not delay investment? It's a charge often made by the unions, and unfortunately it does have some validity. The responsibility for the lack of necessary investment is shared somewhere between the management and the finance staff. The latter are charged by the former with presenting a financial scenario that management want to hear. Consequently when the budget is viewed as merely a set of numbers to be juggled to achieve the desired end result, cutting back on necessary investment is a simple device, particularly to a person whose discipline is concerned with numbers and not markets. You want your financial outlook to come up smelling of roses? Then why spend money on unnecessary luxuries like production?

Production is one area, alongside design, where effectiveness can be scientifically measured. Yet, too often, production in Britain is reduced to Heath Robinson absurdity. There is a distinct difference between managers of production in the USA and the UK. In the US, senior production people, when presenting the results of their endeavours to management, invariably use numerical data allied to different parts of the manufacturing process. Too often their UK counterparts present data in a much more empirical form which is, as a consequence, likely to give a more roseate view than is justified.

This springs from the UK view of people engaged in this particular activity. Graduates rarely view it as the attractive or glamorous end of the business. As a consequence, it is more likely that a production manager has worked his way up from the shop floor. He will gain invaluable experience on the way but at the expense of a more academic, analytical approach. To get month-end shipments through the door becomes panic time where all manner of short-term expedients are used. Unfortunately, it is at this time that a lack of a more scientific approach to production becomes all too apparent. In any production environment, the activity level at the end of a month or quarter or half year is increased, but there is a distinct difference between heightened pressure and blind panic. In part, this is a plea to raise the profile, within the management team, of the person ultimately responsible for finally shipping the product. The need to do this would be self-evident if there were accurate records of the equipment returns, i.e. the equipment that has been returned because of faults at the customer's premises – and then to use that information meaningfully. Too often, there is little attempt to close the loop between people responsible for the equipment after delivery, and those in production. With this information, production can improve the defect rate, minimising post-delivery costs. Another vital piece of information is the number of service calls to equipment in the field. Furthermore, maintenance contracts for first class, reliable equipment are a form of insurance for customers – and, because of the resulting low call-out rate, the contracts are very profitable.

'BS' doesn't necessarily stand for quality

Any view of the British production capability would be incomplete if there were no mention of British Standards. There is no question that many major customers demand compliance with a BS or ISO qualification. Thus many companies submit themselves to audit by the British Standards Institute and hope, as a result, to gain the accolade 'BSI Approved' or ISO 9000. From time to time, officials from the Institute will re-visit a company to carry out the audit again to ensure that the company has not deviated from the standards set. Here again, is a classic case of the nation's love of bureaucracy. By all means, let the country adopt a national standard of reliability or quality if it so wishes, the more so if government customers or major commercial customers demand it. But the granting of approval by the BSI should be an indication of the company's dedication to the quality of its products or services, not an indication that it has completed a form of bureaucratic ritual.

No-one in the company should be allowed to regard 'BSI Approved' as an end in itself as far as quality is concerned. One of the conditions of achieving this status is that the company making the application shall employ a Quality Assurance (QA) Manager, and that, in order to reflect the importance given to quality, he must report directly to the CEO. In one British company, the CEO was approached by the QA Manager for an appointment to discuss the non-compliances arising from a recent British Standards audit. The QA manager wanted authorisation from the CEO to carry out certain remedial actions where the BSI had found some shortcomings. Because the company's customers demanded BS 5750 compliance, the CEO duly gave approval for all of the remedial actions necessary, all of them very trivial. The CEO was given assurances by the QA manager that once these remedial actions had been carried out, British Standards would return and grant the due certificate of compliance. The QA Manager was satisfied that his prime task had been successfully completed, and went about his business. Unfortunately for the hapless QA Manager, one of the major customers, who demanded BS 5750 compliance, was less than impressed with the quality of the products he was buying. The QA Manager was both bewildered and upset when asked by the CEO how he could be happy gaining the approval of the British Standards Institute, while the company was shipping junk through the door, particularly when he carried the title Quality Assurance Manager? The QA Manager's concerns seemed to begin, and end, with the gaining of the British Standards sign-off.

It could be said that the shortcomings of one individual, and his bureaucratic way of working, do not invalidate the whole 'Standards' process. The concern of the CEO however, was that the whole company should not preen itself on this accolade whilst paying far too little attention to what the gaining of the accolade should have meant. Faith in the bureaucratic process had replaced thought for the real task in hand.

12

The General Manager

General Manager, Managing Director or Chief Executive – what's in a name? Actually titles tend to indicate different responsibilities on both sides of the Atlantic. In the UK, titles still carry a certain cachet that denotes more where you are deemed to fit in society, than an indication of your corporate duties. Thus, if the employer is an American company, the term General Manager is adequate to define the job to be done. The same American may be uncomfortable allowing a relatively junior European executive to style himself Managing Director because the title implies that the employer has bestowed rather more authority than was intended. By its very nature, the title General Manager implies an employee, a senior one perhaps, but still an employee. But it is a fact that, in the UK, the title of Managing Director will, in a customer's mind, indicate that the holder of such a title carries considerable power in his company. In many instances, the title Managing Director will gain an audience with a customer; whereas the title General Manager might not be deemed senior enough.

All of this is of passing interest, except when it conditions the thought processes of the holder of the title. If the title-holder sees the bestowal of the title as providing an opportunity to 'do' something, rather than to 'be' somebody, then the title is worthwhile. Unfortunately, even to this day, the title seems, in the UK, to show that the carrier of the title is now in a position of unassailable power. Once upon a time this was, indeed, the case; and although this fact has passed into history it is surprising how many people, even today, once they have reached this illustrious position, cease to function in any contributory fashion. They enjoy the deference and sycophancy extended to them, the perks of office, the unquestioned power, the way in which their wisdom is accepted without demur, at least to their face. At the very time when all of their experience acquired over years can, and should, be used to maximum effect, the very title of Managing Director seems to instil a feeling in the fortunate individual that he can coast down to retirement or his next automatic promotion. A General Manager was once quoted in a trade journal as saying: *'Business is an observation of things you have seen that you like, things that you see that you don't like, an attempt to retain a memory of both and then hopefully put the good bits together and minimise your own mistakes'*. This is still sound advice for any person with aspirations for management, at whatever level, in whatever discipline. At general management level, the advice is particularly relevant.

One man and his dog

A General Manager, Managing Director, or CEO – or whatever title is given to the position at the head of the company is called – should behave like a corporate sheepdog, knowing exactly when to head up, or lie down, or turn the flock. For the purpose of this exercise the title CEO will be used. The CEO is likely to have achieved his position by practising and achieving a level of success in one particular discipline only. He is now charged with managing other disciplines, with whose practice he is not so familiar. It is at this stage that many CEOs fail. They see it as imperative that they display an expertise in an area of activity in which, until they were promoted, they had only a passing knowledge or interest; this of course means that those who report to him and who have a particular expertise must now, because of his power, defer to his new-found but superficial expertise. CEOs who adopt this method of management are not being as effective as they could be. They should use, in a meaningful way, all of the expertise available to them. They should listen to their direct reports who will have an expertise in a given area. This, of course, assumes that these direct reports are still practising their expertise, and that they have reached their senior position by so doing.

Perhaps the CEO, using his experience, or with the benefit of inputs from a wider variety of sources, can bring a wider perspective to the issue. Perhaps the subordinate needs help collecting his thoughts, and collating his data, such that he can make a decision with which the CEO can concur. Whatever the circumstances, decisions made are more likely to benefit the company if they arise from a collaborative effort, with each subordinate bringing his core skill to the foundations of the decision. Just as important, is the fact the subordinate is much more likely to promulgate the decision positively, if the decision has arisen from reasoned collaborative discussion. The decision remains, ultimately, the responsibility of the CEO, but the means of reaching his decisions is much more circumspect, and less likely to be prone to risk. If the CEO continually, and the term 'continually' needs to be stressed, disregards his subordinates, or overrides them, simply to assert his authority, the company performance will either degrade or stagnate. A company will stay dynamic longer when the expertise within the company is used to its fullest extent; hence the description, 'corporate sheepdog'.

The CEO should know where he wants to take the company. He should consult with his, presumably respected, subordinates, to fine-tune this direction, and to assure himself as to its viability. Then to return to the sheep-dog metaphor he should just 'nip' each executive in the heels to make sure all are headed in the agreed direction. This should be true of a manager of people at any level. Any manager that does not have the self-confidence to defer to the particular expertise of his subordinates, should not be in the job, and probably will not have a long-term future in the position. This said, it is undeniable that the task of a CEO is a lonely one; indeed it needs to be if the function is to be carried out properly. Thus there is a very difficult stance to adopt, that of being friendly toward and approachable by everyone, yet maintaining a distance that allows the CEO to be objective about the performance of everyone.

Many decisions that others, using their reporting relationship with the CEO, will urge him to make, may be impossible to make either because many other factors must be taken into consideration. The decision may be impractical or it may be a sound decision but the timing does not allow it to be made for some time. Whatever the reason, it may not be a subject on which it is wise for a CEO to reveal his thoughts. He may be constrained by his knowledge of the plans of the board of directors or the views of City analysts. It is unfortunately part of the job of a CEO to live with the knowledge that, whoever is trying to persuade him and has been unsuccessful, will be of the opinion that either the CEO is indecisive or he does not value the opinion proffered.

Nevertheless, it is only by having a structure that allows dependence on subordinates, individually and collectively, that a CEO can give due attention to the overall direction and performance of the company. It is imperative that the structure is both disciplined and agile, a difficult combination. It needs to be disciplined in order that a change in direction, or an adjustment to an established direction, runs through the entire organisation. The agility is needed to ensure that changes in the market can be reflected rapidly by changes in the manner of the company's response to that change. The company may be vulnerable to a sudden change in the market, and need to make adjustments. Alternatively, a sudden upswing may provide the company with an opportunity to bring forward expansion plans. Whatever the cause, it is vital that a company does not have such a ponderous organisation that it cannot respond quickly to changes, for good or ill; nor can there be so much autonomy at lower levels of the organisation that a necessary change cannot permeate deep enough into the organisation to create any lasting response at all. Without any doubt, whatever the structure, an organisation will reflect the energy and commitment of the man or woman at the top. If he or she is seen as invisible, and decisions never appear to emerge, then the company will lack energy and enthusiasm.

There must always be an awareness of there being a 'captain' of the ship. If for that reason alone, it is imperative that a CEO must swing his vision between looking outwards at the market, and inwards to assure himself that his staff and structure are geared to meet the challenges of that market. It's an almost daily task. A corporate and reporting structure that allows management to spend time with staff, wherever they may be geographically, and with customers likewise, is invaluable. It is another marked difference between American and British executives. Sometimes executives from the States will arrive unannounced at the premises of their overseas subsidiaries, and make a point of meeting non-managerial staff. This is rarely a social call, but an informal means of checking that local management have the confidence of local staff; by such means and however unwelcome, the visiting management reassure themselves that the operation is on track. In a more cynical vein, such visits were often jocularly referred to as the 'corporate seagull syndrome', which translated, means that executives, behaving like seagulls, 'flew in, defecated over everyone, and flew out again'. Nevertheless, it enabled messages of concern to be carried back directly to senior corporate management.

Although such visits can be unnerving for the local management, they do enable local staff to identify and relate directly to senior management. This is markedly different from the way most senior British executives behave. They are often either afraid to meet subordinate staff or they feel that their own status is being undermined by doing so. As a result, the only information very senior management receive is that from their direct subordinates; this information will of course be conditioned to reflect whatever view the subordinate is trying to impart. A CEO will miss an invaluable source of intelligence about the internal condition of the company, or the state of the market and the competition if he does not make it his business to hold impromptu direct conversations with staff at all levels. A structure, or an attitude, that keeps senior management, locked for days and weeks on end in 'mahogany row' is never going to allow that management the vital time to keep its finger on the pulse. It is this tendency that gives rise to the increasing use of consultants in Britain to advise on the mainstream activity of the company. One British managing director who had engaged consultants was asked: *'Why do we need these people from outside to tell us things we know from our own internal inputs?'* His response was, *'Because we do not listen to ourselves'* – an incredible admission! It is not unusual for a consultant's report to be so extensive that it is never studied by many of the people referred to in it. To have called in the consultant is deemed sufficient.

Many Managing Directors and boards of directors call in consultants merely to indicate to the commentators that they are aware of any perceived problem and that they are dealing with it. If we return to the theme referred to earlier where management have risen to the top by concentrating on climbing the corporate ladder then it is not fantasy to suggest that some will get to the top without really understanding at all the business they are in. They dare not ask their subordinates for advice at this stage so they call in consultants to 'pull their irons out of the fire'. Consultants should not be needed in a company staffed by people who had dedicated their entire careers to the industry – provided they are doing their job properly. It should be a mark of failure by management to retain consultants unless the consultants are people with a genuine experience of a relevant area of the business that cannot be called upon from within the company. There is a less than generous view of consultants that describes their philosophy as: 'Lend me your watch and I'll tell you the time'. There are many others who, less kindly, believe them to be industrial whores – they won't sleep with anyone without money – and they'll sleep with anyone that has money. Some – a very few – have succeeded in their own industries, and their views are always worth having; but they rarely get close enough to a business to make a real difference at operational level.

Topics covered thus far for the CEO to be concerned with include corporate discipline, being aware of where the 'buck stops' and monitoring and measuring the performance of each area of the business. This can be construed as proposing a centralised approach to business, a criticism often levelled, disparagingly, towards the American style of management. Often there is some justification for the charge. Severe centralised management is sometimes very difficult to work with. It does not allow sufficient initiative to subordinate and overseas staff, and it can work against the very agility that is essential for long-term success. Nevertheless, in general the centralised approach is more successful from a business standpoint, than a loose structure that allows individual autonomy to come close to a state of anarchy. But the centralisation can be carried too far, to the point where the business suffers.

A very rigid, centralised approach carries the real danger that the only source of decision-making is the man at the top. All subordinate to that position become automatons, too afraid or even mentally incapacitated to veer from the edicts issuing from on high. Senior staff managers with brains and experience, who might have meaningful suggestions for adjusting the company's way of doing business, either don't have the temerity to put forward their suggestions, or don't have the authority to carry them through.

It is undeniable that the more centralised form of management favoured by most American companies does have its shortcomings with regard to overseas employees, and indeed, US domestic ones. Although the same management regime is applied to domestic US management, it does not carry the same overtones as it does for overseas management. Carried to extremes, a strict centralised management regime means that all overseas employees of an American company are expected to behave as if they were living and working in the US State where company headquarters are located. The company is not so much a multi-national, more an American company spread all over the world. The more senior the overseas employee, the more difficult for him this rigid, centralised management becomes. It is difficult to convince a potential major customer that he, the overseas manager, has the flexibility to meet the customer's reasonable requirements, if the customer can see that every trivial decision not in accordance with corporate rules has to be referred back to the USA for a ruling. Such a process will tell a customer that dealing with the overseas manager's company is going to be very inflexible and time-consuming. No matter that he carries the title, Managing Director or General Manager, or more likely, Senior Vice-President, the perception is that he is little more than a cipher.

More importantly, such a method of working and reporting, for all its strengths as far as maintaining a single corporate strategy is concerned, does prevent a senior man using, in the interests of the company, the judgmental

The General Manager

skills that gained him that seniority in the first place. It is not always appropriate to insist that the business practices of one nation, however successful in that nation, will achieve identical success if copied slavishly in another.

At one management-training seminar, a guest speaker spoke of his experiences working at senior level for a British company and an American one; the story he told is a familiar one to those who have worked for both British and American employers. The British one was ICL, a computer company now owned by Fujitsu. The American one was Data General, a very successful computer company in the 1970s and 1980s but now owned by EMC^2. For a brief time, the Chairman of ICL was Sir Michael Edwardes, of British Leyland fame. He was unfamiliar with the computer industry and so, to acquaint himself with the way the industry worked in general, and ICL in particular, he interviewed senior executives. He had also read the book about Data General, *The Soul of a New Machine*, mentioned earlier in this book. Knowing that the speaker had previously been employed by Data General, Sir Michael asked him, *'What is the difference between ICL and Data General?'* His response, not couched in the most formal management terms, was that in Data General, if he had wanted to deviate from extremely rigid corporate rules, he had to work through nine layers of management from his senior position in the UK, via European Headquarters in Paris, to the Data General worldwide headquarters in Massachusetts to ask, in effect, the question, *'Please can I spit?'* Sometime later, the response would come back. The answer was usually 'No', used as a deterrent to asking such a question. But sometimes, on very rare occasions, the answer would be 'Yes', in which case he would go back with a second question, *'Please, in which direction?'* he told Sir Michael that in ICL, on the other hand, everybody seems to be spitting without let or hindrance. He then went on to state that, in his opinion, neither method was totally satisfactory, but that if a worldwide corporate strategy was to be observed and effective, and he had to select between Data General or ICL, then he personally would opt for the Data General way of operating.

He felt that, as a senior manager, he was undoubtedly more professionally comfortable in ICL, because he held more personal responsibility; but this autonomy was dependant on his own sense of personal discipline, not linked to a demand that he behaved in accordance with any overall goal or objective. This was true for both line and staff managers. The contrast with Data General was most marked in this regard.

Unlike Data General, the line managers in ICL also enjoyed an extraordinary level of personal autonomy; so that any policy changes, product changes, etc., devised by staff management at any level could be completely disregarded by line management. The speaker therefore believed the corporate success was prone to being sacrificed at the expense of professional freedom of individuals. An army could not allow it, why should a company? By contrast, as a direct result of its corporate discipline, Data General, from its start date, was the fastest company at that time to become a Fortune 500 company and did so without a dip in its yearly profits of more than 20 per cent before tax in any year, on its way to joining that elite band of companies. It was known and respected all over the world.

ICL, on the other hand, had been in business twenty years longer than Data General, and still drew most of its business from the UK. For all of its long history, ICL was still relatively unknown outside the 'ex-empire' countries. The speaker opined that there was no difference in the intellectual talents employed by the two companies or the commitment of the staff of each of the companies. It was only ICL's poor corporate discipline, together with a lack of vision stretching back over years that had prevented the company from fulfilling its considerable potential. In the late 1970s, a new Chief Executive, Robb Wilmot, joined ICL. He was a man of very considerable vision about the future of the high-tech sector of industry. However, this lack of a disciplined corporate structure, compounded by the fact that most of the staff and management had no experience of a disciplined structure, meant that ICL could not be the company to take the lead in pursuing his vision. By the same token, the very rigid discipline in Data General that had made it so successful for the first twenty years of its life was to lead to its decline as a leading force in the high-tech world.

The speaker also gave an opinion about the working atmosphere in the two companies. He felt that despite its rigid management structure, there was an intoxicating air of excitement in the early days of Data General, engendered by success, growth, winning against major competition. There was a feeling of belonging to a winning team, taking on all-comers. It has been said that Microsoft enjoys, across the world, that same air of excitement. The speaker said that ICL for all of its flexibility and laissez-faire attitude, perhaps because of it, never created that same atmosphere; the company was so inward looking that there was never engendered a feeling of beating the competition. A profile of the weaknesses and strengths of both of these companies is included later in the book.

The General Manager

If it is accepted that neither of the two methods employed by ICL and Data General, as evidenced by their eventual demise, are ideal, then a different way of operating needs to be found. Perhaps reference here to IBM is appropriate in order to find a role model. To the outside world, particularly the high-tech industry, this company has appeared for many years as invincible. By the very imposition of a strict corporate discipline it became, by far, one of the most powerful companies in the world, both within and outside the high-tech arena. Over the years, changes in technology brought incredible challenges to the might of IBM from a multitude of competitors, and it withstood every one of them, and became even stronger. When a company is that big, that successful, in the face of enormous onslaughts, it can only withstand the attack by being disciplined and agile, and by having a highly inclusive form of management.

So, a number of factors determine the success, or indeed the failure, of a company; and these factors need to be examined individually, collectively and comprehensively, as early as possible in the life of the company. The longer the process is delayed, the more difficult the process. It is never too late; but internal resistance to any proposed change to the way of working of a long-established, large company can be daunting to all but the strongest CEO. Trying to change things retrospectively is doubly difficult, because the day-to-day business still has to be conducted. To coin an earlier phrase, 'the rent always has to be paid'. It is just not feasible to say, in effect, 'Stop everything while I reorganise, and we'll restart when I'm done'.

Almost all of the individual factors that need to be considered by a CEO when seeking an ideal management structure have already been touched upon but it is worth examining these factors collectively in order to produce the most effective form of corporate governance. Whatever structure is decided upon, the examination of Data General and ICL, together with the observation of methods used IBM would indicate that a method of corporate governance should be found that allows the talents of all individuals in the organisation, whether they be national or international, to be used to the full in the observance of an overall corporate strategy and goal. Conversely, it is imperative that a structure, together with a reporting regime, is put in place that does not allow those same talents to be used to thwart an agreed strategy or tactical approach to the market place. Companies are comprised of people. These people do not leave their personalities or emotions at home when they go to work. Ideally, one needs to create a structure that allows features like energy, enthusiasm and creativity to be harnessed positively, but does not permit other characteristics such as envy, jealousy, sloth, incompetence and a tendency to indulge in departmental and personal politics to impede corporate progress.

So we come back to the same word – discipline. There needs to be a reporting mechanism that all sections, and all levels, of the company community can understand and abide by. It is a not uncommon practice, particularly with highly centralised American organisations, for headquarters staff at home office; i.e., in the States, to work through the headcount list of an overseas territory, and select those individuals the local general manager must dismiss, in order to meet some necessary cost reduction. The local general manager not only has little or no influence over such a decision but, more importantly, he is seen by his staff to have no influence. If he is consulted on the problems facing the company and asked to contribute to the solution, then his local knowledge is being used effectively. His staff and his customers both will accord him more respect.

Customers, in particular, can be averse to dealing with a supplier where they see local management has no autonomy nor any influence over head office. Another danger of not using his talent and local experience is that the local general manager is encouraged to be, in effect, the 'leading mutineer'. In other words, his very isolation, geographically and managerially, from the corporate senior management means that, for his own day-to-day survival, he will inevitably ally himself to his staff in any adverse attitude they may have to the company and its management style. Only by using the full local expertise to achieve overall corporate goals can a company be deemed a genuine 'multi-national'. To describe itself as multi-national is not, of itself, important to a company; but if it is to maximise profits, then the full use of the talents of a multi-national workforce is essential. As business becomes more and more global, the effective use of local talent will become more crucial.

Despite the tendency, strongly expressed earlier, that the Americans manage their business more effectively than their British counterparts, it is unquestionably a fact that both the Americans and the British could improve their approach to international trade. Both American and British companies when abroad, are often perceived by customers, staff and governments as displaying arrogance, the Americans of wealth and the British of history. The Americans, despite their adventurous approach to business, still view foreign employees in foreign lands with a good deal of apprehension, sometimes amounting to suspicion.

This suspicion arises out of the cultural differences between the American employer and his overseas management. Unfortunately, with time and distance differences, overseas executives do often misconstrue the easy-going nature of most Americans as licence to establish their own autonomous management regime. To counter this, many American companies take the view that the only way to ensure compliance to the corporate will is total and absolute control. Once those same foreigners go to America to work for the company, the suspicion recedes. The British, on the other hand, have rather more exposure to 'things foreign' in their educational and cultural mix. Nevertheless, historically, the British are renowned for their low opinion of, and tendency to speak loudly to, foreigners, as if Britannia still ruled the waves. For many British executives, a visit to overseas locations, particularly those of the former empire, is not so much a business trip, more a 'return of the raj'. The young, with their increased opportunity to travel, both for business and pleasure, seem much less conditioned by history. Provided Britain continues to shake itself free of these cultural inhibitions, then a closer business alliance with Europe, and indeed Asia and Africa, provides an excellent opportunity to use our historical ties in our national business interest. But such advantages will never be maximised, or they will be eroded if the alliance is conducted with little or no sense of corporate discipline.

A suggested way forward

Each company, when deciding how to establish an appropriate regime, will have to make its decisions based on the industry that it is in, the history of the company, its current size and its ambitions for growth, its people, indeed its very psyche. One structure does not fit all. Nevertheless, some or all of the criteria explored above, together with others that will contribute to the forward and upward progress of the company, will have to be considered. Unfortunately it is a truism that many companies under-estimate the industrial and competitive market knowledge possessed by their staff. So how can this knowledge be harnessed in the corporate interest? One method that appears to work effectively is for the CEO to form a group of all those in the company concerned with the marketplace. If the company has overseas staff then those based overseas must be included in the group; for the purposes of this exercise the group can be called The Strategic Marketing Group or SMG (see Appendix III).

The SMG will thus comprise all the senior, domestic and foreign executives who had any dealings with the market, direct or indirect. Included will be the engineering director, marketing director and production director, together with regional general managers from the various regions say UK, Europe, USA, Australasia etc. The inclusion of the engineering director means that he knows directly the thinking behind marketing decisions; he can also interject with a reality check where necessary. Similarly the production director will know immediately what demands may be made on him. The SMG can meet monthly and can be held anywhere in the world. It is always good for morale for such meetings to be held on occasions in regional offices; it removes a good deal of the paranoia that is almost always a feature of the thinking of those with responsibility for overseas regions. Those participants unable to attend in person can participate by conference call or video link.

For the SMG to be really effective, it is important that the regional directors conduct their own 'mini-SMG' with their staff, prior to the main SMG meeting. Thus all staff can play their part in determining the future direction of the company. By the same token, it was expected that each participant in the main SMG de-briefs their staff after an SMG meeting, so that everyone knew what decisions were made, and why, regarding the company future technical and marketing direction. If it is felt, after consultation by the CEO with the proposed participants, that decisions made at one main SMG are still adequate a month later, then the subsequent SMG can be cancelled. By the same token there should be no reason to believe that significant decisions must come out of every meeting; it is vital that the company does not get enmeshed in a series of meetings for their own sake. No minutes of meetings need to be kept but major decisions should be circulated; by this means unnecessary bureaucracy can be avoided. Since major decisions only are circulated, the circulation document can be very brief to be used solely as an aide-memoire. Thus all of the people involved in design, marketing, production and sales knew at the outset where the company was going, and with what goods and services.

SMG meetings need to be as brief as possible. The CEO's role should be that of Chairman ensuring that SMG meetings do not become 'knitting circles'. The meetings should never be allowed, through endless debate, to slow the company down in its main aim – the pursuit of business. Another main feature of the SMG should be that unless there is an overwhelming reason to change, a decision made is a decision to be adhered to. A company cannot afford to endlessly re-visit the same issues, to make yet another decision on a previously settled issue. If it transpires that a poor decision has been made the company will have to live with the consequences and attempt to work its way out of the consequences. Living with the consequences of decisions, good and bad is what all management is being paid for; constant re-examination creates enormous inertia and inhibits spontaneity. So, the first aim of a management structure, to make all sections of the company inclusive in its goals and objectives, can met by the formation of an SMG or similar.

The second main aim is to construct a measuring and monitoring regime that will meet the purpose of allowing the regional directors as much autonomy as possible, commensurate with meeting overall corporate objectives; recognising, effectively, where the 'buck stopped', i.e with the CEO. To meet this second aim, a set of corporate operational procedures can be issued. The aim of these is to give profit and loss responsibility to each of the regional directors, but there should be an independent reporting line within the worldwide financial staff to ensure adherence to the procedures. A copy of suggested procedures is included at the rear of this book as Appendix 2. It is important that, although the financial staff are ensuring that the procedures are adhered to, the executive responsibility for running the operation stays with the line executive. Furthermore, the procedures must be observed, and adhered to, by the entire company worldwide, to the most senior level in the company. It needs to be said that if such procedures are to be put in place in an already existing company as will more often be the case they will not always be universally welcomed by all.

Some of the executives who have previously enjoyed total autonomy will vociferously protest at having what they saw as their autonomy undermined. But by the same token their objections will be considerably weakened by the fact that the procedures are to be observed by all in the company including the CEO.

So, let's assume that the SMG is in place, and there is a reporting mechanism for measuring performance. What remains to be done is to create a forum where the executive management of the company, arising from those reports, can be examined, individually and collectively; a monthly management meeting MMM. Whereas the SMG comprises only those executives concerned with the company's performance in the market place, the MMM will also include directors of finance and human resources. Each of the executives should bring to the MMM their own departmental report, comprising data germane to their specific departmental activities. Thus variance from budget, highlighted by reports from the field could be set in the context of each departmental activity. Perhaps a shortfall in revenues will shown by the report of the Human Resources Director to be caused by a delay or difficulty in recruiting appropriate staff. Perhaps there had been a good deal of absenteeism due to sickness. Perhaps the Engineering Director has had a material supply problem, causing a product development programme to be delayed. On the positive side, perhaps a large order had come in earlier than planned. Sometimes, not very often, the company might be the beneficiary of a 'bluebird', a term given to an order that the company has not planned for, nor was it expected. All such issues can be discussed, such that, where necessary, adjustments can be made to the company's ongoing activities.

We now have in place a forum, the SMG, for discussing and determining the company's marketing strategy and resultant sales results. We have another forum, the MMM, for discussing and adjusting the company's overall management performance.

But there is another requirement of senior management that is vital if the senior manager is to get the maximum effectiveness from his direct reports as possible. He needs to meet once a month with each of these direct reports; let's call them 'one to ones'. Often there are problems and issues, perhaps suggestions, that a member of the team just does not feel comfortable discussing in the presence of his peers or he feels it to be so germane to his activities and to no-one else that he feels he could be wasting their time and therefore does not raise it even though it may be important. One-to-ones can make a vital contribution to the company success as long as the manager conducting the meeting sees it as an opportunity to 'add value' to the task of the subordinate and perceives that 'added value' as making a real contribution, directly or indirectly, to maximising the company's income. In other words the manager conducting the one-to-one should not seek to be 'the boss', but should assist the subordinate to grapple with his problem or problems if there are any. He should use his experience to offer help where it was needed, give a viewpoint if it was requested and give encouragement if appropriate. Sometimes, it may even be necessary to criticise but this too is done in private. Unless the individual is deliberately grand-standing, there is little to be gained by inflicting public humiliation on anyone. Publicly humiliating subordinates just to gratuitously exercise power quells all future debate because all present will not wish to provoke a similar castigation.

The above is just one suggestion of how to put a management structure in place, one that is agile, is not too bureaucratic, allows all staff to participate actively in the company's fortunes and allows for monitoring and measuring performance. It enables the company to acquire a momentum and generate some excitement whilst at the same time positively encouraging the pursuit of profitable business. There is quick and easy access from any level of staff to any level of management so that day-to-day relating between levels of management and between management and staff did not impede the gaining of business. Market intelligence will find its way into the company very rapidly. Chances of there being 'time bombs' ticking are reduced to a minimum. In the case of the CEO, the structure also has the benefit of allowing him time to think. Time to think where the company is going, and needed to go; and time to put in place measures to take it there. It is not necessary for him to be buried in company minutiae. The more senior one becomes, the more important is this process of delegation. It provides him with time to visit staff and customers around the world, without ever losing touch with day-by-day company performance.

Anyone charged with management of any department, or any company needs to put a structure in place appropriate to that department or company. The composition of that structure, by definition, calls for the formation of a management team – always a difficult, time consuming and crucial activity. Sometimes, it requires the moving sideways, or out, of an incumbent; or in due course, the moving on of one of those recently installed. It is always painful to all involved, but the process is no different to that of creating a successful soccer team that must succeed or perish; very often, the supporters will scream loudest and first for the removal of the player deemed to be the passenger. In a similar manner, it is often staff who first detect that their task is not being helped, or is being impeded, by an inadequate manager; passengers cannot be carried. If the team does not produce results, then those members of the team not up to scratch, and not able to be brought up to scratch, must be changed.

This is one of the aspects of the task that particularly highlights the loneliness that is, of necessity, part of any manager's job. It is extremely unwise to lose the element of distance between a manager and those he is called upon to manage. It is always dangerous to generalise but Americans manage this much more easily than the British, not because they are less caring, but simply because their culture enables them to more readily make the separation between their professional tasks and their social lives. It is for this reason that Americans gain their reputation for being more carnivorous! For those unaccustomed to American companies, it can come as a surprise to witness the sheer aggression displayed between senior executives at management meetings, but in the context of the health of a company, it can be refreshing. People who do not perform their allocated tasks are replaced by others who then have to prove they can live up to their new responsibilities. However unpalatable it may sound, such a regime is more likely to create dynamism for the company and opportunity for individuals. It also compels incumbent individuals in any managerial position to constantly re-evaluate their own competence and to be aware of the dangers of complacency.

Another manifestation of the managerial isolation that must be accepted is that subordinates will always know the solution to what they perceive to be his, the manager's, problems. However, they have the luxury of being able to be single-point thinkers. They are unaware that, from their viewpoint, looking at the manager above them is like looking at an iceberg; they will see only the one-eighth protruding above the surface. The manager will, at his peril, enlighten the subordinate about the other seven-eighths. The manager might very well concur with the subordinate's opinion, when judged from a single viewpoint. But more often than not the true picture will be multi-faceted and this will affect the decisions to be made and the timing of them. To reveal such criteria to a subordinate at the wrong time could adversely condition the activities of the subordinate, and even negatively impact the whole department or, in the case of the CEO, the whole company. Despite the fact that the subordinate might believe you do not really understand the problem, or you are out of touch, such isolation must be accepted as a consequence of the managerial position.

The obligation on the manager or CEO to add value to his department or company is always there; therefore some, or all of the issues outlined above need to be addressed, if the individual is to move from being a 'do-er' to the position of being a manager of 'do-ers'. The manner in which this division of effort is managed will largely determine the degree of leadership contained in an individual's managerial capability.

PART 3

CONCLUSION

13

Can You Get There?

It is not everyone's desire to be in management of any sort, nor is it within everyone's capability. Furthermore, the criteria for success in an industrial society should not be based purely on a judgement of whether people are ambitious enough, or capable enough, to be managers of people or processes or departments. However, it is reasonable to expect people to manage themselves, or to understand why they are being managed. This means using every legitimate means at one's disposal to maximise one's value to an employer (or to oneself, in the case of the self-employed).

To coast along, secure in the knowledge that someone will provide that management, and provide one with lifelong employment, is to fly in the face of today's reality. So the term 'getting there', as used in the title of this chapter, means the process of maximising one's value in any employment regime such as to produce longevity of employment. Of course, for those with ambition and capability to succeed in management, the adoption of some of the techniques outlined here and an awareness of some of the issues one might encounter during a career will undoubtedly help.

Along with the knowledge, there needs to be an awareness of the inherent dangers and threats. Paradoxically, if a wild animal drinks at a pool while keeping his ears pricked for approaching danger, it is called survival; yet when a human does the same thing in the jungle of commercial life, it is called paranoia! Yet both are trying to prolong life in an environment where such an eventuality is becoming more difficult to achieve. To occasionally take a bird's eye view of the working environment beyond the confines of one's own immediate task, is invaluable – to keep crawling through the undergrowth and not pop up occasionally for a look around can be injurious to one's corporate health.

When a voice, managerial or otherwise, brings wisdom and experience to bear upon an issue, that voice is invariably listened to and valued. That wisdom comes from absorbing the various inputs that have been brought to bear on other problems in the past, and using them, modified or otherwise, on the current issue. These inputs will not be restricted to one's own core skill, but will have come from a variety of sources, all of which have a bearing on the problem. It is only if one can be this circumspect, that one can claim to have five years experience, or ten or twenty as the case may be. Otherwise, it is quite legitimate for others to claim that your experience is five times one, or ten times one, or twenty times one; in other words age is the only thing that has advanced.

At one time, it was sufficient for an employee to have a core skill, and to gain some experience of how his employer worked and preferred him to work. Armed with such skills and knowledge, advance up the company ladder was pretty much automatic. The only potential impediment was to give in to the temptation to punch the boss on the nose. But 'progress', even of that sort, is no longer guaranteed to those who merely 'hang on in there' long enough; even where remnants of this prehistoric culture exist, it is wise to assume that it will not last for the lifetime of today's career.

The gaining of new experience and fresh wisdom is also vital for staying abreast of market or technology changes. It is in the natural order of things that the young will take over from those more advanced in years. It is quite futile to believe that this order can be changed, or held at bay by artificial means, such as pulling rank or 'anti-ageism' legislation. To advance in later life it is necessary, at least wise, to embrace the enthusiasm, the energy, the ambition of the young, even their impatience. Such experience and wider knowledge, used judiciously alongside the younger, more current ways of thinking and problem solving can produce a truly winning combination to bring longevity to a career. On the other hand any attempt to stem or control or inhibit the tide of new ideas, forcefully presented, will only serve to hasten the demise of a career.

As far as the younger people are concerned, it is vital in today's fast changing world not only to absorb new technology, but to realise that each person is an economic unit, not only in one's immediate surroundings but also globally. Whether we like it or not, we move in a world, whose ultimate recognition of success is based on money and the power that comes with it. Therefore, to make it for one's employer is a pre-requisite for making it for oneself in the form of a long-term income. This is not to be apocalyptic, quite the reverse. Opportunities opening up today, and the way the world is shrinking in the manner of its economic practices, means that there will inevitably be a more egalitarian world, a more meritocratic world, a more exciting world. Unfortunately, or otherwise, it does also mean that those who choose to be bystanders will increasingly be left behind in a world that will no longer be able to support them in a lifestyle that they had earlier become accustomed to. Whilst British nationals are undoubtedly citizens of a major commercial country, there are increasing signs that, on an individual basis, each person will be compelled to become economically self-sufficient. Therefore, each person, whether on a payroll or self-employed, is truly in business for himself. But where can individuals learn this?

Many demands are made on pupils by the 'core curriculum' imposed by successively more nervous governments on schools. It is almost a mantra that such a concentration on education, education, education as manifested by increased literacy and numeracy will bring forth national economic success; the author of this book questions this assumption. A British education may teach you that the Industrial Revolution began here, in the 1760s, at the heart of Empire. What it does not teach you is that, unless the nation radically changes its way of thinking about and doing business, and soon, it is likely to end here too.

APPENDIX I

Comparing Companies

The author been employed by British, American and Canadian companies at various management levels in many different parts of the world; it is an observation of such companies that gave rise to this book. There is no question that companies in one country will behave quite differently to their counterparts in other countries even if they are in similar industries; this difference arises from the culture in which they exist. The differences in behaviour by both the companies and the employees and management in them enable comparisons to be drawn. This, in turn will suggest ways in which Britain's indigenous professional behaviour can improve and thus bring some benefit to individuals and companies. To look at some of these companies specifically, and to examine their overall management style, might help the reader to define his own management philosophy, or the type of philosophy that he might find it most comfortable for him to contribute to. Throughout the remainder of the book, specific instances from various companies have been related in order to illustrate a certain point or to highlight a danger or potential advantage.

So this appendix is confined to providing an insider's view of company philosophy; indeed of company personality, since it is almost undeniable that companies do indeed acquire, over the years, a personality almost as tangible as that of a person. It is advisable that anyone working for, contemplating working for, or even contemplating doing business with, any company should first acquaint himself with the stated philosophy and, more advisedly, the tangible personality of that company. Some of the companies described below have not survived in their original form. Some have been driven into receivership and others acquired by more successful companies. Yet to include them is still valid because in many respects the demise of these companies serves to illustrate the very real risks that every company is subject to every day, risks that management must do its best to foresee.

The first company is described only briefly, simply to illustrate the origins of some of our stranger attitudes that defined a company philosophy and personality.

Unquestionably, such a company philosophy would be difficult to detect today in such stark terms. Yet some vestiges of the behaviour still exist, most easily observed in large utility companies trying, not always successfully, to drag their way of working away from being a quasi-government monopoly into a 21st century privatised company. Furthermore, even where there has been a greater degree of success it is not too difficult in many companies to detect the origins of today's company philosophy. Engaged in heavy electrical engineering, this first company (which shall remain nameless) to be examined was founded in the mid-19th century. The Chairman still wore a frock coat – this is the 1950s, remember – and paternalistically employed many thousands of workers and staff, some of them graduates, together with several hundred apprentices, none of whom were graduates. Any qualifications the latter might achieve were to be gained at evening classes, or on day-release to the local technical college.

There was a huge divide between 'workers' and 'staff'. The former were hourly paid, punched a clock to start and finish work (and were docked a quarter of an hour's pay if they were more than two minutes late), and wore overalls. The staff were monthly paid, had longer holidays, signed to clock in (no penalty for lateness), and wore lounge suits and ties. In the works at tea-break time, denoted by a whistle, the workers were given tea, made in the works canteen, from an enormous enamel jug. The staff on the other hand, were offered biscuits and tea, coffee or cocoa, made in the office by a lady specifically recruited for the task. The selected refreshment could be consumed at any time. The workers, usually working in very dirty conditions by the very nature of their job, could wash their hands in the washroom labelled MEN, and use a roller towel for drying them, one roller towel to every 200 men. The staff were issued with individual hand-towels and toilet soap and washed their hands in a washroom entitled GENTLEMEN. If a worker was promoted to the staff it would be made very clear that he should on no account, 'fraternise with the workers' who had been his colleagues hitherto.

The above divisions meant that no-one would expend one minute more than they were compelled to, to assist their employer. Workers literally lay on their stomachs, ready to roll under the rising factory exit door when the whistle sounded at the end of the working day. Hours of effort were wasted in time studies for specific jobs, such that a worker could extract the maximum payment for a job. The shop steward would oversee every such study. Many years later, these practices still in place in many organisations – and jealously guarded by both sides. Even if, over time, some of the harsher manifestations have faded, these bitter divisions still remain at the root of many of the nation's current industrial ills.

When one still hears arguments between the Secretary General of the CBI and the Secretary General of the TUC over European legislation concerning information that should be given to a worker regarding the activities and plans of his employer, one wonders how long it will take to remove these damaging divisions. Even today there are conferences held at which the President of the CBI and the Secretary General of the TUC will be involved in disputes concerning the place of the unions in today's society. Given that such conferences are often conducted by the Department of Trade and Industry, and usually attended by the Minister, to explore how the country's competitiveness might be improved, it is dispiriting to see how little the nation has changed fundamentally and as a result plays into the hands of international competitors.

This is not to suggest that the management of our more successful foreign competitors wholeheartedly embrace their staff, but their management style is not so quasi-paternalistic. There is a more adult view that recognises that all staff want their efforts to be rewarded financially. One often hears the call for a 'partnership' between workers and management. These calls, from unions, politicians and industry representative bodies, by their very nature suggest a rift, which can be healed by some form of accommodation; the term 'partnership' is one that is rarely heard in American firms. British management still instinctively holds to the view that non-managerial staff, i.e workers, can be rewarded by keeping their jobs, whilst directors get financial rewards comparable with the best of overseas executives.

Ferranti – the 'commercial university'

In the book *Ferranti: a History* (John F Wilson, published by Carnegie Publishing Ltd) there is a foreword by Sebastian de Ferranti, the grandson of the founder of the company. In this foreword (page xv) Mr de Ferranti makes two statements that in a sense confirm the themes running through this book. Firstly he says, *'It took just over 100 years to build the company, and by Alun-Jones's unfortunate judgement, and that of his board of directors, it went into receivership in the same number of months'.* Secondly he says, *'Above all, my grandfather, father and I had a long-term commitment to engineering vision. All too often this defied conventional methods simply because we were not driven by stock market valuations'.* Perversely, since earlier in the book there is a recommendation that companies should run the business and let the city take care of itself, it would have been beneficial if Ferranti had taken more notice of the City simply because the devotion to the 'engineering vision' as Mr Ferranti calls it, meant that Ferranti was run like a ' commercial university' with much more emphasis on 'university' than 'commercial'. The mis-judgement of Alun-Jones referred to in the first of Mr Ferranti's quoted statements arose from Mr de Ferranti's view of Sir Derek Alun-Jones's stewardship of the company after he (Mr de Ferranti) and his brother were removed from executive positions.

As a former Senior Engineer at Ferranti, the author of this book is qualified to say that the demise of Ferranti arose because it was symptomatic of the problems elucidated through much of this book. Engineers were expected to be that and nothing else. They were positively discouraged from making themselves aware of the commercial imperatives of the business. Furthermore, those that were promoted to the board were also former senior engineers, all fighting for their divisional survival while denying the financial realities. It led to a senior accountant appointed by NatWest to point out a fundamental weakness, *'This is a good business but it must be properly run, and while it has been well led, it has been badly managed'.*

To be employed as an engineer (this title meant professional designer) called for at least a polytechnic qualification, more usually an electronics or physics degree. As a consequence, some of the brightest engineers in the country were snapped up on graduation. Many others, similarly qualified were then employed by Marconi, Pye, Racal, the Atomic Energy Authority, ICL, Sperry Gyroscope and other leading-edge companies with copper-bottomed defence industry contracts. National Service had ended, so that few of these very bright young people had experienced any form of structure or discipline in their environment. It was hardly surprising that the whole working atmosphere was akin to being at university. Golfing competitions were arranged, camping and hiking weekends, orienteering expeditions, soccer and rugby leagues, all discussed at great length in company time. Tea breaks lasting an hour, days off were taken without question. A truly marvellous working atmosphere, very stimulating – provided you were on 'the staff' and not one of the workers on the actual shop floor. Wilson confirms this in his book about the company (p534) '----*This philosophy created an environment in which engineers and managers could follow their instincts, giving rise to the widespread belief among employees that Ferranti was a 'fun place' in which to work'.* This 'fun' turned to anger many years later when extremely bright people realised that their early retirement was due to a badly managed company that had kept them in total ignorance of the commercial realities.

There is no question that, with fine brains working on stimulating projects, it can be counter-productive to constrain such creativity – particularly, as was often the case, where some engineers were working on pure research. Nevertheless, Ferranti was a commercial concern, and some form of structure to give the creativity a common direction would definitely have been useful, even vital. There was absolutely no sense that engineering efforts had any financial consequences whatsoever. Engineers were rarely called to account for the time being expended to bring a specific design project to a conclusion. Engineers would be asked by an estimator how many printed circuit boards did he, the engineer, believe it would take to perform a certain function? The engineer would give a number, and would not find out for many months that this off-the-cuff response of his was the only input he was expected to give to a bid set that was being submitted to the government to win a future project!

Compare this with a situation that obtains in North America. A project engineer is totally responsible for preparing a bid to the US government. If the bid is successful, this same project engineer will probably get to run the multi-million dollar project. All departments will submit their total costings, including staffing levels, estimated hours, materials, capital equipment, overhead (known as G & A – General and Administration), etc. An example of how the bidding process works can be given by examining how the drawing office bid might be handled. The project engineer might believe that the costings bid by the drawing office are unacceptably high. Further, he suspects that the drawing office are using this particular bid to recover losses on a previous job. Typically he will demand a re-submission of the bid set and threaten that, unless the bid is substantially reduced, he will approach an outside drawing agency for a bid. If the outside bid is substantially lower, he, the project engineer, will leave it to the drawing office to explain to management why it had been necessary to approach an outside agency, and why this agency can, given their profit motives, produce a more favourable bid. Almost inevitably the internal bid will be reduced. This is to point out that all engineering staff engaged in the bidding process will know the financial imperatives and by so doing will have gained a very necessary commercial education.

In its heyday, Ferranti had almost a monopoly on advanced, automated weapons systems for the Royal Navy. These systems incorporated Ferranti's own computers. During those halcyon days, surprise was expressed in the City that Ferranti could make substantial profits one year to be followed by equally substantial losses the next. For those working in the company, and observing its ways of working, it should have been no surprise at all. Some years later Ferranti was to form an association with an American electronics company, which terminally damaged them. Ferranti, with its marked dependence on brilliant graduates working without constraint or question, appeared to have been so insulated from the realities of the commercial world that, without a drastic cultural change, such damage from some source or another was almost inevitable. An exclusive 'cost-plus' arrangement with the British military leaves a company ill-equipped for dealing with commercial predators. Since the Ferranti demise, more commercial, more competitive, form of bidding has been introduced for IT and other government projects, but despite this the record of cost over-runs and failure to meet time deadlines and performance criteria is appalling. It would be immensely gratifying to say that the demise of companies like Ferranti, together with the introduction of more commercial practices by government, that the poor management that brought about the demise is a thing of the past. Regrettably, as indicated by the profile of ICL below, corporate indiscipline was still in evidence as recently as the late 80s and probably contributed to the company being driven into the arms of Fujitsu.

Xerox

Xerox was, and is, a successful company. The inclusion of such a company here is to describe one aspect of Xerox at a certain time in its history. Although this aspect has now passed into history, it remains illustrative of the problems that can ensue when there is no 'top to bottom' control of the company. Prior to the mid-1970s, Xerox had a monopoly on patents for photostatic copiers and copying. The technology was marketed brilliantly and the company was very successful and very rich. It had a hard-driving, but even-handed attitude to its employees worldwide. However, the product line was so successful that the major task of managing the company was confined to adding up the income. The company appeared to have money to burn. Countless executives drove luxury cars, air travel was first class down to relatively junior management levels. Expense accounts seemed limitless. At some future date, not so very far off, the patent monopoly was to come to an end, and an invasion by the Japanese into this hugely lucrative market, with its even more profitable leasing contracts and consumables spin-offs, was inevitable.

Outside of the USA, Xerox and the Rank Organisation had a cross-stock ownership and the Rank Organisation had the rights, outside of the USA, to sell the products exclusively. The organisation engaged in this activity was called Rank Xerox.

Investors put their money into Xerox because it was a high roller. It was an exciting stock, turning in brilliant performances year after year, and investors were not enthused by the idea that Xerox should become 'respectable'. If 'respectability' was what they wanted, they would typically choose IBM. So, in effect, Xerox, for all of its undoubted success, had many potential problems ahead. It had huge staff numbers, people who had known only uncontrolled success and spending profligacy, a situation not enjoyed by many companies. It was going to be very tough to change that mentality, to get the genie back in the bottle. Although there were undoubtedly people who could see the problem, how do you get concentrated effort on dealing with it? No-one wants to sacrifice their place on the gravy train.

This is what happened when Xerox bought a computer company. Many of the shareholders protested at the price paid, and many of the existing staff perceived a threat from 'these clever computer people'. Because of the Rank Xerox connection, the management of its Xerox's overseas business was in foreign hands. Local management autonomy in each of the European countries under the Rank Xerox umbrella was absolute. Consequently Xerox was not in control of Rank Xerox and Rank Xerox had given total autonomy to its country managers, known by staff as 'the barons'. It is not difficult to see how taking care of the threats on the horizon from the imminent loss of its monopoly would be an enormous problem. The Americans, as usual, have an expression for it, *'If you're standing up to your waist in a swamp, surrounded by alligators, it's difficult to remember you went there to empty the swamp'*. Xerox was forced to sell the computer company after being in the business for less than 10 years.

Some time later, Xerox bought the majority share in Rank Xerox, the name of which is now history. Thus management control passed into the hands of the parent and a homogeneous structure could be put in place worldwide. Technology changes meant that some time later the entire company had to venture into the computer world again, whatever the shareholders or staff wanted. But the point is made: how difficult it is to marry short-term expediency to long-term planning for a company in a highly volatile market. It is doubly difficult if the company structure militates against a uniform, agile response from the entire company acting in unison.

Data General

Frequent references have been made in this book to Data General, to illustrate the strengths and weaknesses of certain management practices. The general company philosophy, and the demands it made on staff and customers alike have been alluded to in the book *The Soul of a New Machine* referred to earlier. When the company was founded in the 1960s, its impact was almost immediate. Founded in Massachusetts, in a building that had formerly been a pizza parlour, the company set out to challenge the influence and market of the hugely successful computer company Digital Equipment Co., later to be known simply as DEC (both Data General and Digital Equipment have been since swallowed up by other companies.). The companies were fierce rivals from the outset, the rivalry becoming extremely acrimonious and, between the two founder Presidents, very personal. Because of its later foundation, Data General had to bring something new to the market. It is not overstating the case to say that DEC was a technology-driven company and, as a result, created a fierce loyalty for itself within its customer base, and the scientific market place. Data General, on the other hand, was almost immediately known for the ruthlessness with which it pursued profit. Even in this increasingly sophisticated market, the company established a unique reputation, both in the United States, and in the rest of the world, not all of it favourable. D.G. wasted few resources on cultivating the regard of its customers, or indeed on buying the loyalty of its staff. The philosophy was that customers purchased the company products because they were state-of-the-art, top quality and competitively priced. They were also launched at a breathtaking rate. These factors, and nothing else, would command customer loyalty. Similarly, if the development staff were working on leading edge projects, and well rewarded; and if the sales and marketing staff were being equally well rewarded to sell these up-to-date products in a sellers' market, the company did not have to provide anything else to command staff loyalty. This meant that staff had to be very self-sufficient to stay with the company. Any form of paternalism was absolutely alien to the D.G. philosophy. Similarly, the customers either had to be on a very tight budget, or they were also very independent, profit-orientated businesses, well able to take care of themselves in the harsh Data General climate.

The company published price lists of equipment, and the sales force worldwide had absolutely no choice but to abide by the price list. Discounts were based purely on product quantities, and again there was no deviation permitted without higher management approval. Any form of deviation had to be justified, at length, on a form called a P.V.R. (policy variation request). All of these finished up on the President's desk for final approval – and almost all were denied. The reasons were quite simple from a financial standpoint: the company had shaved its margin, and factors loading that margin, absolutely to the bone. If there had been any fat in the margin for further reductions in price, it would have reflected in the original selling price. Any contractual deviation had a price implication; so, they too were usually denied. It is sometimes difficult to sell this rigidity to a demanding customer, but the policy had the saving grace that there was no discrimination between one customer and another, a very strong selling point.

Adopting these policies, the company grew at the rate of 40 per cent per annum. It was the fastest company up to that time to enter the ranks of the Fortune 500, and the only company, up until then, that had done so without a single drop in profits on its way to entering these illustrious ranks. It was impressive that, once all staff recognised and accepted the way the company did business (and if they didn't, they didn't stay), there was no time wasted, arguing for relaxation of the rules. As a result, there was very rapid forward progress. The company was very exciting, and held up as a true American success story, much as Microsoft has been since. It was also impressive that the company disciplines were put in place almost from the day of its founding, and these same disciplines were still functioning fully when the company turnover was exceeding $1bn per annum.

However, it was at this stage that the weaknesses in the system began to show. Such a rigid pricing policy is beneficial when a company is getting off the ground. During a time of rising market, the President can, without a noticeable change in company fortunes, determine every allowable price deviation, every product introduction, every change in company structure and every policy change. Unfortunately, even in good times, such a system is also, in reality, only workable to the full when the company attracts people who thrive on excitement and personal self-sufficiency. As the company grows, those original founding ideals fade, but the disciplines that underpinned them are still in place, and neither are really understood; nor is there a great deal of empathy with them from employees at all levels who later joined the company when it had all the appearance of maturity. By the same token, a company of substantial turnover attracts more and more mature customers with more choice and clout, and these are also unlikely to accept without demur, rigid rules dating from another era.

So here is a successful company, where all meaningful decisions are made by one man who inevitably, without input from people who are listened to and have the courage to impart unpopular messages, will be more and more distanced from the market place and the enormous changes rapidly happening there. It's probably not the case that the President always insisted on being the only management voice to be heard, but he had created a regime where such a belief was inevitable. One senior country manager whilst in a meeting in Beijing in China personally agreed a set of terms and conditions at variance with the company standard. It was just not feasible for him to suggest to the Chinese government that the meeting be suspended while he attempted to wake the founder of the company back in Massachusetts, to ask if he, the founder, would allow an amendment to clause 14 of the company terms and conditions. So the country manager accepted the amendment and the contract was agreed; Data General, after examining the end result, accepted the outcome without demur. Under normal circumstances the country manager would never have been allowed to commit the company to changes of contractual terms, without prior permission. But many people used the company's veto as an excuse for not making any decisions of their own. Such a rigid management regime, so valuable and vital in the early days, inevitably attracts such risk-averse people, and the company stultifies as a result. It is difficult to deny the observation, that it is the ability to meet new challenges, yet adhere to its core disciplines, which has made IBM the unique company that it has been over the years; it is still there whilst many others have, like Icarus flown for the sun and perished

ICL

It is the rigid corporate discipline of Data General that invokes comparisons with ICL, now owned by Fujitsu but still Britain's major computer designer and manufacturer. The origin of ICL, compared with that of Data General, could not have been more different. ICL did not enjoy the luxury of starting from scratch with a homogeneous product line and corporate discipline. ICL, as a company, was the end result of a series of mergers and acquisitions stretching back over twenty or thirty years. ICL itself was to be the subject of an unwilling take-over by Standard Telephones and Cables (STC). The ICL culture, if indeed there was one, was an amalgam of those from ICT (International Computers and Tabulators), Power Samas, Hollerith, Ferranti (which sold its commercial computing interests to ICT) and Singer (which also sold its computing interests to ICL). ICL had never managed to shake off the effect of the various influences on its resultant shape.

There is no question that a shrewd merger or acquisition can bring overnight growth to a company that would take years attempting to grow organically However, unless care is taken to adopt one culture or another of those involved in the collaboration, or unless a completely new culture is invented which can be observed by everyone, then it is almost certain that the joining together will never work effectively, if only because the inevitable conflict between the parties will just absorb so much management time and energy. Reference has already been made to the heavy technical orientation of Ferranti. Even in its commercial activities (its involvement in the Atlas programme for example) the Ferranti elements still pursued universities as customers primarily, because that is where the company was comfortable; its staff, conditioned by the poor Ferranti management, once in ICL, still pursued their own goals unhindered by any stricter management regime. The American company, Singer, on the other hand, were mercilessly commercial, chasing the financial market. Its machines were designed to appeal to the financial community, and its staff were a totally different kind of person from those one would find in Ferranti. Signs of both of these cultures were still visible in ICL many years later. Furthermore, ICL, because of its national flag carrier status, seemed to have gathered these various companies in order to take on all comers, particularly IBM.

ICL's favoured history with the British government (the government used to be a major shareholder), going back over many years, gave the company a distinct advantage on many fronts. Those advantages have long since disappeared. So, for the past twenty years or so, the company has had to forge a new way forward. It is difficult to escape the conclusion that ICL's inability to devise a single culture, together with its corporate parochialism and its lack of discipline made its demise almost inevitable – hence its Fujitsu ownership. ICL has been caught between its technical origins, together with the shackles of its patronage from government – and the harsh commercial climate in which every other company has to operate. The government, by its very nature, is ponderous and deliberate in its decision making process, and this inevitably constrained the speed with which ICL could operate. It also led to a form of company complacency which, instilled over years, was difficult to shake off; it's even more difficult if there is no concerted attempt to try.

Beating ICL for an order always gave rise to unbounded joy and celebration in almost every other competing computer company. Undoubtedly, the company had some superb technical intellects at its disposal, people who were, beyond question, loyal and talented and committed. But the endless debate, and the desire to always have the 'clever' solution seemed to inhibit forward progress. The lack of a core discipline gave extraordinary latitude to middle management, particularly in sales and marketing, to make autonomous decisions in their own personal and departmental interests. This appeared to give rise to a disconnect between commitments made to a potential customer by the commercial interests of the company, and the ability or understanding of the technical people to fulfil that commitment. This corporate culture stretched back over many years. In fact it is quite possible to detect, twenty years on, the same cultural instincts that gave rise to Ferranti Inventors Club mentioned in the preface to this book. As has been explained in the main body of the book, it is terribly difficult to change a culture to provide a common purpose, while at the same time not rocking the boat too violently, in order that the revenue streams can be maintained to 'pay the rent'. But unless the task is undertaken, and the earlier in the company's life the better, the eventual outcome is almost unavoidable.

The history of ICL goes back to the original days of the computer industry, and the undoubted depth of its early and subsequent technical talent, had the wherewithal to be a major player in the world. The fact that it was founded in a country more dedicated to pushing back the frontiers of science than to real commercial success, has allowed its technical and geographical parochialism to prevent the company ever realising its full potential.

Dataproducts

A West Coast American company, Dataproducts was for many years the largest independent computer printer manufacturer in the world, with revenues reaching in excess of $1bn. The company provided large, fast-impact line printers to IBM, DEC, Burroughs, Wang, Siemens, Olivetti, Honeywell Bull and many others. Founded by engineers, the company duly prospered on the basis of its excellent engineering skills, with factories and laboratories on both coasts of the United States as well as in Dublin and Hong Kong. The company's fortunes were made as the result of a unique break-through in line printer technology. Customers would buy Dataproducts printers, suitably modified to interface with the customer's particular computer family and then sold by the customer as part of their own product line. There were few large computer rooms in the world that did not contain a Dataproducts printer badged under another name.

As the mainframe computer and, later, the mini-mainframe began to lose its prominence in favour of the personal computer, so did the need for huge line printers specifically, and impact printers in general. The company could see this decline clearly in its financial data, which were exhaustive and detailed, and yet the company was frozen in a time warp. It could see the rise of the dot matrix printer, from people such as Epson, and the onset of laser printing from people such as Hewlett Packard. Hewlett Packard was not even known as a player in the computer printing business, but by adopting a Japanese laser engine from Canon as the core of its laser printing offering, Hewlett Packard came from nowhere to be the dominant player in this new, lightweight printer market. It was obviously thinking 'outside the box'.

Dataproducts, on the other hand, was very much boxed in by its history. It had financial analysis, together with inputs from all of its field staff, that told the company that the days of impact printers were numbered, yet it could not bring itself to face the reality in any practical way. New staff were employed to introduce the new laser technology, but were never given the prominence or the audience that their skills called for. New methods of marketing were tried, but with only the minimum of commitment, which would immediately disappear if a more traditional type of customer was to give the merest hint that they might want to buy a number of the old-style printers. The company was, to all intents and purposes, like the proverbial rabbit, paralysed by the headlights of approaching cars.

The eventual solution was to try to repeat its earlier success and bring a completely new type of print technology to market. Unfortunately, the company did not have the financial clout needed at this time to undertake such a brave venture, when other forms of technology had already been established and accepted. The company was eventually taken over by Hitachi.

So survival is not guaranteed to a company, founded on sound engineering principles, well organised and with an unmatched knowledge of its sector of a huge industry as well as a first class reputation in it. The staff were, to a man, incredibly committed to the company and very knowledgeable about the industry and the competition. But they couldn't change. The threats to a company are many and varied and there is little forgiveness for the unwary. It is vital that those responsible for the stewardship of a project or department or company do all in their power to be aware the threats, be they technical, financial or cultural. It has been mentioned earlier in the body of the book, that all the financial detail in the world, for all its undoubted value, cannot of itself save a company. Dataproducts was, in effect, almost the exact opposite of Xerox. Xerox made a key decision, but could not get it implemented. Dataproducts would have had no problem getting any decision implemented, but the management could not relinquish its loyalty to an outdated paradigm. It is an example of a company that had great engineering skills and a disciplined structure, but lacked the agility to respond to market and technology changes.

Case

Case (Computer and Systems Engineering) is another British company founded by entrepreneurs. Founded, together with others, by a former British IBM employee, Case dedicated itself to the business of connecting computers to each other via the telephone networks. Although a commonplace activity nowadays, the company was very much the pioneer of this particular industry back in the 1960s, particularly in Britain. From humble beginnings, Case grew to be a substantial company. Unfortunately, the company, as it grew, gained its share of organisation people, and the entrepreneurial spirit of the founders was diluted. When the company was enjoying outstanding success, this problem was easily disguised. The company tried to repeat its British success in the United States, by employing the same tactics as in the UK but again giving too much autonomy without control to people sent to create the enterprise. The company got its fingers burned, and did not have the necessary management talent combined with deep pockets, to assist a recovery. It too was purchased; this time, rather bizarrely, by a British industrial dinosaur, Dowty, seeking to diversify out of heavy engineering into a high-tech business.

EMI

Entry into the United States is always difficult for foreign companies as they tend to lag behind their US competitors in most areas. Those that succeed tend to do so as a result of being 'more American than the Americans' – but not all. Many case studies have been written about EMI and its unfortunate experiences in the brain and body scanner market place; it is often used as a case study by British business schools. With its British inventor, subsequently a Nobel prize winner, on the payroll, EMI enjoyed phenomenal success at the outset of bringing these non-invasive medical scanning techniques to market, particularly in the USA. Because of the in-depth nature of the many published case studies detailing how EMI lost control of this lucrative market, the author of this book will confine his comments to his own observations, gained as a significant supplier to EMI.

Not unreasonably, given the market size, EMI set up a fully-fledged American operation – perhaps too fully-fledged, as there was little control from the UK Instead of responding to an incredibly rapidly expanding market, the company seemed to be spending an enormous amount of time trying to control the monster it had created. Frustrated by the British way of doing business, and without proper controls, the Americans were running at their own speed. They had their own production facility in the US., they had their own sales and marketing and technical people – so who needs head office? It is quite one thing to create a presence in a foreign country in order to do business in that country. It is quite another to create such a presence that all control is lost. Whilst infighting was consuming the larger part of management time on both sides of the Atlantic, the competitors were circling and, not impeded by sufficient patent restrictions, eventually wrested the market from the inventors, EMI. It appeared that, once again, while the company was fighting internal trans-Atlantic battles, focus on the political moves being made by medical insurance companies, and competitors, was lost. In many respects the EMI story has parallels with the case of Xerox in that it is another case of the parent company losing, or being out of, control of its overseas operations. As has been said earlier, risks to a business occur almost daily and such risks are many and varied. It is a prime task of senior management to attempt to detect the risks, be aware of their consequences and take measures to deal with the consequences. To do so will assist with survival whilst to not do so can be fatal.

All of the above examples are not recounted here to point fingers or make judgements, good or bad. Hindsight is always 20/20. The examples are included so that the reader can adopt certain practices where he perceives those practices to be beneficial, or to detect fault-lines running through corporate philosophies. To resolve to correct them, if appropriate, or to be determined never to be a victim of them. It is hoped that the inclusion of American companies will serve to illustrate that American companies do not have a monopoly of success or that British companies are doomed to failure. However, it does seem, from the examples above that, in general, American companies succeed, or fail, on their responses to circumstances in the market. The British, on the other hand, seem to fail by being too intent on examining their own corporate navel. To characterise Americans as extrovert and British as introvert is possibly to oversimplify the case, but history has a lot to answer for.

APPENDIX II
Corporate Operational Procedures

These guidelines have been included to illustrate a simple mechanism for the control of a company. They cover most of the activities that occur in most companies. They have the advantage that they are not over-complicated so that almost all staff can understand them. They can be used by staff and management in one country if the company operates in only one country but they can also be used in a number of countries. The guidelines thus provide a means of imposing a company discipline and this discipline can be observed by the entire company at every level of management. It avoids the problems that can arise when such a discipline is imposed from on high to subordinate levels of staff.

For sales regions:
Asia Pacific
Mainland Europe
UK
USA

Contents
    A.   **Introduction**
    B.   **Quantifiable goals**
    C.   **Guidelines – financial**

General
1. Pricing
2. Advertising and Promotion
3. Contracts
4. Third Party Vendors
5. Premises
6. Capital Expenditure
7. Outside Services
8. Travel

D Guidelines – human resources
1. Headcount Levels – AOP
2. Recruitment – within AOP.
3. Recruitment – not within AOP.
4. Promotion and Changes in Role
5. Termination
6. Remuneration
7. Non-Periodic Reviews
8. Benefit Programmes
9. Sales Quotas
10. Training Programmes
11. Performance Appraisal and Development Programme

APPENDIX A   Expenditure Authorisation Limits
APPENDIX B   Human Resources Approval Levels
APPENDIX C   Weekly Finance Report

A. INTRODUCTION

It is intended to give autonomy to Regional Directors for driving profitability within certain constraints that recognises that each Region is part of the worldwide Corporation and therefore, management of the Region must be in accordance with overall goals, strategies and disciplines of the Corporation. Therefore, your management should be determined by two criteria:

1. The meeting of your quantifiable goals as defined by your Annual Operating Plan (AOP) and as reflected in your personal remuneration incentives for the year in question.
2. The observance of the Corporate disciplines and guidelines issued by the CEO's office.

An audit of the observance of the above can be carried out at any time at the instigation of the CEO's office.

B. QUANTIFIABLE GOALS

1. The Regional Directors will draw up an acceptable Profit and Loss Statement for their area of operation prior to the start of the fiscal year. This, in due course, will go through the normal review process with the CEO's office and Group Management. Such management reserves the

right to modify the plan throughout the year to meet financial or market demands and to reflect changes in product status. The Plan is to indicate:-
i) Bookings and Revenue by Product
ii) Operating Expenses in detail
iii) Headcount Plan: increase in headcount will always trail, justifying increase in revenue by at least one quarter.
iv) Profitability will be Profit/(Loss) before tax as shown in your AOP. Excluded will be any central management fee deviations from the AOP figure. Regional Directors will be expected to make adjustments in their selling prices to compensate for changes in costs of product caused by currency movements.
v) A monthly review, usually telephonic in the case of Asia Pacific and USA. But occasionally face to face, will be held with the CEO's office. Dates for these reviews will be communicated six months in advance and will usually be timed to accord with submission of all monthly results to Group HQ. All criteria of AOP will be examined. Suggestions, and in some case instructions for improvements of performance will be given where appropriate. financial controllers will be expected to submit to the Commercial Director, a weekly flash report of financial data, the control and timing of which will be determined by the Commercial Director (see Guidelines – Financial below).

C. GUIDELINES – FINANCIAL

General
It is the duty of the Regional financial controllers to ensure adherence to these guidelines. The Controllers shall have an independent reporting responsibility to the Commercial Director at the CEO's office.

Occasionally there will be charges incurred by CEO's office for activities involving staff from all countries and where this staff needs to meet at one venue, i.e. product launches, some training courses etc. It is expected that where possible this decision would be made by agreement between CEO's office and the Regions. In any case, at least one quarter's notice of such an event will be given and total charges incurred will be allocated to the Regions.

A Controller's flash report will be required on the Monday of each week.

This report will take the form given in Appendix C of these guidelines.

1. Pricing

All Regional Directors will compile a regional price and discount structure which must be adhered to by all sales staff. Variations can be approved only by Regional Sales Directors/Managers within agreed boundaries and or Regional Directors. Giving of discount does not qualify for any relief of bottom line. Regional price lists will be submitted to CEO's office. Approval is expected to be automatic although obvious inconsistencies may be queried.

2. Advertising and Promotion

Promotional spend to be in accordance with AOP unless extra expenditure can be justified by savings elsewhere on operating expenses. Additional promotion expenditure can only be incurred if all goals – revenue and operating expense to revenue ratios are at or better than AOP in the preceding quarter. Such additional expenditure must not adversely affect profitability for the remainder of the current fiscal year. Centrally incurred charges will be charged to the Regions in accordance with the opening paragraphs General above.

3. Contracts

All contracts to be signed in accordance with the level of authority outlined in Appendix A attached to this document. There are to be NO exceptions.

4. Third Party Vendors

No responsibility is to be accepted by Regional Management for a systems bid where third party added value to that bid exceeds 10% of the total bid. Approval for programmes where the added value exceeds 10% may be given after consultation with CEO. Even if the added value is of a content level that is acceptable for the company to take responsibility then two further criteria must be satisfied:
  i) the bid can only be made in the country of origin of the added value and when the source company has had its financial well-being examined and signed off by the Regional Finance Director. His signature indicates his personal endorsement
  ii) the bid must be signed off by the appropriate Regional Technical Director/Manager. His signature indicates his personal endorsement. No added value is to be included in a bid where the added value is

from a country other than that of the bid unless and until that added value has been ratified by the Engineering Director/Manager in the country of origin of the company's own equipment forming part of the bid.

5. Premises
No new lease or refurbishment contracts will be signed without CEO's approval.

6. Capital Expenditure
Will be in accordance with Group policies and procedure (see Appendix A).

7. Outside Services
Will not be retained without approval of Corporate Management.

8. Travel
All travel outside his/her region by a member of staff should have the express approval of the Regional Director. Regional Directors planning to leave their region of responsibility should inform the CEO of their plans before travel is undertaken. All air travel should be coach (economy) class.

D. GUIDELINES – HUMAN RESOURCES
It is the duty of the Regional Human Resources Managers to ensure adherence to these guidelines. See attached Appendix B for approval levels.

1. Headcount Levels – AOP
Headcount levels will be approved in line with the AOP Operating Expenses.

2. Recruitment – Within AOP
Replacement – Regions are authorised to replace staff already approved in the AOP as per classifications.

Additions – Regions are authorised to recruit additional staff up to the approval AOP levels provided the preceding Quarter is on target both for Revenue and Expenses. If the Revenue or Expense to Revenue Ration decline more than 10% from the AOP for any quarter then all hiring will be frozen until new staffing levels are agreed with the CEO.

3. Recruitment – Not Within AOP
All additional staffing will need approval of the CEO. No such approval will

be given where YTD (year to date) performance at the time of the request is below AOP. Approvals are more likely to be granted where the additional heads can be shown to a Business Plan to be self-funding i.e. training personnel for revenue generating training programmes etc. It is unlikely that requests for additional sales personnel in Q4 of any one year will be approved.

4. Promotion and Changes in Role
Promotions, changes in role etc, are the responsibility of Regional Directors. Up to date organisation charts must be with the CEO. The CEO reserves the right to query organisational structure.

5. Termination
All involuntary termination can only be implemented after observance of local industrial relations laws. Any alleged infringement of these laws by a dismissed employee which leads to legal action being taken or a national tribunal calling the company to account must be informed to the CEO's office.

6. Remuneration
Details of remuneration levels of all staff on commission and bonus plans must be copied to CEO's office. Annual reviews are the responsibility of the Regional Director but these must be shown to not adversely affect the bottom line.
Remuneration for Regional Directors will be established by the CEO.
Salary structures will be established by Regional Human Resources based on survey data. Approval levels are shown in Appendix B.

7. Non-Periodic Reviews
High Performers should be looked at every six months to ensure they are adequately compensated in line with their performance. It will be Company policy to reward and retain high performers. Regional Directors should also identify key people for promotion/training and special award in line with appropriate Recognition Award Programmes.

8. Benefit Programmes
It is the responsibility of Regional Human Resources to Review annually all Benefit Programmes to ensure they are competitive and in line with market trends.

9. Sales Quotas

Sales quotas for the sales force will be set by the Regional Directors in line with the AOP but details must be submitted to the CEO's office. Those for the Regional Directors will reflect the AOP and be set by the CEO.

10. Training Programmes

It is Company Policy to improve the skills of all employees in line with Company objectives. To achieve this, training needs should be identified prior to the start of the fiscal year and training programmes established for the Region. It is the responsibility of the financial controllers to ensure all Training expenditure is in accordance with the operating expense plan.

11. Performance Appraisal and Development Programme

It is the responsibility of the Regional Human Resources Department to introduce a Performance Appraisal and Development Programme and ensure that Performance Assessment interviews for Sales employees should take place in Q4 prior to the start of the new fiscal year.

APPENDIX A
AUTHORISATION LIMITS

SIGNATURE AUTHORITY	CEO	REGIONAL DIRECTORS	REGIONAL FINANCE CONTROLLERS	DEPARTMENT MANAGERS*	SALES EXECUTIVES
Quotations/Proposals	Copies of items >£1m annual value	Up to £1m es t annual value at standard price book			Price book
World-wide contracts	All agreements				
Local agreements	Non-standard	Standard	Non-standard	Standard	
Purchase requirements for standard inventory	Unlimited	£100k	£25k	£25k	
Purchase req. for non-standard inventory (3rd party product)	Unlimited	£25k	£10k	£10k	
Capital eqpt approved in AOP	10k	<£10k	<£10k		
Not approved in AOP	£1k	<£1k	<£1k		
Lease contracts:					
Equipment in AOP	£10k	<10k	<10k		
Eqpt not in AOP	£1k	<£1k	<1k		
Motor vehicles (annual lease)	As defined by group car policy				
Premises	Require corporate approval				
Outside services	Require corporate approval				
Promotion (PR)	As defined in corporate operational procedures				
Travel: Expensed items:	Outside territory	Within territory			
Purchase requisition*	>£25k	>£25k	£5k	£1k	
Expense reports	>£ 3k	£ 3k	£2k	£1k	
Invoices**	£>25k	£25k	£5k	£1k	
Cheques as per bank mandate.					

* Proposal only
** Excluding building rent/rates/services and insurance/communication costs-regional director expense reports to be submitted periodically to CEO.

Appendices

APPENDIX B

HUMAN RESOURCES APPROVAL LEVELS

Approval level	CEO	Regional Directors	Regional Finance Controllers	Human Resources	Department Manager
AOP headcount levels	4	4	4	4	4
Recruitment within AOP		4		4	4
Recruitment Not within AOP	4	4	4	4	
Promotion and role changes		4	4	4	4
Termination Involuntary		4	4	4	4
Remuneration					
Commission Plans	4	4	4	4	
Bonus Plans	4	4	4	4	
Annual Review - Staff		4		4	4
Annual Review - Directors	4				
Salary Structures				4	
Non-Periodic Reviews		4		4	4
Benefit Programmes		4		4	
Sales Quotas		4	4		
Training Programmes			4	4	
Performance Appraisal and Development Programme				4	
Special Recognition Award Programme			4	4	

APPENDIX C

WEEKLY REPORT

REGION:
PERIOD:
WEEK ENDING:
WEEKS REMAINING:
CURRENCY:

		CURRENT MONTH				CUMULATIVE TO LAST		
	To date	Expectation	MD report	Budget	(Under)/over	Actual	Budget	(Under)/over
Order Input External	x	x	x	x	(x)	x	x	(x)
Inter-Co	x	x	x	x	x	x	x	x
	xx	xx	xx	xx	(xx)	xx	xx	(xx)
Revenue External	x	x	x	x	(x)	x	x	(x)
Inter-Co	x	x	x	x	x	x	x	x
	xx	xx	xx	xx	(xx)	xx	xx	(xx)
Order Backlog	x	x	x	-	(x)	x	x	(x)
Cash Balance	x	x	x	-	x	-	-	-
Cash Flow	x	x	x	-	x	x	x	x

Major orders won/lost in month to date:
Key dependencies in achieving order/revenue/cash expectations:

Appendices

NOTES ON WEEKLY REPORT

1. Timing

The report should be faxed to Corporate HQ by 8.00 am (UK time) on the Monday morning of each week.

2. Definitions

Period	Current month.
Week Ending	Date of last day of current month
Weeks Remaining	Number of weeks left in month.

Current Month:

To Date	actual achievement in month to date. Note: for order backlog and cash balance the figure should be the actual amounts (not movement in month)
Expectation	latest view of month end result
MD Report	for orders and revenue only. As stated in MD report issued at the beginning of the month.
Budget	AOP
(Under)/Over	difference between current expectation for month and budget.

Cumulative to Last:
All figures are for the cumulative to the end of the previous month as stated in Day 7/Day 14 reports.

APPENDIX III
Strategic Marketing Group (SMG)

Strategic Marketing Group (SMG) nominally meets monthly but only if there are substantial matters to be discussed or decided or reviewed.

SMG is not allowed to slow down company momentum.

No minutes of SMG meetings are taken. Only major decisions are circulated.

SMG process means that all contributing departments to company marketing thrust participate in establishing the direction. In summary, it is an inclusive process.

All members of the SMG are fully aware of their individual responsibilities, including the responsibility to ensure all SMG decisions permeate down through their respective departments.

APPENDIX IV

Bexley Business Academy Presentation

Because the author was raised in South London, he was invited to address some teenage students at the Bexley Business Academy; despite its name the school is a state school that does not require any qualification to be a pupil. The creation and worth of these business academies, sponsored by wealthy individuals, is still the subject of considerable controversy from politicians and educationalists. None of this is of concern to the author as far as the presentation was concerned.

Given that in the book the author appeals for some form of business education to be given to the young before they leave school, the presentation (details of which appear at the end of this appendix) provided an excellent opportunity to see if the young would respond to such an education. To see if there was indeed an interest, or was business to be a total turn-off to the youngsters aged between 13 and 17 years of age and numbering about 250 in total; the result was extremely gratifying. There were no interruptions for the 45-minute duration of the four identical presentations, and each presentation was followed by some very searching questions. Much of the presentation used professional football (soccer) as an illustrative means of describing the imperatives of a business.

It was important to catch and hold their attention but then that is true whatever the age group and whatever the subject. Since Bexley Business Academy is in a socially deprived area of London, it is probably true to say that the percentage of pupils that will go on to university is probably small, although this is the author's perception and not based on any data given him by the school. Accordingly the author attempted to catch the student's attention by first displaying names of famous businessmen with whom the students are likely to have been familiar. All of the businessmen have one thing in common – none of them is a graduate (although some of them quit university before graduation). The reason for this was to illustrate that success in life is not dependent on graduating, and that leaving school without graduating does not mean inevitable failure or a life of drudgery.

A second display showed a list of famous individuals with whom the students were familiar and who are famous for quite different reasons. All of them are from the world of sport or entertainment, some known domestically in the UK and others of more world-wide renown. The reason for this list was to show that although these people are famous and some of them rich, their success arises out of three quite distinct criteria – Timing + Luck + Talent. Many of them, talented as they are and hardworking as they undoubtedly are, have also been blessed by an element of luck that, together with timing, forms a constituent part of their success.

Nigel Kennedy, the classical violinist would have enjoyed far less success 50 years earlier when his demeanour and his dress would have been far too outrageous to be accepted by the then audiences of classical music. Tiger Woods would have found many golf clubs and courses closed to him 50 years ago. The purpose for this list was to illustrate that there might be people in the school audience who might well have a talent and who might equally be the beneficiary of luck and these two criteria might coalesce at the right time for them to be successful. But the list begs the question, what happens to those people who do not have the aptitude to be entrepreneurs and do not have the attributes that will make them successful in the world of entertainment or sport? It is a reality that the people who fall into neither of the successful categories form about 99% of society. It was to these people that this presentation was aimed. The fortunate 1% will need no help from any form of presentation.

Although this book is primarily about business and wealth creation for individuals and for companies, it is a fact that many people are not concerned with material wealth when selecting their career or manner of earning a living. People will make a very personal choice. Some will decide that their social life or sporting activity is far more important than actively pursuing success in their chosen way of earning a living. Others will pursue a vocation such as entering the medical world or teaching or social work or the church and this is a perfectly valid choice to make and it was felt that this should be pointed out in the presentation. Having made the choice to enter into the world of commerce then it is imperative that the individual realises the stark reality. No one should be more interested in the development of the individual than the individual himself. It is not suggested that the individual will be able to observe this reality to the same extent as the footballer, David Beckham. However, he is a good illustration of an individual who has had to make very significant decisions in the interest of his own short-term and long-term career.

Individuals in industry and commerce also need to do so and this will increasingly be the case, as the support given by employers and Government will inevitably diminish in the future. He may be an employee but this does not mean, and it is imperative that the individual does not see it as meaning that he hands over responsibility for either his life or his career to an employer; he's likely to be disappointed. Furthermore, he will increasingly find that any skill or aptitude he had when joining will be of short-term value, the more so in these days of rapid technological change. Therefore in the same manner that a company must launch and offer more and more up-to-date products to retain existing customers and gain new ones, so much an individual constantly undergo a process of personal renewal if he is not to render himself redundant. Redundancy whilst still employed, is where the individual is not making a contribution to the profitability of the company or where the contribution he is making is one that can be sacrificed by the employer – it's only a matter of time before the employer comes to this conclusion, usually the time when a company is going through a bad spell. It is worth bearing in mind that when a company makes this unpalatable decision it is almost certain that the company will make the decision based on parameters that go beyond salary but will take into account benefit costs such as health, pension and vacation as well as statutory redundancy costs; it is a very harsh reality.

The remainder of the presentation was concerned with the conduct of business starting with the fundamental statement that all businesses run on the basis that there is an income and a cost of producing that income and that the subtraction of the latter from the former produces hopefully a profit (and less hopefully a loss). To refine this without over-complicating the whole issue a slide was displayed, showing how the income from the sale of products or service as appropriate to any particular company minus the costs of materials, etc creates a gross margin from which the costs of running the company, salaries etc, are further subtracted to produce the profit or loss. The final part of the presentation drew in the soccer aspects of the presentation starting with an outline display of the management structure. Not surprisingly, all of the pupil audience believed that Sir Alex Ferguson ran Manchester United whilst the chart showed exactly where he fitted into the scheme of things. In the Preface to this book there is further reference to Sir Alex's role in the club.

The final two slides of the presentation (see panels IV(11) and IV (12) showed a very simplified spread sheet, an illustration of the main criteria that determine a company's profit and/or loss; it was pointed out that for all of its sporting affiliations, Manchester United is a company. These two slides present a fictional (although not entirely fictional) comparison between two clubs Real Madrid of Spain and Manchester United of

England. The comparison was made for two sets of circumstances. The first is when Davis Beckham is playing for Manchester United and the second is after David Beckham is sold to Real Madrid. It assumes that Manchester's sponsorship and merchandise sales drop as a result of the sale and Real Madrid's income from the same two criteria commensurately increases as a result of the acquisition of Beckham. Since this sale of Beckham did take place from one of these clubs to the other it is not unreasonable to say the presentation was not entirely fictional. Furthermore, since the sale had taken place very shortly before this presentation, the pupils were all very interested.

For the purposes of the presentation it was assumed that Real Madrid's stadium is twice the size of Manchester United but that the Spanish Club played half as many matches as Manchester; thus income from seat sales is the same for a sell-out crowd. Similarly to keep it simple, all other criteria were assumed to be identical. It was a very simplified but illustrative way of showing schoolchildren, albeit teenagers, how a business works, how judgements are made, or should be made, and the consequences of such decisions. The presentation turned out to be quite accidentally prescient as discussed in the Preface to this book.

Appendices

BEXLEY BUSINESS ACADEMY
BUSINESS DAY

Appendix IV (1)

- MicroSoft
- Virgin Atlantic
- Tottenham Hotspur
- Federal Express
- Walmart (ASDA)
- Hutchison
- Bill Gates
- Richard Branson
- Alan Sugar
- Fred Smith
- Sam Walters
- Li Ka Shing

Appendix IV (2)

- David Beckham
- Paula Radcliffe
- Tiger Woods
- Paul McCartney
- Elton John
- Nigel Kennedy
- Lennox Lewis
- Charlotte Church
- Serena Williams
- Frankie Detori

TIMING + LUCK + TALENT

Appendix IV (3)

A Very Personal Choice

VOCATION vs WEALTH CREATION

Appendix IV (4)

TODAY

David Beckham
 – a one man business on a payroll

You – a one man business on a payroll

Appendix IV (5)

- Improvement of Current Skills
- Personal Renewal
- Adoption of new skills
- Contribution to the Bottom Line

Appendix IV (6)

Product Renewal – Can we afford it?

Personal Renewal – Can we afford not to?

Appendix IV (7)

INCOME – COSTS
= PROFIT (LOSS)

Appendix IV (8)

Income
Manufacturing Costs
Gross Margin
Operating Costs
Profit (Loss)

Appendix IV (9)

Shareholders
Board of Directors
Chief Executive
Manager (Ferguson)
Players

Appendix IV (10)

225

Comparison
Real Madrid v Manchester United
David Beckham playing for Manchester United

Real Madrid				TOTAL	TOTAL				Manchester United
Income									Income
Ticket Sales	seats	cost per seat	Matches			Matches	cost per seat	seats	Ticket Sales
	120000	40	20	96000000	96000000	40	40	60000	
	No. of members	cost P/A				cost P/A	No. of members		
Supporters Club	100000	20		2000000	2000000		20	100000	Supporters Club
Merchandise				10000000	10000000				Merchandise
Sponsorship				20000000	20000000				Sponsorship
Total				128000000	128000000				Total
Cost of Stadium				84000000	84000000				Cost of Stadium
Wages of Players				32000000	32000000				Wages of Players
Profit approx 10% of A				12000000	12000000				Profit approx 10% of A

Appendix IV (11)

Comparison
Real Madrid v Manchester United
David Beckham sold to Real Madrid

Real Madrid				TOTAL	TOTAL				Manchester United
Income									Income
Ticket Sales	seats	cost per seat	Matches			Matches	cost per seat	seats	Ticket Sales
	120000	40	20	96000000	96000000	40	40	60000	
	No. of members	cost P/A				cost P/A	No. of members		
Supporters Club	100000	20		2000000	2000000		20	100000	Supporters Club
Merchandise				30000000					Merchandise
Sponsorship				30000000	10000000				Sponsorship
Total				148000000	108000000				Total
Cost of Stadium				84000000	84000000				Cost of Stadium
Wages of Players				37000000	27000000				Wages of Players
Profit approx 10% of A				15000000	-15000000				Profit approx 10% of A

Appendix IV (12)

Index

Accountant's speak, 65
Acquisition, 61
Ageism, 16
American graduate, 48
American way, 81
Annual operating plan, 210
Apple computers, 44
Apprentice, The, 7
Attitude, 82
Awareness days, 36

Beckham, David, 11
Blair, Tony, 40
Board of directors, 61
Brain-power, 22
Branson, Richard, 26
Britain's decline, 15
British Airways, 10
British Standards, 171
British way, 13
Bureaucracy, 39
Business Academies, 49
Business angels, 64
  education, 53
  health, 72
  studies, 48

'Can-do' attitude, 42
Capital, 63
Capital goods design, 90
Car manufacturers, 50
Career, 55, 64, 84
Case, 206
CBI, 52

Change, 53, 66
Changing perspective, 80
China, 56
City, 50, 60
Civil service culture, 56
Clinton, Bill, 43
Colonialism, 56
Commercial awareness, 51, 74
Commission plan, 97, 121, 154, 162
Comparing companies, 193
Competition, 30
Competition Commission, 70
Corporate discipline, 89
Corporate ladder, 54, 57
Cost of sales, 94
Cradle-to-grave care, 67
Creativity, 43

Data General, 106, 179, 200
Dataproducts, 205
Decline, 15
Dell computers, 26, 44
Design engineer, 93, 106, 112
Designer, 87
Discipline, 11, 20, 65, 78, 81, 89, 103, 112, 156, 177
DTI, 52
Dummer, Geoffrey, 56
Dyson, James, 26, 46

Educated approach, 58
Education, 8, 13, 14, 25, 27, 30, 42, 53, 79, 98, 143, 192, 198
Elitism, 69

EMI, 207
Engineer, 54, 69, 79, 94, 106, 112, 194
Engineering, 54, 88, 99, 105, 110, 130, 146, 161, 184, 196,
Engineering day, 90
Enron, 160
Entrepreneurs, 20, 26, 46, 64, 148

Ferranti, 72, 74, 195
Finance, 61, 74, 161
Finance people, 65, 159
Financial Controller, 159
Football, 10
Ford Motor Company, 34, 88, 119
Foreign competitors, 78
  manufacturers, 50
Further education, 44

Gates, Bill, 26, 44
General manager, 173
Germany, 14, 30, 33
Glazer, Malcolm, 11, 12
Global market place, 37
Goals 37

'Hail to the Chief', 82
Honours system, 55
HR, 164
Human Resources Manager, 164

IBM, 45,110, 181
ICL, 72, 125, 203
Image, 49, 71
Industrial culture, 84
  leaders, 45
Institutions, 52
Internet, 70

Japan, 14, 36, 38, 42, 47, 53, 73, 169
Jobs, 26, 44

Knowledge, 92
  workers, 35

Lloyds, 50
Lorenz, Andrew, 62

Making money, 21, 53
Management culture, 43
Manchester United, 11
Manufacturing, 24, 44, 50, 61, 75, 87, 109, 137, 169
Marconi, 8
Marketer, 109
Marketing, 11,27, 60, 69, 78, 83, 88, 93, 98, 109, 113, 122, 160, 169, 183, 184, 201 135
Marks and Spencer, 9
Massage, 72
Meetings, 144
Microchip, 57
Microsoft, 6, 22, 44, 70, 82, 99, 106, 135
Mobility, 58, 68

Non-competitive nature, 58
Not made here, 75

Obstacles, 37
One-man business, 146
Operational procedures, 209

Post Office, 10
Post-sales, 137
Prince's Trust, 64
Product cycle, 133

Index

Product introduction, 117
  launch, 44, 100, 106, 118
Production, 21, 34, 50, 54, 61, 75, 76, 107, 110, 160, 169, 170, 182
Production Manager, 169

Qualifications, 38
Quality, 52, 101, 110, 121, 171

Recruitment, 98
Rejuvenating, 79
Relegation zone, 66
Resources, 33
Responsibility, 124
Retirement, 22
Ring-fencing, 62
Risk takers, 55
Roles, 78
Rolls Royce, 34
Ryannair, 10

Sales manager, 148
Sales order processing, 157
Salesman, 142
Sandbagging, 104
Self-assessment of income tax, 128
Self-development, 23
Selling, 142
Sense of purpose, 44
Service, 137
SMG, 183
Society, 54
Spending targets, 132

Start-ups, 63
Status quo, 79
Strategic Marketing Group, 183, 220
Structure of industry, 49
Sugar, Sir Alan, 7, 45
SWOT, 118, 130, 134

Talents, 32
Teaching business studies, 48
  the young, 26
Team player, 78
Technical snobbery, 69
Tesco, 10, 50
Them and us, 30, 34
Trade unions, 34, 57, 59

Unions, 57
Upward mobility, 58
USA, 6, 10, 12, 16, 24, 38, 41, 53, 58, 68, 70, 102, 113, 123, 140, 169, 178, 199, 207

Venture capital industry, 63

Wal-mart, 50
Way forward, 183
Wealth, 32
Who runs industry? 62
Worldcom, 160
Worker, 60
Workforce, 27
Working overseas, 30

Xerox, 125, 198